מסורה

ArtScroll Series®

Rabbi Nosson Scherman / Rabbi Meir Zlotowitz

General Editors

From My Father's

Published by

Mesorah Publications, ltd

Table

Stories of warmth and inspiration

S. M. Tenenbaum

FIRST EDITION
First Impression . . . January 1998

Published and Distributed by
MESORAH PUBLICATIONS, Ltd.
4401 Second Avenue
Brooklyn, New York 11232

Distributed in Europe by
J. LEHMANN HEBREW BOOKSELLERS
20 Cambridge Terrace
Gateshead, Tyne and Wear
England NE8 1RP

Distributed in Israel by
SIFRIATI / A. GITLER — BOOKS
10 Hashomer Street
Bnei Brak 51361

Distributed in Australia & New Zealand by
GOLDS BOOK & GIFT CO.
36 William Street
Balaclava 3183, Vic., Australia

Distributed in South Africa by
KOLLEL BOOKSHOP
Shop 8A Norwood Hypermarket
Norwood 2196, Johannesburg, South Africa

Typography by Compuscribe at ArtScroll Studios, Ltd.

Printed in the United States of America by Noble Book Press
Bound by Sefercraft, Quality Bookbinders, Ltd. Brooklyn, N.Y.

ספר זה מוקדש לזכרו של אבי מורי

הר"ר יצחק צבי מנחם משה מאיר רוזנבורג זצ"ל

נפטר ד' שבט תשנ"ד

איש החסד והמתן בסתר, נדיב לב ומאיר פנים לכל אדם. יוקד
אמונה ובטחון, ומרבה לספר נפלאות הבורא להחדיר בלב צאצאיו
רגש קודש.

This book is dedicated to the memory of my father

Yitzchak Zvi ben Menachem Moshe Meir Rosenberg

A man of chesed — who gave charity freely and quietly, and
loved to tell stories of emunah and bitachon to instill the feeling
of spirituality in all his children

Introduction

The Shabbos table was set with a crisp white cloth and adorned with fine dishes, gleaming glassware and cutlery. At one end of the table the women exchanged news; the little children laughed and played. At the other end, a debate among the men was in progress. The Gemaras and other *sifrei kodesh* were open and my two grandfathers, my father and others were arguing heatedly. As the discussion became more intense, they rapped on the table, causing the pages to fly and the chandelier to quiver. The children stopped playing and stared spellbound at the scene before them. The women fell silent and watched in respect, for surely, they reasoned, no one can be engaged in such a lively discussion unless the subject truly matters. Such a debate ignites the Jewish soul and awakens the spirit.

In this environment, richly imbued with Torah and the holiness of Shabbos, stories that were told at my father's table were not mere words. They were sweet delicacies such as have been served to Jewish children at countless Shabbos tables throughout the generations. These stories are either true or based on truth with some literary license. All of them aim to impart the same warmth and Jewish values that were lovingly given over to me by my father.

Contents

The House on
Belilius Street

very stone of every building in Jerusalem's Old City lives and breathes and has a story to tell. Each house constructed from these stones is much more than merely a dwelling place for Jewish families. It is a center for *gemilus chasadim*, doing good deeds, and the learning and living of Torah.

No less was the house of the Tenenbaum family on Belilius Street. It had been said that "the Yerushalmis were of a special breed" — where strife and jealousy never appeared. All of Jerusalem was one big family which married within the community

— and many can still verbally relate their genealogies dating back many generations. We all know that when it comes to family one tries hard to please. The Tenenbaums treated everyone as family and worked to please one and all in a way that was special. HaRav Moshe Dovid Tenenbaum was the *Rosh Vaad HaYeshivos* of Israel, the umbrella organization representing the yeshivos to the Government. It was established in Europe under the aegis of the Chafetz Chaim, R' Chaim Ozer Grodzinski and others, to provide financial support for the yeshivos. In *Eretz Yisrael* its function served to delay or exempt the conscription of yeshivah students into the military, and act as an intermediary to the Government. R' Tenenbaum worked not only on behalf of the yeshivos, but on many vital issues involving the religious population and the Jewish people at large.

The Tenenbaum home on Belilius Street was approached from a shaded garden from which a flight of stone steps reached high up — physically high to the apartment where the family lived, and spiritually high to a world of *chesed* ... "*Olam chesed yibaneh* — A world of kindness will be built." Together with his Rebbetzin Rivkah Liebe, the house evolved into a warm welcoming home and shelter for many of *Am Yisrael* who needed it. Whoever entered this home — whether it be a man of prominence who needed wise counsel, or a simple stranger in need of lodging — found a haven. The great personalities of Jerusalem, from Torah and secular sectors alike, found a warm and patient reception here. *Roshei Yeshivah*, the Brisker Rav, famous Rebbes, spiritual leaders and giants, influential politicians and other distinguished laymen came to consult with R' Tenenbaum. From the political and military sectors came Yitzchak Navon, Shimon Peres, Teddy Kollek and others; Ben Gurion was in contact with R' Tenenbaum, though he did not visit Belilius Street in person. Many prominent statesmen and personalities from varied fields came to seek counsel.

People were always welcome and the door rarely closed. There was the porter from Salonika who could hardly speak but came to collect leftover *cholent* on *Motzaei Shabbos* — enough to last him through the week; the deranged girl who had survived the ravages of the concentration camps; the Yemenite boy who had arrived in Israel, one lone member of his family, on the "Magic Carpet." He no longer knew his father or mother for they were images buried in the deepest crevices of his mind, but he sought them in every Jew he met. He was brought up by Rebbetzin Rivkah Liebe and it was she who prepared his *tannaim* (engagement party) — even when she was weakened by illness. These "living history books" that entered into the heart of the family numbered so many that one could have filled a library with them. There was even another small Shabbos visitor, a cat, who would wait faithfully in the garden each Shabbos afternoon for her portion of whatever crumbs were tossed away.

Rivkah Liebe rarely set a table for only her family. Having a houseful of guests was an everyday event in her home. However, one Pesach, on the night of the *seder*, she suddenly realized that the family had neglected to invite guests, something that in her mind was unthinkable. "*Kol dichfin yeisei v'yeichol* — All that are hungry should come and eat." She and her husband interpreted this invitation to include both spiritual and physical nourishment. "We are not beginning our *seder* until you find some guests!" she announced. So the boys went into Meah Shearim and returned with a young couple, American tourists, with their baby, who gratefully accepted the invitation. Now the Rebbetzin was content knowing that she was providing a home to needy people. The *seder* finally leaped to life, complete with the newcomers.

Rebbetzin Rivkah Liebe was an energetic "community worker" in her own right and a warm human being whose efforts sprang from a true love of people. She was active in many charitable institutions and other important causes — with refugees, orphans and new immigrants. She worked with the healthy and the sick, and she did it all in a modest and discreet manner. She never divulged any of the deeds of *chesed* that she performed in the hospitals to anyone. These only came to light by chance after her passing, when the heads of various departments of hospitals for the chronically ill and incurable contacted the family to ask, "Where is the Rebbetzin? Why have her visits stopped?"

The entire Tenenbaum family had earned a reputation for their *chesed* work, and for their patient listening ear. They loved people — they had great *ahavas Yisrael*. People of all ages and walks of life ascended those steps on Belilius Street carrying a burden and invariably went away lighter and happier. It was almost a "natural" occurrence then, that Dorit, the would-be *giyores* (convert) from Switzerland, found her way to the Tenenbaum home.

Dorit was immediately attracted to this family. They were her model, her ideal of what a Jewish family should be. Through them she learned of the beauty of Shabbos and Yom Tov, and what it meant to be a Jew. They shared with her their vast treasure house of stories and traditions of Jewish life, of the *tzaddikim* and ordinary Jews of the olden days, whose histories shed beacons of light for all future generations.

In the company of the Tenenbaum family, Dorit felt she had "come home" without knowing why, and she did not want to leave. So, through the *beis din*, she underwent a formal conversion and was given the name "Ruth," as is often the practice in renaming female converts to Judaism. Dorit learned that the first Ruth was a Moabite princess, a noble soul who clung faithfully to her mother-in-law Naomi and to the God and the Torah of Israel. In demonstrating sincerity and commitment, Ruth merited to become the great-grandmother of David, king of Israel! The Swiss girl from the border town in the Alps had traveled this long road until she, too, could say with all her heart, "Your people are my people and your G-d is my G-d" (*Ruth* 1:16).

Great was the excitement and joy for Dorit/Ruth when she came to Belilius to share the wonderful news that she was a *kallah*. She had met a young *chozer b'teshuvah* who was studying to be a *sofer*, a scribe, and they had become engaged to be married. The neighbors were thrilled at the good news and enthusiastically joined in the celebration. The young couple was elated, but before wedding plans could proceed, Ruth approached R' Tenenbaum to ask his advice. "My mother in Switzerland asks that I go home to visit her and the rest of the family before my wedding. I feel a little strange now that I have converted, knowing that we are so different in our ways and that they do not wish to attend my wedding. Should I go?" "Go by all means," answered R' Tenenbaum with his usual tact and wisdom. "Your Swiss family deserves it! For was it not they who brought you up and nourished you throughout your tender years? You must be extremely careful not to hurt them. Come to see us when you return."

Dorit/Ruth embarked on her long and difficult journey. Air travel, still in its infancy, was generally regarded with great trepidation. And so Ruth set out to face the rigors of the voyage by sea and rail. She left Jerusalem, the Holy City that had drawn her close to Yiddishkeit and had brought her under *kanfei haShechinah* — the wings of the *Shechinah*. She left *Eretz Yisrael*, where she had found her foothold and direction, to return to the little town in the mountains of Switzerland where she had grown up.

After being away for over six weeks, Ruth's first stop upon her return to Israel was the house on Belilius Street. She embraced Rebbetzin Rivkah Liebe warmly, feeling her tenderness, and accepted the Rebbetzin's offer of a place at the dining room table. Rivkah Liebe gazed intently at Ruth, not saying a word, but worrying about her. Ruth looked wan and tired and something in her eyes indicated that all was not well with her. Ruth remained silent and shy for a few minutes, but after a warm glass of tea and a few words of encouragement, she began to speak:

"My family was pleased to see me, but they found it very hard to accept Ruth in place of Dorit. They saw a Christian girl leave their house, and a Jewish girl return — one who could not eat with them, whose way of dressing was different, guided by the laws of *tzinius*, and who was soon getting married to a young Jewish man in the Land of Israel.

"Things were somewhat awkward at first, but when I began to speak of my wedding, the atmosphere became very tense. Suddenly a strange silence fell over the room. All of them were eyeing me and looking at each other in a way that I could not understand. Mama even began to cry and Grandmama shook her walking stick at her, warning her to stop. Then Grandmama stood up from her chair, straightened her glasses and hobbled out of the room. When she came back she was holding a package in her hand. It was this one!"

Ruth took a brown paper package out of a shopping bag and placed it on the table. All eyes were riveted with intense curiosity on the crinkled brown paper bundle as Ruth continued, the words rapidly pouring out. "Grandmama told me that this package was mine and that my real mother left it for me many years ago, just as the war broke out. She begged them to look after me, and asked that no one but I should open this package — and only when I was engaged to be wed. They did as she requested — they are very honest people. They did not want to tell me any more. I tried to ask more questions — I would have loved to know who my real mother was and what she was like. I never knew anything about this until now — but they all remained silent; it was very hard.

"When it was time to leave them I could feel their pain at losing me, and I felt the same way about leaving. But I sensed that they were relieved to finally be able to unburden themselves of their secret. I am still in a blur, my thoughts are very unclear; I do not understand all this completely." Ruth's expression was one of confusion and distress. "And I have been frightened to open the package."

The Tenenbaum family sat in a circle around Ruth and her parcel. The mystery was too great to bear and everyone was eager to find out what was in the package. R' Moshe Dovid, with his keen intelligence, assessed all facets of the situation and acted with strength and conviction. "Open it!" he said. "Go on, open it now! It will be okay!" Ruth did not need further coaxing; she hurriedly tore open the old brown paper, and revealed a leatherbound volume which she placed carefully on the table before her. R' Moshe Dovid smiled one of the warm smiles that were so much a part of him, picked up the volume and read the title aloud. "*Siddur Korban Minchah!* The *Siddur Korban Minchah* — the *siddur* traditionally given to a Jewish bride as a gift at her wedding!

"Ruth, as you must realize by now, your mother was a Jewish woman," R' Moshe Dovid said gently to her. "Either the Nazis were close behind her, or perhaps the Swiss authorities were threatening to hand her over. Seeing this and fearing for her life, she placed you with this Swiss family — to bring you up as their own child. They were surely *Chasidei Umos HaOlam*, Righteous Gentiles. Think about it — here was a Jewish mother believing that her last days in this world were approaching. This woman had to take a courageous step — giving her precious child to gentiles to raise as their own. At the same time, she had to think of some way to send her daughter an all-important message in the distant future — to save her from marrying a non-Jewish man and thus becoming lost to the Jewish people forever. How could she apprise you of the truth? Do you now see the message in front of you? Do you see, Ruth? You had a wonderful and caring Jewish mother and you were born a *bas Yisrael,* a Jewish daughter!"

Great was the merit of this unknown Jewish woman and her gift of the *siddur.* She gave her life *al Kiddush Hashem* — but left behind a daughter who, seemingly on her own, found her way back to the Jewish fold, even before her wedding day. There really is no such thing as "circumstance — purely by chance" to our way of thinking. It was surely in the merit of the gift of the *Siddur Korban Minchah* that Ruth returned to her true roots.

Anna

This is the story of Anna, the bitter-sweet tale of a proud and noble woman with many memories. She remembered that she had come from a traditional Jewish family near Odessa, and she had learned to speak Yiddish in her parents' home. Her father owned a small vineyard where he made his own wines which he stored in large vats in the ground. He was considered an important businessman. Since he was self-employed, the Bolsheviks, at the advent of the Revolution, claimed that he was an enemy, withholding funds from the "true cause." On this pretext, they sent a mob of soldiers to the vineyard. The soldiers had with them a fire engine, which they used to pump the wine out of the vats. The confiscated wine would either be drunk on the spot or carted away as best they could. Much of it was carelessly spilled and ruined on the way. Worse yet, Anna's poor father was tortured, forced to stand in ice—cold water for days, to compel him to reveal the hiding place where he had supposedly hidden his fortune. Haplessly, the poor Jew cried, "But I have no fortune, no money! You have already destroyed my whole livelihood, everything that I owned! Please let us be, let us be! Please!" His protestations fell on deaf and cruel ears, for not only was property smashed and ruined but, as the peasants became increasingly drunk, even human life was trampled underfoot. Only little Anna, running to and fro amid the chaos and mayhem, went unnoticed. But her childhood memory registered enough bitter images for her to subsequently present an accurate portrayal of the Communist "heroes."

Years later, as a married woman, Anna was involved in the baking of Passover matzos. Under Communist rule, the religious practices of the Jews in Russia were stifled. They were forbidden to observe Torah and *mitzvos*, and subsequently forgot a great deal of their Jewish traditions. Still, Anna never forgot how to bake matzos for Pesach. This had to be done in great secrecy, for fear of discovery by the authorities. Even the children could not be let in on the secret lest their teachers in school elicit this information from them. Once the matzos were baked, it was Anna's task to distribute them among several Jewish families. She secreted the matzos in a pillowcase and warily climbed the steps to the roof of an apartment building. She did not dare to carry them openly in the street for fear of the KGB. If she were caught carrying them, the penalty would be extremely severe.

As she reached the roof of the building, she heard footsteps behind her. She did not dare to look around to see who was following her. Her feet moved faster and faster until she broke into a run. Stealing a furtive glance backwards, she saw a shadowy figure pursuing her, and with pounding heart, she jumped from roof to roof, her precious bundle still tucked under her arm. Finally, with great help from Above, she slipped breathlessly into a narrow hiding place, watching in fearful relief as her pursuer ran past her. "*Ha lachma anya* — This is the bread of affliction that our fathers ate in Egypt." And with great devotion and courage, in our generation, Jews eat it with longing under the most difficult circumstances, relishing every bite. Acts such as these were surely one of the *zechusim*, the spiritual merits, for the redemption of Russian Jewry in later years.

Anna, the courageous one, was a doctor. "A specialist of the eyes," she would say. She had money, status and many patients, and was highly respected. Her husband was also well established and successful. Sorely absent from their lives, however, were children. They had no children until, miraculously, at the age of 40, Anna conceived! She spent most of the nine months of her pregnancy lying in bed, and as a reward for her prudent caution a beautiful baby boy came into the world. They named him Michoel. It was Michoel who would change the lives of Anna and her husband forever.

Anna was finally a mother, but her tribulations were far from over. Her little boy grew and the family decided that for his sake they would emigrate to *Eretz Yisrael*, far away from the Communist threat. They applied for an exit visa from Russia, knowing full well that this would mean an instant dismissal from work, as well as other hardships. Retribution was swift in coming. Anna's husband was arrested on a trumped-up charge and sent to Siberia. He, among others, became one of the famed "Prisoners of Zion," incarcerated for wishing to emigrate to the Holy Land for the love of Zion. "*Tziyon, Tziyon, halo tishali* — ask for the welfare of those imprisoned ones." Anna, using her maiden name, moved with her son to Siberia, to be near her husband, to provide support for him in any way she could. Bribery and influence could sometimes ameliorate the lot of a prisoner, and just knowing that his family was close by would provide encouragement at such a trying time.

The political wheels turned slowly, but with pressure from behind the scenes, they turned. Anna discreetly bribed officials, and made herself known in high places where she cajoled and coaxed until her husband was released and the coveted exit visa procured. A sick and broken man returned to his family. They quickly prepared to leave the hated stepmother Russia as soon as possible!

Arriving in transit in Vienna, the halfway point for Russian *olim*, Anna asked her son Michoel, then aged 13, "Should we not go on to Switzerland, where Papa can receive the best medical care?" Michoel was shocked at the suggestion and would not hear of any such thing. "Papa suffered for Zion, not Switzerland!" he exclaimed. "He was an *Assir Tzion*, a Prisoner of Zion!" So the family traveled to the Land of Israel, and eventually settled in Jerusalem.

There, misfortune struck once again. Anna's husband was too weak to withstand any further adversity. He had merited to bring his family to the Holy City, but he soon passed away. Still, he was more fortunate than many of his Russian Jewish brothers whom he left behind, as he was brought to *kever Yisrael* in Yerushalayim.

Time passed, and Michoel grew up. His mother Anna had begun to work intermittently in the medical profession and he went to a yeshivah in Yerushalayim. Little by little, Michoel, now a young adult, became attracted to Torah and *mitzvos*. For a Russian orphan growing up virtually on his own, this was a major accomplishment, especially since his mother knew very little about the Jewish religion. Any change for her, especially at her stage in life, was extremely hard. In the past she had suffered untold pain for the sake of this son and for the sake of an ideal.

Now for his sake she made her kitchen kosher and did her best to keep the *mitzvos*. She became known for her *chesed*, her acts of kindness. Neighbors would relate, for example, how, despite financial straits, Anna took the only meat she could afford that week — a pound of turkey — and prepared it for the mourners sitting *shivah* in the adjoining apartment.

It is not our place to question why events unfolded as they did. Why, after so much struggling throughout her life, did Anna fall victim to cancer? We can only weep at the thought, for it hurts. But we cannot ask "why," for our human comprehension is limited. Can we possibly understand the ways of Hashem? Is it not better to accept the decrees of our Heavenly Father the way young children accept the directives of their parents?

Some of Anna's neighbors met her at the *Kotel* and urged her, "Anna, come *daven* with us here, in this wonderful holy place, for the *Shechinah*, Hashem's Presence, has never left this spot." But Anna barely responded except to admit that she had never learned how to pray, that no one had taught her. Her kind neighbors tried to explain about the greatness of the Creator of the Universe, of never despairing of Heavenly mercy, of pouring out one's heart first in praise and then in petition, like a child before its father or a subject before the king; she listened but did not reply.

Friday night arrived and some of those neighbors came to help Anna light the Shabbos candles. Suddenly she broke out in a cry that shook the roots of the soul — "*Di neshamah veint! Ich vill davenen!* — The soul weeps ... for I want to pray!" When in this generation did such a *tefillah* rise to heaven? Anna was truly a noble soul.

A large crowd is assembled in a beautiful hall in Jerusalem. Many years have passed, and Anna, long deceased, is doubtless sitting among the righteous women of the generations. Surely tonight she and her husband are here among the guests, for *Chazal* teach that the souls of the departed relatives will join with their children on the day of their *simchah*. "Do you remember Anna?" one woman asks another. Thus, they begin to talk and re-member. They do not reminisce for very long, however, for the young *chasan* — serious, bearded, a strictly observant young man in every way — is coming towards his *kallah*, a special joy radiating between them. He, accompanied by two *Rabbanim* who stand in place of his father and father-in-law (for the bride's fa-ther is also deceased), approaches to make the veiling ceremony, or the "*bedekken*" as it is traditionally called. Students whom this young man has been instrumental in bringing from Russia to learn Torah in *Eretz Yisrael* are following behind him, clapping and singing. All the assembled guests are caught up in the hap-piness of the moment and are tapping and singing, smiling to one another and rejoicing at the wonderful event before them — Michoel is about to be married. *Rabbanim* from the yeshivah where he learned and also taught others are surrounding him and singing his praises. The atmosphere is electric. Everyone is laughing as well as crying, for the *chasan* has no parents. But he is far from alone in the world, lacking neither friends nor good deeds; he has become an outstanding person. Anna, do you see all of this, your work, your son who is continuing what you start-ed? Your heartfelt prayer was not in vain!

"*Di neshamah veint! Ich vill davenen!*" Anna's words echo on-ward. Anna, Anna — your *tefillah* was surely accepted.

As a Deer Pursued by the Hunter

The Jewish communities of Syria have ancient roots which can be traced back to the Second Temple. These communities flourished for a long time, with many of their residents becoming wealthy and established. Their *chachamim* and yeshivos also enjoyed rapid growth and academic success. Many years ago, the Muslims were fairly tolerant towards the Jewish community, for it was the Jews who brought financial acuity, prosperity and progress to any community in which they settled. At the time of Cromwell, the exiled English Jews were even invited to return to England from their new settlements in Europe, "for they were good for business!"

The tide turned, however, when the Arab countries — Syria, of course, among them — would not tolerate the existence of a Jewish State. The world witnessed waves of immigration to the Land of Israel from all areas of the Middle East, but the communities that remained in the Arab countries and did not go up to the Land were subjected to great animosity, especially in times of local political unrest or war with Israel.

Although the Jews in Syria could still function, attend schools and colleges, and succeed in commercial life and in social circles, their activities were carefully monitored, with each community member under careful watch. All were regarded as potential spies for Israel and subjected to many degradations. The media was full of distorted news broadcasts regarding Israel, especially during wartime. If the Jews of Syria wished to hear the truth, they had to listen to radios while hidden under their blankets, tuned in to *Kol Yisrael*. Letters from relatives in Israel had to travel via the United States where friends and relatives would assist in rerouting them. Syrian Jews were not permitted to leave the country, for the authorities suspected that they would make their way to Israel. If they left for other countries, they had to sign over to the government all their possessions — including businesses and homes. A family member was usually left behind as a "hostage," and would suffer tragic repercussions if the rest of the family failed to return. If a Jew wanted to travel to another city within Syria, for example from Khaleb to Damascus, he needed written permission from the Security Police in both the city of his origin and of his destination, and had to report daily to the Security Police. When he wished to return home, a second round of bureaucracy ensued, with official documents issued, in the reverse.

The Syrian Jews' identity cards were stamped "*YEHUD* — JEW," in large red letters. Sometimes, a Jewish householder would answer his door in the evening to find a government official pushing his way into the house. The family members would be counted, other information registered, and then the government agents would leave, the family peering after them in fright. The Jews lived in mortal fear, knowing that the long arm of the hostile government and its police was poised to find a scapegoat, a victim among them. It has been noted that as a group, the Jews of the Syrian community are frequently introverted in their personalities, guarded in what they say, and in public their manner is quiet and reserved, even terse. They certainly had reason to exercise self-control. Without intending to, the Muslim authorities and their regime had become prime educators in the subject of *middos* — a Jew simply had to adapt himself and learn to "guard his tongue" on a permanent basis in order to survive.

Many grim accounts are told of those who were either caught trying to escape to the Land of Israel themselves, or were trying to help other Jews to safety. Their fate often involved being taken without trial to a padded cell, where for months they were subjected to cruel torture, starvation, merciless beatings, and the crushing of their teeth as well as their spirit. Their families had no access to them, and there was no possibility of intervention from "Amnesty International" or other such agencies to help them.

When one young man who had spent a period of time in a government jail — with all its attendant horrors — was released, he went to work in his father's shop. While he worked there he observed how his father would stealthily meet with different people, and without a word to him, disappear into a small room somewhere behind the market and speak in subdued tones. One day the truth dawned on him. "Father! Take care! I know that you are helping people to escape." His father raised a warning finger to his lips, hushing his son into silence. Soon afterwards, he and his family were also off on the trail to freedom, but it was forbidden to publicize that fact even among one's own kin!

Thus the Jews, who lived in their own separate districts, knew that whatever the cost, it was better to flee, even if it meant relinquishing one's last penny, than to be subjected to the terror of the Security Police who held them accountable for their every action. When a member of the community did succeed in getting away, his relatives or other Jews who knew him had to inform the authorities of this, for fear of retribution. Upon receiving this information, the Muslims would move into the missing family's house, and publicly auction off all the property.

Moussa, or "Moshe" in Hebrew, now a married man with children, who is learning in a Kollel in Jerusalem, described how he made his escape:

It was almost 25 years ago, when I was a teenager of about 16. My older brother, David, approached me secretly and told me that he was planning to escape, taking along Savta, our grandmother, whom we called Se'uta in Syria. My father's mother had been dreaming for years of seeing the shores of the Holy Land with her own eyes. As she aged, she yearned for the privilege of living in the Holy City of Jerusalem and enjoying freedom among Jews — freedom to live as a Jew and breathe as a Jew without fear of what each day would bring.

The risks were considerable. I could not inform my parents or sisters of the plan, not to mention friends or outsiders. There could be no good-byes or farewell parties, and we could take with us only what a person would carry on a typical outing.

I was quite tense and frightened, and feared that someone might glance at my face and guess that something was wrong. My brother encouraged me, and surprisingly Se'uta was the bravest of us all. "We are all going on a summer holiday!" she joked, and handed out good things to eat, although she must have been petrified inside.

We made the trip in a taxi which undoubtedly had traversed the route on numerous previous occasions, and the driver drove quickly and in silence. Our destination was Lebanon and the papers that had been issued stated that we two boys were going on an overnight trip supervised by our grandmother. We saw the checkpoint at the border looming ahead of us and I felt my mouth go dry. Se'uta was watching me and she drew some peanuts from her bag saying, "Go on, eat some!" Grateful for something to do, I made a *berachah* and obeyed her instructions. At the checkpoint the guard put his head in our window and scrutinized us for a few painful minutes, then handed back our documents and we were on our way. It surely looked harmless enough: two youngsters with their grandmother on an outing.

Our taxi sped on into the growing dusk. We were happy that it was now evening, for the dark offered a shield of security for us. One of the main Jewish communities of Lebanon was awaiting us. There was no reception committee and no fanfare, but a secret room had been set aside in one of the houses. We got out, carrying our small bags, all that had been possible to take with us, and were enveloped in the pale light of the room. We were boys from religious homes and our *tefillas Minchah* and *Maariv* of that evening had the power of the *Kol Nidrei* of Yom Kippur. We were grateful to our Heavenly Father that we had arrived safely so far, and we prayed that the remainder of our escape would be as smooth.

From then on, until we moved from the small room, we lost track of time. I doubt if others in the community knew that Jewish fugitives from Syria were holed up in that room, or even knew of its existence. Food was brought to us by a man named Nissim, who acted on behalf of the Lebanese Jewish community and was responsible for refugees. He did his utmost to make us comfortable, and this was no small feat under the circumstances, but we were prepared for discomfort.

It was around two days later that we received the O.K. to make our next move. Contact had been made with Israeli authorities and a rendezvous had been arranged.

By now, the excitement was mounting and we were anxious to be on our way. Nissim warned us to calm down and control our feelings. "You two youngsters, settle down! We are not there yet! Better that you *daven* a bit that you should make it with the help of G-d."

Quieter now, we, together with Se'uta, followed him, as he showed us which direction to take. On a side street were two sanitation men standing alongside a large truck filled with garbage. We eyed each other partly in amazement and partly in disgust: *This* was to be our taxi to freedom?

There was no arguing, and no other way. We bid a warm farewell to Monsieur Nissim, who had so thoughtfully cared for us in our time of need. My brother embraced him and showered him with blessings, "May Hashem bless you and all of yours in this world and the next for this *gemilus chasadim* that we can never repay!" Nissim in turn wished us a safe journey and added a request that we remember him at the *Kotel HaMaaravi* when we arrive in Jerusalem.

Then we climbed into the trash-filled truck. It was a re-lief to find that a corner had been set aside for us where no smelly refuse would fall. The engine grunted and churned for a minute, sounding like an old man reluctant to start his day, and then roared to life.

So we chugged down the road on a route that none of us could envision. We, who were seated on the bottom of the inside of the truck, suffered more from the stench than from the journey. Anyone looking in our direction would see only an old garbage truck with worn-out shock absorbers bumping up and down on its way to dump its contents. Nobody could begin to imagine that precious human cargo was concealed within. Time passed, and we saw the gleam of sunshine above our heads as the sun rose in the sky. It was nearly noon by the time the truck ground to a halt.

"Everyone out!" called the driver, and we stiffly climbed out of our "limousine." More surprises awaited us, for now we found ourselves on a deserted beach. Following our guide, we walked along the seashore to a natural harbor where a small boat was tied. Seated near the outboard motor was an elderly crinkle-faced Lebanese seaman who rose to help Se'uta get into the boat.

"David!" I cried. "You don't think that we are going to sail to the Land of Israel in this 'saucepan'!" To my mind, the boat seemed very tiny, although it had more than likely ferried more Jewish refugees to safety than I could ever imagine.

But my brother comforted me, "Don't worry, Moussa. I know that the Israelis are picking us up in midsea. This is the last leg of our journey — we are nearly there *b'ezras Hashem*!" Seeing my doleful eyes and last-minute panic, Se'uta comforted me with a smile, "Don't just look at the outside of the pot, try tasting the contents! Not everything is as it seems from the outside! Get in the boat, my child." We looked at one another and began to smile, despite our fear. We were indeed nearly there, but we had been through some rough times over the last few days and the stress was still weighing on us.

As we set out, Se'uta tried to be brave again, "See? I promised you a summer holiday." It was a small boat but a sturdy one. Slowly the waves rose higher and the current became choppier. The old boatman remained silent and held on tightly to his rudder keeping his face turned toward the water. The swell of the waves became even greater as we moved out of territorial limits, and we all felt a pathetic feeling of helplessness as the boat sailed between the seas and the open expanse on the sky. I felt my stomach churn with the rolling tide and wondered if we would indeed make it this time. Where was the promised Israeli vessel? I glanced sideways at Se'uta. So much had passed between us in the last few days, more than we would willingly admit outright. There was only one consolation to which we all could turn. Se'uta's lips were moving and a tear rolled down her cheek. I turned my face so that she would not see my eyes full of tears, and began to *daven* that we should reach safety.

Suddenly we saw it. In midsea, between the Heavens above and the blue carpet of the seas, a stately ship was coming towards us. It had cut its engines so as not to capsize our little boat, and was awaiting us — a boat of the Israeli forces. We were home! *Baruch Hashem,* we had made it! We clambered aboard and grabbed the hands of the crew to thank them and embrace them with affection. "Whoever saves a soul in Israel is as if he has saved a whole world," and for sure that day they saved our world.

We arrived in Jerusalem at the beginning of Elul, and made our way to the *Kotel HaMaaravi.* We arrived there with a burning desire to pray at the remaining tangible fragment of the Holy Temple. Even more important, we came with the knowledge that we had a debt to repay. We had to pray on behalf of our parents and family, and also to remember Monsieur Nissim as we had promised, and all the other Jews still in danger in the Arab exile. It was about 5:30 in the morning when we, along with our valiant grandmother, arrived at the Wall, and the excitement we felt was almost palpable. The swallows, mentioned in *Jeremiah,* often circle the *Kotel* at that time of morning. They serve like an honor guard, twittering and rapidly circling again and yet again. At the end of the *Shacharis* prayer, the different *minyanim* sounded their *shofaros* one after another in a rising chorus, triumphant to the King of all kings. *Baruch Hashem,* we had arrived!

Soon afterward, my brother and I enrolled in a yeshivah program and began our lives in the Land of Israel.

Much time passed — over 10 years in fact — before other members of the family joined them. One of Moussa's uncles with his wife and eight children planned to escape.

All the neighbors in the apartment complex where the Cohen family lived were Arabs. On the surface, the Arabs maintained cordial ties with the family they knew to be Jewish, as the Cohens made no secret of their religion. However, these neighbors were silently observing and waiting to see if perhaps one day these Jews might decide to escape. If the Arabs would be able to pass on this information to the authorities, they would be given considerable monetary rewards. And besides, just imagine, if there would be one of those public sales ... the Cohens had such a lovely lamp in their front room ... and good carpets, and a mahogany table. Yes, there was much to gain!

The Cohens made their plans with care. They had young children, and this made matters more dangerous. After consulting with one of the Jewish agents experienced in these matters, they contacted professional guides and chose a relatively difficult escape route. Huge sums of money had to be paid out in advance to the "guides" who were responsible for supervising the operation. Great care had to be taken in selecting them, for they were Arabs and many of them were neither reliable nor trustworthy. Some had been known to stop halfway over the mountains and demand extra money, knowing that the Jews had additional cash hidden in their belongings. They would threaten that if they didn't receive more money they would simply abandon their charges in the middle of nowhere and disappear. Inevitably, the Jews on the run were captured by the Syrians.

Other families described what they experienced when tramping across the mountains in great danger. One young father held his small baby tightly in his grasp. To his horror, his foot slipped on the mountainside, and his little one fell out of his arms and down into a muddy indentation in the cleft of a rock. He immediately began to climb down into the hole to rescue the infant, who had previously been given drugs to induce sleep. "Leave her there!" hissed the guide. "There is no time for lost children — we can be caught if you slow us down!" But the father glared back angrily at the Arab, his heart weeping for his child whom he loved and would never leave behind. If Hashem willed them to live, then they would all live. "You may be callous enough to forget your child, but I'm not!" he retorted. "I will find you. You go on ahead!" The guide turned his back and bounded on ahead, the group following him. The father, ignoring the guide's warning, clambered down the rock, recovered his baby, and looked up ahead to see the group rapidly disappearing into the trees. With the infant held tightly in his arms, he ran as fast as he could after the group, shortened the gap between them and, thank G-d, he made it!

⊙⇥⥆⊙

To allay their neighbor's suspicions, for several weeks before the Cohen family was due to leave, they made a point of going out each evening together with the children. Once they went shopping, once to the park — just so that their neighbors would grow accustomed to seeing the family going out as a group. They would nod to their neighbors on their way out, and it became a regular sight to see this family taking their evening "stroll."

It was on a midweek evening that they had arranged to leave. By then all family members had been rehearsed and trained as to precisely how they would move and conduct themselves — as if they were involved in a military operation.

At a prearranged signal, Mother put a small bag over her shoulder and the children each took similar knapsacks and tote bags, as if they were going on a family outing. Father, who remained at home for a short while, opened all the lights, turned the radio on high volume, and sat down to listen. At least he appeared to be listening, but how could he possibly pay attention to the radio while he was in such a state of anxiety? His thoughts were flying in a hundred different directions, but most definitely were not in tune with the evening's broadcast. The children followed Mother quietly down the stairs in pairs, the younger ones holding each other's hands, and the youngest, about six years old, holding onto Mother. They all knew what was expected of them, and mentally reviewed the instructions that had been drilled into them over the past few days. Now it was for real.

Reaching the outskirts of town, each child took a different route. Mother clutched the youngest one tightly, praying that he would not start to cry or complain as the "baby" of the family could sometimes do, and she cautiously set out on her way, walking along as the houses thinned and the forest began. They were going to make their way by foot over the high mountain range to Turkey and, with G-d's help, to the safety of the Land of Israel.

Mr. Cohen checked his watch. It was now time to move. He gazed longingly one last time at his home, left the lights on and the radio blaring, kissed the *mezuzah* concealed in the doorpost, and rapidly disappeared into the dusk. He walked along yet another route until he left the town and joined his family anxiously awaiting him in the forest. There were others yet to come — some Jewish youths with the sister of one of them, and the guide. As night fell, these others appeared from among the trees. And so they started their journey, a difficult and dangerous trip at the onset of the winter months. However, as there were so many people in the group, it was the only way to go.

Hours upon hours of trudging on foot passed — around 30 hours in total on the grueling trail. They sensed danger all around, and each crackle of a twig startled them. Despite the frosty weather conditions, the Cohens and their children persevered and kept going, although the smaller ones often had to be carried. The Arab guide kept pressuring them to keep up the pace and to go even faster. Heaven forbid that anyone should be caught. The youths gritted their teeth and strode on firmly through the night, but the young girl, the sister of one of them, began to gasp. She cried out in fear, "We are like deer pursued by the hunter, without mercy and with no relief in sight." They eyed her anxiously and encouraged her, "Soon we will be there, G-d willing. Do not give up — you must keep going!" "I don't feel well!" she wept. Her eyes began to roll back, and then, to everyone's horror, she fainted. Her brother did not wait for unsolicited advice, but scooped up her limp body in his arms, gritted his teeth and continued to trudge across the rough terrain.

The first subtle shades of morning were appearing through the trees and the scenery began to change a little. They were still in the mountains, but the few houses and settlements in the distance looked different. Suddenly voices, in an unfamiliar dialect, were heard ahead of them. Soldiers appeared, with rifles cocked and bayonets pointed at the group. "Halt!" came the obvious command.

Mrs. Cohen began to cry and the children, grabbing tightly at her skirts, began to sob too. The guide turned rapidly on his heel and disappeared like steam evaporating in air. As *Chazal* state, "There is no one that we can rely on except our Father in Heaven!" And so it was with them.

"We've come so far — and yet it's like leaping out of the frying pan and into the fire!" exclaimed the young men in dismay. "Wait, don't be hasty!" retorted Mr. Cohen, as he took a hesitant step forward and approached the patrol. He spoke a classical Arabic, and they understood, for they were Turks.

"We are weary and in need of help!" he explained, taking the initiative. "None of us is armed. We are only civilians, a family with young children, as you can see, and we come in peace. Please help us now. Whatever you do, don't send us back, we beg you!"

They followed the Turkish patrol that directed them onto a narrow road and then called for transport. The group, footsore and weary, soon found themselves seated in military vehicles, being driven to the offices of the Border Police.

After consultation with officials, they were held in custody in a Turkish jail for a period of six uncomfortable weeks. The group produced papers and names that proved they had family ties and relatives in Israel who would help them if the Turkish authorities would contact the Israelis. The tension was palpable. They had no way of knowing which way the tide would turn, or what the Turks would finally decide to do with them. The Jews waited and prayed fervently that they would not — *chas veshalom* — be sent back to Syria!

Finally, the miracle that they had prayed for happened. The haggling between the Turkish authorities and the Israelis bore fruit. The negotiations for their release were successful, and with great joy and relief they at last set foot on the soil of the Land of their Fathers.

We were pursued as deer before the hunter, without mercy, without relief, but with the help of G-d, we merited to be among those saved.

The Impenetrable
Shield

Robert, a Jewish businessman from England, travels frequently — all across Europe, to the United States and to Israel. His life story is a fascinating one, including how — at a relatively advanced age — he became religious, but that is perhaps for another time.

On one of his first trips to Israel, he met the Tenenbaum family who live in Jerusalem. They struck up a friendship, and whenever he had business in Israel, he made sure to contact them. On one of his recent journeys, he asked them for a favor.

"I have a good friend living in Detroit," began Robert, "who was married last week. I was visiting with him and his wife and I told him that you had gotten some unusual *mezuzos* for me, written in Jerusalem by a very worthy Rabbi who writes with *kavanos* for each individual case. Although my friend Jonathan is not an observant Jew, I attempted, to the best of my ability, to explain the importance of the *mitzvah* of *mezuzah* and the concept of *mezuzos* providing *shemirah*, protection, to a Jewish home. He was receptive to the idea and agreed to put *mezuzos* on some of the doorposts of his home. I know that all *mezuzos* written by reliable scribes are acceptable and bring protection," continued Robert, "but what I would like to do is give Jonathan those extra-special ones for a wedding gift. It's something that I truly want to do for him. He may not yet keep any of the *mitzvos*, for he has not had teachers or role models from whom to learn, but he is a good soul! Would you be able to get four *mezuzos* for me to give him?"

R' Tenenbaum happily agreed to Robert's request. He went to the venerable R' Fischel of Yerushalayim, *Rosh Yeshivah* of Shaarei Shamayim, and ordered special *mezuzos* which Robert took with him to America.

On his next trip to Detroit, Robert presented his friend with the gift of the *mezuzos* and helped Jonathan affix them to some of the doorposts of their newly purchased home. As he left, he wished the young couple health and happiness as they started their new lives together.

Jonathan and his bride Sally had longed for a large family and were disappointed that children did not arrive as quickly as they had wished. Finally, their hopes were fulfilled and the happy moment arrived; Sally gave birth to a beautiful baby girl whom they called Vicky. The little one filled their home with the love and pure joy that children bring. The young couple eagerly took to the task of raising her.

All was fine, their lives full of love and contentment, until one evening when they were sitting outside in the garden, the baby fast asleep in her crib upstairs. Sally suddenly heard a crackling sound coming from within the house.

They ran inside and, looking up the stairs, found to their horror that the entire second floor was swathed in black smoke. Jonathan let out a bloodcurdling scream that was heard by the next-door neighbors, "Fire! We've got a fire! Quickly, somebody, call the fire department! Vicky is up there! G-d help us! Our precious baby!"

Perhaps an electrical short had sparked the fire, no one could be sure, but the flames had set fire to the woodwork and were spreading rapidly from place to place. Sally stood momentarily paralyzed, but then she joined in and began to scream, "Fire! The baby! Get me my baby! Fire!" Her husband tried desperately to battle the choking smoke and rising inferno, to blindly climb the seemingly endless flight of steps to rescue his beloved child, but there was no way to penetrate the flames. Within minutes, neighbors arrived on the scene, and dragged the young couple outside the house. People seemed to be running in all directions, fear and foreboding etched on their faces. Within minutes the young couple's world was turned upside down.

The fire engines arrived with great speed, the sound of the alarms piercing the quiet of the neighborhood. Sally and Jonathan remained outside their home, attended by good neighbors who sought to calm them, but they were unable to be comforted. Tears rolled down their cheeks as they watched the firemen hurry to put out the fire. Neither of them was concerned about the loss of the new house they had just bought or its furnishings that had been chosen with such enthusiasm. They both knew that the heavy streams of water being pumped into the house would probably do more damage than the fire itself, but they hardly cared. Their thoughts rested solely on their little sandy-haired baby Vicky who was trapped upstairs in her room. "Please, G-d, let my baby live!" the young mother sobbed.

When the firemen succeeded in putting out the flames, the fire chief beckoned to Jonathan to follow him back into the house. Not needing further encouragement, Jonathan ran back into the house and bounded up the stairs, or what remained of them. The house was a wreck. But as he reached the top of the stairs and surveyed the scene, he was overcome by amazement. The doors of both Vicky's bedroom and the master bedroom were the only ones not destroyed. They were charred, but intact. He had not put *mezuzos* on all the doorposts. He had agreed to only two *mezuzos* at the time, refusing to take the matter too seriously. He had affixed one to the master bedroom door and one to the doorpost of the baby's room. He raised his hand instinctively to Vicky's doorpost and examined it for a second. The fire had not penetrated through the doors where there was a *mezuzah*, for the doorway, door and the *mezuzah* itself were unscathed. He burst into baby Vicky's room and, to his relief, heard the infant crying weakly. Running to her, he bent over the trembling little body and picked her up, cradling her in his arms. She had inhaled some of the smoke and had cried long and hard from fear and distress, but otherwise she was safe.

Jonathan emerged from the smoldering house, grime and soot on his strained face, holding his baby bundled in his arms. The fire chief was close behind him. A sudden fearful hush fell over the small assembly of neighbors who had gathered outside the house. No one was quite sure what to make of the situation until they heard the baby cry; little Vicky filled her lungs with fresh air and gave a good hearty yell! A ripple of excitement passed over the crowds. Sally jumped up and ran towards her husband and took the little one from him.

Some weeks later, Robert arrived in Detroit on business. By that time the worst physical evidence of the fire had been cleaned away, although the events would be indelibly imprinted on the minds of all concerned for a lifetime.

Robert visited with the young couple and listened to them retell the events of that evening. "It all seems so long ago and yet is so vivid in my memory," Sally told Robert. "And all I keep thinking is, thank G-d for the gift of my baby! A miracle was performed for us — only by a sheer miracle could she have survived those flames. It was surely those *mezuzos* that you brought us! Please, next time you visit us, bring us more so that we can really feel that G-d is protecting us."

Because of the Fathers the Children Will Be Redeemed

Zalman was known in his Polish hometown as a "*macher*," a self-made philanthropist and community worker. He was a person who cared for his fellow man, and helping a Jew was, in his eyes, a holy duty.

Zalman remembered once seeing his grandfather poring over a particularly difficult passage of Gemara, totally absorbed in his studies and then elated when he was finally able to unravel the intricacies of the Sages' word. Evidently his grandfather was seeing the cycle of life beginning and ending like a flower that opens in the morning and closes at dusk, and Zalman asked him, "Zaida, what is life all about? You work so hard every single day. Each day you learn a bit more, carrying out the same chores day in and day out — and then ... what? What is the purpose of it all?" The old man replied crustily, shutting his Gemara with a snap which caused dust to rise, "I am preparing for my *Olam Haba*, for my portion in the World to Come. And, at the same time, Zalman'ka, I am providing for my *Olam Hazeh*, This World, which means that I am trying to provide sufficient sustenance from which my descendants will be able to nourish themselves, spiritually and materially, until *Mashiach* will come — so that they not fall to ruin and their lives go to waste, Heaven forbid! Work, Zalman, work! Provide for all those around you. With every *mitzvah* that you perform, with every tiny effort, to make provision for yourself and your descendants after you ..."

Zalman cast his eyes down in thought. Even after he left his grandfather's presence, the impression these words made remained with him throughout his life. "Zalman, work!" So indeed he did, working for each and every Jew, to assist him in any way he could.

Zalman and his family lived in one of the hamlets neighboring Warsaw. He had a wife and three children, the eldest was nine years old and the youngest five months. It was then that the Jewish world was called upon to face the Nazi threat.

Zalman would see and hear things that he did not like. He heard that in places where the Nazis had gained a foothold, Jewish lives were endangered, not only by the Germans, but also because of the cooperation of other Jews with the Nazis. He grieved sorely, to the point of depression, but did not know what to do. By this time Poland had been overrun and the Nazis were in control. Zalman was a good soul, "*A gutte neshamah*," and the troubling times took their toll, for he was struck by a heart attack and died suddenly, leaving his wife a young widow and his children orphans.

Zalman's funeral was remembered by everyone, for it was almost symbolic of the times. Zalman was one of the first victims of the crisis, and since he was everyone's "do-gooder," his friends' mourning was double-faceted. He was borne in sorrow to the Jewish cemetery and laid to rest beside his learned grandfather.

Despite all of this, Zalman was very fortunate. He was one of the last Jews in that town to merit being brought to *kever Yisrael* (afforded a kosher Jewish burial), with a grave and a tombstone to mark his grave. Shortly thereafter, with the arrival of the Germans, such "taken for granted" amenities ceased to exist. Thus, Zalman was one of the first casualties of the German invasion and one of the last Jews to be buried in the Jewish cemetery of that town.

The Germans arrived in Zalman's hometown, as they did in every Jewish settlement. Too familiar was the scene — the roundup, the killings, the horror. Zalman's wife Breindel, in the furor, took her children and started to run. She gave no thought to where she was running, but she headed for the countryside. With her infant son in her arms and her older children running beside her, she fled. After a while, she turned towards the two older children — but they were nowhere to be seen. She stopped, and began to scream, "Aharon — Arele — Chaya Leah! Where are you?" But in the frenzy, they had become separated from her and had vanished. Sheer terror overtook her and, fearing that they had already been murdered by the Nazis, she continued to run for her life.

Breindel eventually found a place of refuge. She recalled a farmer from whom her husband would purchase produce, often in large quantities. As it was Zalman's nature to perpetuate goodwill towards all men, he had in the course of his transactions done several favors for the non-Jewish farmer, and the two had a good relationship. Now, Breindel asked a favor in return — that he provide a hiding place for her and her baby in their hour of danger. In return she would work for him in the small factory that he maintained on the grounds of his farm, where he prepared pickles, preserves and other cooked foods for the local market. The farmer, remembering Zalman with respect, agreed to Breindel's request, and gave her a small shed where she and her baby could stay.

❧❧❧

Many years passed. The war was long over and Poland became part of the Communist bloc. The borders to the West had been sealed. Breindel, having suffered so much anguish during the war, was traumatized by her experience, but she was finally able to tolerate with what happened and accept her lot. She had no money with which to escape, and no strength to change matters, so she stayed where she was and her son grew up as a Polish gentile.

❧❧❧

Still more time went by and Breindel began to feel the infirmities of old age creeping in. In her heart, she began to reflect on her life — she had abandoned the ways of her ancestors and had lost all ties with her people. Now, looking death in the face, she shuddered. Soon, she knew, she would stand before a mighty tribunal — and what would she be able to offer as a defense? Her only son was to all appearances a non-Jew, without even the slightest connection to his Jewish roots.

"Pietter!" she called him, using his Polish name. "Come to me a moment ... I need you. There is something I have to tell you ..." Pietter, by now a middle-aged man, entered and sat near his mother, a gray-haired old lady in her late 70s, still somewhat vibrant and in full possession of her faculties. In her mind Breindel mulled over how best to broach this subject.

"Let me tell you a story," she began. "Before the war, in a small town near Warsaw, there lived a Jewish man and his wife. This man was everyone's friend, for he was kind and gentle, a wonderful person. They had three small children. G-d was good to them, life was pleasant, and it seemed that it would always be so. But it was not to be, for tragedy loomed on the horizon. The sufferings of Job struck this woman. First her husband was taken from her when he suffered a fatal heart attack; and when the Germans came, the two oldest children were lost as well."

Continuing her story now as a personal account, Breindel went on, "Maybe it was better that my husband did not suffer, that Zalman was the last or nearly last to be buried in the Jewish cemetery before the troubles really began. Pietter, you are my sole surviving child, and I want you to know that you were born a Jew. We remained here and although you have grown up believing that you are Polish, I want you to know that you have a Jewish father buried in the Jewish cemetery several kilometers from here. His name was Zalman."

Pietter stared at her in near disbelief. In all her years, she had not once referred to any of this. In fact, she had brushed aside any mention of the years of her youth, choosing instead to assume the role of a gentile peasant woman. For a long time he stood staring at her, in shock and disbelief. Finally, he demanded, almost accusingly, "Why did you not tell me before?" But she declined to answer him. "One request I make of you," she begged. "For your own sake, and so that you will see that I am telling the truth, go visit your father's grave!"

Pietter agreed. Although he had never known of this man he had to see things for himself. Was he really the good man that his mother described? He must find this grave and try to make sense out of this predicament.

Pietter made the journey to Warsaw not long after his mother's "confession." From there he traveled to the small town, now expanded and changed from the time when his family had lived there. Once there, he made inquiries about any remaining Jews, or anyone who could help him to uncover information about the town's Jewish cemetery. Someone directed him to Menashe, an old pensioner, who had survived the war and was knowledgeable of the past. Answering the knock at his door, Menashe appeared, hobbling a bit. Walking on old legs was painful. "Do you know something about the Jewish cemetery?" asked Pietter. Menashe peered suspiciously at the *goy* before him. Maybe he was up to no good, he thought. "Why do you need to know? It's all broken up anyway! Not of interest to you ..." Pietter answered Menashe and explained that he had personal reasons for wanting to see the cemetery. Something about his manner convinced Menashe to oblige, and so he began to walk, painfully and with effort, with his visitor following closely behind.

When they reached the cemetery, Pietter stood in stunned silence. The place was in a complete state of ruin. Many old gravestones were reduced to rubble, and most had been deliberately vandalized. "Who could have done this?" he asked out loud, and when Menashe began to explain, about the Germans, the Poles and others, the visitor waved his hand to indicate he had heard enough. "I want to visit a grave — Zalman was his name. One of the last to be buried here." Menashe did not remember the name, but he did remember the area where the last ones were buried. He led the visitor to the place and, sure enough, there was the gravestone — or the remnants of one — marking Zalman's resting place, the Hebrew inscription still visible. Menashe read it out loud.

Pietter knelt down and ran his hand over the grave. Blood is thicker than water, and he was visibly moved. He looked up at Menashe, almost revealing his secret, but then he held back. He cupped some of the earth from the grave in his hand and let it run through his fingers. He wanted to weep, but did not want to be seen. "Can you fix up this grave?" he asked suddenly. "See how smashed and broken the stone is? This is disgraceful! Nobody attends to the repair of the gravestones!" Menashe shrugged a bit. "There is no money!" "I will give you some!" replied Pietter. "Do you have someone who can set up a new gravestone with proper engraving?" asked Pietter, feeling a magnetic pull to perform an act of love for his father who lay buried before him. Menashe nodded and acquiesced, accepting the cash that the Polish man produced from his pocket. It seemed a bit odd to him that the stranger should display such interest, but he asked no further questions. That was how matters were left. Pietter went on his way, and Menashe complied with the request. He found a stonemason and arranged for the refurbishment of the grave.

☙❧

About a year later, as the gates of the Soviet Union were opened to tourists from Israel and the West, advertisements began to appear in the Israeli press. "*Tour Poland and Russia, the holy places of Eastern Europe. Visit the graves of the holy Baal Shem Tov, and other great Rabbis in Cracow, Warsaw and other cities ...*" It had now became possible to visit not only the holy places of Eastern Europe, but also to make one's way to *kivrei avos,* the burial sites of parents and relatives. Many took advantage of the opportunity and traveled to these places. On one particular tour were a brother and sister from one of the distinguished families of Bnei Brak.

They arrived in a small town near Warsaw, having left the tour group for the day. Their thoughts were focused on a place vaguely recalled from before the war. The brother, a man approaching his 60s, remembered a little of his father's funeral but not where he was buried. He also remembered wandering together with his sister, not knowing where they were going, hiding where they could and constantly being on the run throughout the war. At the end of the war, together with many other Jewish children who had been left wandering on their own, they were sent on a "Kindertransport" to Israel, where surviving relatives helped them.

Now that they had reached their destination, the small town near Warsaw, the brother and sister too were directed to Menashe — the unofficial "caretaker" of the Jewish cemetery — in an attempt to find the grave of their father Zalman. Once they reached the old cemetery, they stared in shock and disbelief at what had become of the graveyard, and their eyes filled with tears when they remembered what the years before the war had been like. When they saw their father's grave, they were in for yet another surprise. For among all the graves, neglected and overgrown with weeds, Zalman's grave remained the only one intact and readily identifiable. It was clear that it had recently been restored. With overwhelming emotion, they *davened* at the site. Peering closely at the inscription on the monument, they realized that their father's *yahrzeit* was two days hence.

They then hurried to the house of the old Menashe, "Tell us, that grave that has been restored — who did it? Who else has been here recently?" queried Aharon. Old Menashe scrutinized the face of this man, obviously a Jew, with beard and *peyos*, speaking to him in Yiddish. His sister, wearing a *sheitel*, stood by his side. Menashe was worried for a minute — perhaps he had done something wrong and they were angry. But a small bribe persuaded him to tell the truth. "About a year ago, a Polish man came here — not a Jew I think — and gave me money to fix up that grave!" Chaya Leah became excited, her innate curiosity prompting her to probe further. "Who was the man? Think, what was his name? Do you have an address, a telephone number? Please, try to remember!"

Menashe painstakingly went into the cobwebbed room to search among his papers. He was too tired these days to maintain even minimum standards of cleanliness. "Here, I found it!" he called out exuberantly. Adjusting his cap, Menashe returned to the entrance where his visitors waited and gave them the name and phone number of the man who had paid him to fix up the grave.

Chaya Leah and Aharon phoned the number they had been given. A man answered, but he spoke only Polish. They found someone who could interpret for them and then they tried again. This time, they met with success. Scribbling down the directions they were given, they hired a taxi and were soon on their way to the farm. They approached the house and knocked apprehensively. The door was opened by a middle-aged man. Following a gasp of surprise, a teary-eyed Chaya Leah walked right past him and headed straight towards old Breindel seated in the corner of the living room. Speaking to her in Yiddish, she said, "Mama — it is me, Chaya Leah! And this is your eldest son Aharon! Do you remember us?" The old woman looked unbelievingly from one to the other, examining their faces. Then she rose from her place, overcome with emotion. The children hugged their aged mother and then turned towards the man who was standing quietly by, observing the scene being played out before him. The puzzle pieces suddenly fell into place and Aharon and Chaya Leah realized that this was their younger brother! At long last the family was reunited!

Undoubtedly the good deeds their father Zalman had done did not go to waste — not while he was living and not now. It is written that the righteous pray for the living even from the next world. The *mitzvah* of restoring Zalman's grave had been instrumental in reuniting the family.

It was the day before Zalman's *yahrzeit*. His eldest son went to great lengths to gather a *minyan* from among tourists and the few other Jews there, in order to say *Kaddish*. When the family arrived at the cemetery, Aharon put his hand into his pocket and pulled out a black *yarmulke* which he handed to his brother, indicating that he place it on his head. "Ezriel!" he called him softly. "Your Hebrew name is Ezriel!"

"*Yisgadal v'yiskadash shmei raba*!" began Aharon as the brothers stood side by side before the grave. The age-old *Kaddish* melody resounded through those forgotten burial sites for the first time in forty years. Aharon's eyes met those of Ezriel, his brother. Ezriel was weeping.

The Gold Pocket Watch

A beautiful 18-carat-gold pocket watch on a chain was the apple of his eye. My zaida, Moshe Rosenberg, had purchased it from a German Jewish lawyer who was emigrating to the United States and was in need of cash and thus compelled to sell his family heirloom. Its harmonious chime made you feel that life was not so bad after all, and it had a dial recording the full moon and half moon, as well as the calendar date and a stopwatch, among other features. Zaida had formed a strong attachment to his watch, which reminded him of times for *davening*, for *shiur*, for his work at the slaughterhouse, and for all the other events of his life, both great and small.

❧❧❧

I can still see Zaida's face in front of me — a warm, intelligent face, despite the blindness that afflicted him in the last five years of his life. He was somewhere between 93 and 97 years old when he passed away; nobody could really be sure, for many Polish Jews had, in their youth, concealed their true age from the Polish authorities in order to avoid conscription into the Polish army. When Zaida died, a part of a mighty generation died with him. Many of his peers were like him in their strong adherence to Torah and the Jewish way of life, and each one had a story.

Moshe Rosenberg was a *chasid* of Gur, who had twice beheld the holy countenance of the *Sfas Emes*, and whose father and grandfather before him had also been *chasidim* of the Rebbes of Gur. Orphaned when young, he learned Torah in *Beis Midrash Gur*, and like so many of his contemporaries, his love of Torah was his paramount joy. Indeed, his face would light up brightly whenever he spoke *divrei Torah*. Even towards the end of his life, when he had lost his eyesight, he could remember clearly all that he had learned, and frequently related his own *chidushei Torah*. In *shul*, he would correct the *baal korei* from memory, his head swaying appreciatively to the rhythm of the melody of the Torah reading like one enjoying the performance of a fine orchestra.

❧❧❧

Moshe Rosenberg had lived in Poland until August of 1920, when he and his family moved to Berlin. Life in Poland was difficult for its millions of Jews who for centuries had called it "home." Crushing poverty was rampant, anti-Semitism and danger of forced military conscription were a part of life, and an adequate *parnasah* was hard to come by.

Chasidism, with its many streams and rivulets, flourished in Poland. At the times of the Jewish festivals, *chasidim* would crowd the roads and trains, even clinging onto the roofs of the carriages in the rush to reach their Rebbe in time for the holiday. Prior to World War II, the *chasidus* of Gur was almost an empire, numbering some 250,000 followers of various backgrounds. Although many very learned men, indeed Torah giants, were counted among the Gerer *chasidim*, not all the *chasidim* were *talmidei chachamim*. Many were simple Jews (not that it's simple to be a Jew!). Farmers, or businessmen, some more worldly than others, and ordinary pious Jews, all found their way and their place in the Court of Gur. All these Jews found that their service of Hashem was strengthened by both the individual guidance each received from the Rebbe, and the *achdus*, the wonderful unity, they shared with one another.

In Berlin too, first on Dragonenstrasse and later on Linienstrasse, the Rosenberg family joined other *chasidim* who lived in their section of town. Life was fairly good there for "Moishele *Shochet*" and his family. The girls attended the Jewish school, while the boys eventually returned to yeshivah in Poland. Moshe's wife, Bubba Shaindel Cyrel, was a tall fine-looking woman, with a warm disposition who ruled her small "kingdom" on Dragonenstrasse with wisdom and an iron hand. In Berlin the family enjoyed a security that had been lacking in their lives in the stark poverty of Poland. However, their bliss was short lived, for the tides were changing in German society and the gates were opened for the rise of Hitler, *yemach shemo*, may his name be blotted out, a direct descendant of Amalek.

Many *gedolim* — great Jewish sages — expressed unease at the changes on the political front. Among them was the *Imrei Emes*, the renowned Rebbe of Gur. In 1933, upon Hitler's rise to power, the Rebbe remarked to his son-in-law, Rabbi Yitzchak

Meir Levin, "Our brothers in Germany have not understood what being in exile means. Now they are going to experience it. Without a doubt they will flee to *Eretz Yisrael.*" His words were to have great import in the years that followed.

It is a well-known precept that Esav hates Yaakov. Anti-Semitism was not born with Hitler, but was exploited by the Nazis to its ultimate, in political and ideological terms. Everything that was wrong with Germany was suddenly the fault of the Jews. From 1933 on, with his "five-year plan," Hitler proposed to "cure Germany of all her ills" including, as it subsequently became clear, a "final solution to the Jewish problem." Hitler despised the Jews for giving the world a conscience; he hated the Torah values of piety, humility, and holiness that formed the very essence of the Jewish personality. This monster would conquer the world with brute physical strength and establish a "Master Race" of creatures who were unencumbered by human emotions or ethics.

We are G-d's people, and Hashem has forged a covenant with us, a bond of love, for all generations, that we keep His Torah and guard His ways, with the unique purpose of spreading holiness in the world. To what degree must the Jews guard this love! How great is the jealousy of the nations of this pledge between Hashem and His people Israel. What threat could a *sefer Torah,* a Jewish school, or the practice of *shechitah* and *bris milah* and other bastions of Yiddishkeit pose to the Germans? Why did they make the Jews and Jewish institutions primary targets for destruction when they entered a town? Even at the end of the war, when it was blatantly clear that the Germans were losing, instead of concentrating their final resources on their military effort, they wreaked vengeance on those Jews remaining in their grasp. The *Haskalah* movement had begun in Germany, centuries earlier. It promised the Jews that if they deserted the beloved holy bonds of tradition for the universities and secular life, and if they appeared to be like the gentiles in all ways, then they would be accepted by the gentile world and would no longer be subject to persecution. Such beliefs were proven false however. No Jew in the Nazi era escaped, no matter how assimilated he was.

✦

"*SHECHITAH* FORBIDDEN ON PENALTY OF DEATH!" Part of Hitler's infamous "five-year plan" dictated that anyone caught practicing the Jewish ritual form of slaughtering and preparing meat would be executed. No one could possibly claim that this "act of treason" could harm Germany in any way — economic or otherwise. This decree was outright malice and would cause grave hardship, and even a potential spiritual danger to those who would be tempted to eat *"treif,"* G-d forbid.

There were those among the general Jewish community and also among the *shochtim* who refused to "wait and see" what would happen. Instead they grabbed whatever they could and fled across the borders, calling behind them, "You will see ... this is only the beginning; there is much worse to come!" Yet others among the *shochtim* took a stoic view, claiming that it is wrong to abandon a ship that is in trouble, for "*kol Yisrael arevim zeh lazeh* — all of Israel is responsible one for the other," and they were still needed. Out of this argument grew the plan for a form of Jewish resistance to the enemy: They would form an underground *shechitah* network to sell meat on the black market. My grandmother, Shaindel Cyrel, went along with my grandfather in this decision. "Such things have been known to occur in our history; many of them pass like a rainy day!" she stated, and both surveyed the fruits of a lifetime, both material and spiritual, arrayed before them. Four small treasures were sleeping in the next room, and their security and happiness hung in the balance. Here in Berlin, life had proven stable. "Dear G-d," she whispered, "let us choose the right path both for the sake of these children that You have given to us and for ourselves, for I sense danger ahead." From that day forth, a *Tehillim* was always at her side, day and night. Like many women of her generation, she could not readily translate from the Hebrew, but she would read *Tehillim* and *daven* with great fervor, tears running freely down her face. "*Mamme*, why do you cry so much when you *daven*?" her children would ask her. "*Kinder, kinder,* when you get to be my age, and know what I know, then you too will cry to the *Ribono shel Olam*," she would reply.

For several months, the *shochtim* would go secretly at pre-arranged times by day or by night to a farm out in the country, where the meat would be ritually slaughtered, koshered and prepared. It would clandestinely appear on the market, where those in the know could purchase it.

To build and maintain this undercover network, it was necessary to bribe some of Berlin's top officials and even a number of the ministers in the growing Nazi Party. Daring and dangerous, the operation seemed assured of success by virtue of this official involvement. The *shochtim* and their families warily walked this precarious tightrope, praying day by day for yet another safe dawn.

❦❧

It was a very long night. Shaindel Cyrel went back and forth to the window, gazing out onto the dark, bleak street. Her husband was normally home by this hour. The clock on the wall chimed, shattering the thick silence. She returned to her chair, picked up the *Tehillim* again, and continued to plead: "*Shema tefillasi* — hear my prayer — *al tastir Panecha mimeni b'yom tzar li* — do not hide Your face from me in my day of anguish."

Dawn was breaking, and the first bird's song could be heard — like the earliest prayer of the morning. By now, Shaindel was filled with dread. Moshe had not returned all night — nor did the others who had gone with him. Someone had talked; there had been an informer. Such a ghastly deed is looked upon in the blackest terms in *halachah*. One who informs on his brethren to secular authorities loses his portion in *Olam Haba*. "*V'lamalshinim al tehi sikvah* — To the slanderers there should be no hope." This "informer" had endangered many lives, and Shaindel and all the others who were involved shuddered at the thought of what was yet to come.

The main jail in Berlin was a grim-looking building in the best of times. Now that it housed Gestapo headquarters, numerous stories were told of what transpired within, stories that make the blood chill. Merely nearing this place made one pause and wish to flee. It was there that Zaida Moshe was taken with the others. His money was taken from him, and his clothes were exchanged for prison garb. Then they found his faithful companion, the gold pocket watch. As he followed the greedy eyes of the warden examining his watch, he remembered with sadness the last time his watch had been scrutinized. On his last visit to Gur, the Rebbe had also admired the gold watch, but had promptly handed it back to him. Since then, this timepiece, which was so important to him, had taken on added significance. He had to get it back. Moshe gathered courage and spoke. "I need that watch — one must know the time of day!" But the warden in charge answered him with a rude guffaw and sneered, "You won't need to by the time we are through with you here! Here, WE make the times of day! Sign here, that you have deposited all of this." And under duress, he had to sign, resigning himself that this was the last time he would see his prized possession. Inwardly he prayed that the Jewish lawyer who had sold it to him would forgive him for breaking his solemn promise never to allow the watch to fall into gentile hands.

Upon receiving news of her husband's arrest, Shaindel reacted with the boldness of a leopardess. She had read and heard all kinds of horror stories, cases of trials being staged privately, with no evidence emerging to the public. She had even heard of urns containing ashes being delivered to the bereaved relatives. Shaindel was not going to sit by idly while Moshe was being held against his will. She remembered that the group of underground *shochtim* had bribed some of the German elite, who would now certainly want to silence the *shochtim* and cover up the matter. She decided firmly, however, that this case would be made public. Her courage and initiative played a significant role in those days. Shaindel remembered the name of a good Jewish lawyer, Herr Jaffe, who even in those turbulent times had effective front men and the right connections, and would certainly know how to "wheel and deal" with the German authorities. However, she would do nothing without guidance from the Rebbe. "The Rebbe must be informed, must *daven*, must advise," she told herself. Taking pen in hand, and a blank piece of white paper, as was the custom when writing a *kvittel*, she addressed a detailed and heartrending letter to her son Herschel, who was learning at the time in the *Beis Midrash* of Alexander. Although only 16 years old, he was the one she felt would be best able to handle this business. "Make haste and take my *kvittel* to the Rebbe without delay," she urged him.

When Herschel received the letter he was in somewhat of a quandary. He knew that the crush of hundreds of older *chasidim* at the Rebbe's house would probably prevent him, a mere youth, from reaching the Rebbe. Furthermore, the time allotted to each member to state his case was severely curtailed and the response given by the holy *Imrei Emes* was normally brief, with words chosen with care and precious as pearls. An astute level of clarity and understanding was required to fathom the essence of the Rebbe's words. The Rebbe regarded time as a valuable commodity and words as tools to be employed with great trepidation. Here, Herschel would need time to explain the matter at hand, for his father's life hung in the balance. Despite all these doubts, Herschel was encouraged by his mother's trust in his abilities. The messenger had brought the letter in the middle of the night, and Herschel did not tarry. He immediately left and arrived at the Rebbe's house at dawn. As he entered the door he met the Rebbe's son, Yisrael, who worked closely with his father in all undertakings, and later became known as the *Beis Yisrael*, the Gerer Rebbe in Jerusalem. Herschel, grateful for this encounter, approached him and poured out his heart and, heeding the keen advice of the *Beis Yisrael*, gave over the *kvittel*, including his mother's letter in its entirety. Herschel then went to *daven Shacharis*.

It was well known in Ger that the Rebbe dealt with the pressure of the huge public that sought his help by rapidly noting the contents of each *kvittel* and giving a concise reply. When the time came for Herschel to join the sea of *chasidim* waiting to speak with the Rebbe, he found that he had been maneuvered to the last place in the line, with no one else allowed in after him. As the Rebbe's door opened, Herschel found himself in the corner of a large room with a high ceiling. The holy Rebbe's eyes were scanning his face; he dropped his gaze to the floor for who could withstand the Rebbe's penetrating look? His son, R' Yisrael, was standing in attendance. Watching, waiting, and listening for any comment, R' Yisrael watched together with Herschel, hearing the Rebbe's sighs as he read the *kvittel* in every detail. The Rebbe told Herschel to stay over for Shabbos and, before he realized what was happening to him, unseen hands propelled him from the room. He was finally aroused from his daze by other *chasidim* who asked, "Why are you standing around? Don't you realize you have heard all you are likely to hear?"

Herschel spent a tense Shabbos — waiting — just one among a vast army of *chasidim* whose *davening* rose to the Heavens in a mighty voice. When the Rebbe's *tisch* had ended, a *shamash* called Herschel into the Rebbe's room. Herschel stood stiffly at attention, his eyes partly lowered in respect, unable to meet the piercing fiery gaze of the Rebbe, and partly directed towards the Rebbe who stood by the tiled oven that tempered the sharp cold of the room. At his side, as usual, stood his son R' Yisrael. The Rebbe posed the question in Yiddish, "*Vos is der chait?* What was the chargeable offense?" — to which Herschel replied, "*Er hot geshochten!* He practiced *shechitah*!" Herschel felt the Rebbe's penetrating gaze boring into his soul and quickly lowered his eyes. "*Geshochten?*" he asked, implying

— why, this is a *mitzvah*! Herschel did not dare to speak out of turn as the Rebbe concluded his inquiry and declared, *"Der Aibeshter vett helfen der tatte — vett arois frei!* Hashem on High will help your father — he will go out free!"

The following morning, Herschel went to *daven Shacharis.* When the *chazzan* reached the words *"U'matir asurim —* and releases those who are bound," during the repetition of the *Shemoneh Esrei,* Herschel felt the Rebbe's gaze resting firmly upon him. After *davening,* Herschel received a message: "You can feel confident that your father will go free; and moreover, tell your mother not to worry — he will even retrieve his pocket watch."

The following days were difficult ones for Zaida, with grueling interrogations as the Germans tried to gather incriminating evidence. Their policy was both political and anti-Semitic, and they were fascinated by the fact that their prisoner was a man of Jewish learning. One of the younger prison guards became quite friendly with Zaida, frequently holding lengthy conversation with him. With Hashem's help, Zaida was able to have kosher food secretly brought to him, and even an occasional daily newspaper. These were above and beyond the normal privileges afforded a prisoner in German hands. Zaida was extremely grateful to the Almighty who had allowed this *chesed* to be performed for him.

It was some years after the infamous Beilis trial in Russia that had been publicized throughout Europe. The Beilis trial was a Russian anti-Semitic propaganda attempt and many particulars of this horror story found equal favor with the Nazi prosecutors who gleefully adopted them. None of this was novel to Jewish ears, and when Zaida heard about it, the medieval show trials, or the arguments of the Spanish Inquisition, resounded in his thoughts.

The Nazi authorities summoned Zaida and arrayed before him a group of "experts" on the topic of Jewish learning. "Is it not written in your writings, '*Atem keru'im adam v'ein umos ha'olam keru'im adam*'? This means that the Jews believe that they are in fact the only ones who are called 'men.' All the rest of the nations of the world, including the pure Aryan race, are therefore animals or subhumans in your eyes! You genuinely believe in Jewish superiority. You are dangerous traitors to the entire gentile world. Do you deny this?" Zaida's sharp mind raced. He recalled that there were various references to this, that Israel is called *adam* but the peoples of the world are not called *adam*, and he remembered also the reply given by Beilis at his trial. No doubt these Germans had read about it with glee and, for a moment, Zaida found himself in a mental whirlpool. He pleaded to G-d for heavenly assistance to help him find the best approach in presenting his case and both saving himself and preserving the dignity of the Jewish people.

It was then that his thoughts cleared. He suddenly recalled an article which had appeared in the local newspaper the guard had brought him that week; the story and its purpose in relation to him was now readily apparent. Determined to display Jewish pride and dignity, he drew himself up to his full height and began in his best German, "*Herren*! I know that there was recently reported in the general press a case that rocked all Germany. A young German, in his early 20s, entered a pharmacy in the late evening as the manager, a widow, was totaling the day's receipts. He took out a metal bar, hit her viciously over the head, and made off with the money, leaving her bleeding on the floor. She made a heroic effort to sound the alarm, and in fact the police came, but she later died from her wounds. Who will the police be hunting for, for this foul murder? *Herren*, they will seek one young German in his early 20s. Will they seek to arrest also his mother, his father, his brothers and sisters, or hold blameworthy other citizens of his town? No, they will not. If he were a Jew, however, would this be the case? No, *Herren*, it would not be the case. As many Jews as it would be possible to include in the charge, even the whole Jewish nation — as is presently being done throughout the media — would be held collectively responsible for the crime. Why is this? For, *'Atem keru'im adam.'* We are called a man — a single being, a man that has two hands, two feet, two eyes, and so forth. And if one organ is hurt, the whole body groans and suffers. If one member of the Jewish people falls into trouble, the total Jewish community, by YOUR attitudes towards us, is thus in trouble. We will all feel it and the pain will be felt in the hearts of every Jew! We are *adam* — as one man! The Jewish people are united in their religious purpose ..." Silent faces with transfixed gazes confronted Moshe Rosenberg now. The matter was quickly dropped.

When Zaida was later asked all that he remembered of that period and of the trial, he focused his thoughts and recalled: "It goes back many years and not all is clearly remembered, but I can tell you this much — the political climate against the Jews was dangerous and chilly. To see a Gerer *chasid* with beard and *peyos* stand up in court obstinately refusing to bend was anathema to the Nazi authorities. But the saintly Rebbe was behind us and we received great encouragement from him. The *chasidim* turned to the Rebbe as a child turns to a father — for his guidance, his *tefillos* and his blessings."

The *Imrei Emes* was constantly kept informed of every development regarding Zaida and his case, and his was but one among hundreds. Every Jew was as a child to him. They say that although Zaida could technically have been charged with treason, which would have made his case impossible to plead, some parts of the charge sheet were simply ignored or not even admitted as evidence. No stone had been left unturned. Where it was possible to "buy" an entry into the German offices and procure a "better deal," this was done. So, to their embarrassment, the prosecutors found either that many people in high places were involved in some way or that doors were simply closed to them.

After much investigation and deliberation, they held a hasty "hearing" and offered Zaida bail. In fact, a deal involving a bribe was arranged among the lower officials. The Gerer Rebbe was informed and he gave instructions for Zaida not to return home when freed from the jail. His personal belongings were returned just before he left the prison, but without his documents and passport, and he had very little money. Acting on the Rebbe's orders, he boarded a train that took a rural route across the German-Belgian border at Aachen.

"You might think that this was the end of the story. I crossed the border and that was that," Zaida smiled as he remembered. "No, it was not quite so simple and we could write another megillah with all the incidentals. Briefly, however, this is what happened on the way to safety ..."

Zaida Moshe was obviously terrified of being caught, since he had no papers and since he was a Jew and could not and would not conceal that fact. The country train was filled with peasants, farmers and simple people who took little notice of him, so he was able to quietly huddle up in a corner and recite Tehillim by heart, praying that he would not be discovered. All went well, until they reached the border.

There was the usual squeal of brakes and slamming of doors as the train entered the station, but no one was allowed off until the German officials had passed through the train. Do not forget that this was 1939, only six months before the outbreak of the war. Anti-Semitism was rampant and Jews were already being sent to "work camps" — the precursors of the concentration camps. Zaida watched the border guard pass down the rows of seated passengers and check their papers, until he reached him — the only Jew in the carriage — and with a glaring look demanded, "Papers!" There was utter silence. Zaida Moshe could not utter a word. "Papers, Jew, I said!" the official raised his voice menacingly. To which, as was his way, Zaida answered humbly, "I have no papers," and stared helplessly at him for several silent, chilly moments. Suddenly, the official seemed to "see the funny side." The situation appeared to him as a major comedy and he burst into scornful laughter. "A Jew crossing the

German border without papers? What do you imagine the Belgians will do to you when they find you? That should be interesting! Next stop for you and the likes of you will be the work camp! Be seeing you!" And he left Zaida in his place. Later, the Belgians, as luck would have it, simply ignored him, passing him by as if he were not there. *Baruch Hashem*! Zaida finally got through to Antwerp where a committee of Gerer *chasidim* was waiting to greet him at the train. The Rebbe's orders had been received and followed there as well. It seems that Zaida was but one of many.

"And what became of Zaida's children? Did they all get out?" This time, it was Zaida's daughter, Aunt Channah, who recalled, memories reawakening as she answered. "My sister Pepi was nearly left behind in the rush. As we prepared to leave the halfway house at the border she was sleeping upstairs in her crib; but I suddenly remembered, and gave a shout: 'We have forgotten the baby!' And so she came along! It was a wild journey to say the least. After we heard how Zaida had reached safety we were filled with hope; with Hashem's help we would all get through and we were prepared for any risks. Thus, we openly auctioned off all our possessions, and found a crazy woman driver who promised to get us across the border that night, provided we paid her fee.

"My mother, Bubba Shaindel Cyrel, had firsthand knowledge of the hatred and cruelty perpetuated by the Nazis towards all that was related to the Jewish people and their religion, and she had a clear idea of what was yet to come. She had long before decided that if we were leaving, then our *sefer Torah*, the family *sefer Torah* that had been donated to the Great *Shul* in Warsaw, should leave with us. It was priceless, written on special fine parchment by Zaida's grandfather Binyamin Dovid. Shaindel, on her previous journey to Poland, had visited the *shul*. Ignoring the protestations of the *gabbaim*, she, in her usual style, stood her ground and somehow made them open the huge *aron kodesh* for her. Her eyes immediately were riveted upon the little *sefer*

Torah with Zaida Binyamin Dovid's name embroidered on the *mantel*. There was no time for courtesy or for begging forgiveness for such boldness. She ignored their cries of protest and took the *sefer Torah* from the *aron kodesh* and fled with it. As things turned out, her actions rescued it from subsequent destruction at the hands of the enemy, as was the fate of so many other *Sifrei Torah*.

"My brother Herschel hid it under his coat, and in the dark of the night we flew at top speed over the roads to Aachen, avoiding the checkpoints, and squealing over dirt tracks in what seemed to be constant acceleration, until we arrived safely on the Belgian side. From there, we all managed to reach London just before Poland was overrun by Germany. Today the *sefer Torah* is in the Gerer *shtiebel* in London."

What happened to the Gerer Rebbe? He also escaped — but how? That was a long and miraculous story involving foreign governments and the duping of German officials. The Germans had placed a price tag on the Rebbe's head; they called him the "*Wunderrabiner* — the Wonder Rabbi," for they had heard the accounts of miracles and wondrous happenings that Hashem had worked through him. But the Rebbe stayed behind as long as possible to rescue as many Jews as he could. Each Jew was to him a precious child, and the Rebbe was a fatherly leader. He had labored to bring together all Torah Jews under the banner of Agudas Yisrael in Europe, and spoke repeatedly of the need for unity: "*Tiheyeh lachem agudah echas* — you should be one congregation," for *Am Yisrael* will only be redeemed when they are *agudah echas* among the G-d fearing, especially in the Holy Land. There would be an end to hatred and enmity among Jews, there would be Torah education for Jewish boys and girls, and *shalom* — peace between one Jew and another and for the entire Jewish people. The Rebbe wrote: "*Eis tzarah l'Yaakov shelo hayah kamohu b'Yisrael* — A time of trouble is coming to Israel the likes of which has never before been in Israel," and the only answer is to strengthen faith and belief.

The Gerer Rebbe arrived in *Eretz Yisrael* in Adar 1940, heartbroken at the tragedy that had befallen the Jewish people, but encouraged at the new beginning in the land that he loved. It is a known fact that the Rebbe loved *Eretz Yisrael* and since 1920 had visited there several times. He had even made attempts to settle there and not return to Poland in the hope that his *chasidim* would follow him. But the *chasidim* convened a *beis din* under the leadership of the *Gaon* R' Yaakov Meir Biderman and the Rebbe was compelled to return to his flock in Poland.

Later, when he was asked for the reasons for the Holocaust, the Rebbe wrote in his letters, both to the shattered communities of Europe and to individuals, that the true reasons behind the Holocaust will only be understood in time to come; so vast and terrible a tragedy "will never be again in Israel" — it is part of the birthpangs of the coming of *Mashiach*, and beyond our limited comprehension.

Further, he comforted a Holocaust survivor who had lost his entire family, by explaining the reason why the Tablets which Moshe *Rabbeinu* broke "before your eyes — *l'eineichem*" were still placed in the *Aron*. Why do so, if they were seemingly so shattered and unusable? Similarly, Shimon was imprisoned by Yosef "*l'eineihem* — before their eyes," whereas in fact his brother released him quickly from his chains when the other brothers did not see, and then fed and cared for him. We, too, both in the Holocaust and amid all the troubles of Israel to the present time, do not see or comprehend; but all that we have lost will in fact be returned to us!

This is an example of the detail and care that the Rebbe lavished on each individual, and how far reaching was his holy vision: Zaida made it known to the Rebbe that he and his family had reached safety far from the clutches of the hated Gestapo. With that, the Rebbe sent back the following message to him regarding his precious watch that he believed he had lost forever: "They returned your gold pocket watch to you, didn't they?"

The Postmaster of Jerusalem

odah Ahuvah sat back and sighed. "He was so tall and good looking. He stood up without fear for what was right, no matter who opposed him. Such a wonderful man!" She loved to tell stories of her father.

R' Berel Meir of Jerusalem came from a distinguished family. His father's family was from Kobrin-Stolin, and numbered among the *chasidim* of the *Beis Aharon* of Karlin. His grandfather, R' Dovid Zelig, was a Karliner *chasid* of note, who sent his son Asher at a young age to stay with relatives in Chevron, the holy city of the Patriarchs. There he lived and thrived and eventually married and prospered. R' Osher Tenenbaum was renowned for his vibrant *tefillah*. As was usual among the old Karliner *chasidim* who would cry out in the course of their prayers, R' Osher Tenenbaum would call out loudly and with fervor, his heart embracing the Heavens above with the strength of his supplication to the Almighty. Guests coming to visit on the streets adjoining the *shul* would ask, "What is that voice we hear, rising so mightily?" To this the reply would be, "It is the voice of *tefillah* — R' Osher Tenenbaum who is acclaimed for the piety of his *davening*."

R' Osher's son, Berel Meir, showed great promise even at an early age. The boy's good name preceded him, for Berel Meir was a talented and capable student, with a warm and pleasant way about him.

Guided by the venerable Karliner Rebbe, the *Or Yisrael*, Berel Meir and his parents left Chevron before he was *bar mitzvah* to enter the yeshivah in the Old City of Jerusalem. His parents had always had a longing to live closer to the *Kotel HaMaaravi*, the last existing remnant of the Holy Temple, where the *Shechinah*, Hashem's Presence, still dwells. It was fortunate that they left when they did, for the terrible Chevron riots of the year "TaRPaT" (1929) were imminent, and they were thus spared this horror.

The Jerusalem of the old Yishuv was a kind of Jewish melting pot concentrated into a small area. It was home to Jews from Turkey, Russia, Lithuania, Germany and other parts of Europe, and from the Arab countries as well — all compressed together in the Jewish neighborhoods of both the Old City and the new areas that were now being developed outside the walls. The Turks were still in the land, for *Eretz Yisrael* was a part of the Ottoman Empire.

Berel Meir had an open mind and was a sociable young man. He had become not only a respected *talmid chacham*, but also a proficient linguist, speaking and writing six or seven languages.

He had many varied interests and picked up copious amounts of secular knowledge and understanding of the world around him. He grew tall and handsome, and at a relatively young age married a fine girl named Golda Rochel, who was from a large Yerushalmi family. They began married life in a tiny apartment in the Deutsche Platz in the Old City, where he went to study in Yeshivas Toras Chaim, noted for its outstanding students.

After two little daughters were born, Berel Meir received a request to appear before R' Shmuel Salant, the revered and honored Rav of Old Jerusalem. Such a summons was no small event, and the young man hurried to fulfill his duties so that he would arrive at the Rav's offices on time. "What could be the problem?" he asked himself anxiously. "I hope that R' Salant has not found some fault with me or with someone from my family!"

He need not have feared, for the venerable Rav rose to greet him with a warm smile and a long handshake. R' Salant was not one to waste time with idle talk, and so his purpose in calling Berel Meir was immediately revealed. "R' Berel Meir, we need your help," R' Salant explained. "It has come to our attention that you are not only a *yirei Shamayim* with a reputation as a *chacham*, wise and understanding in all your dealings, but also gifted in your knowledge of languages. I believe you are fluent in several languages — including Russian — in speech, in writing and in comprehension. Is this so?" Berel Meir nodded in the affirmative.

R' Salant nodded back in acknowledgment and continued, "R' Berel Meir, you realize that all of the men of the Yishuv here in Yerushalayim are divided into groups called "*kollelim*," and are engaged in the study of our holy Torah. A vast majority of these *kollelim* and yeshivos are maintained by funds donated by the communities in the Diaspora, especially from Russia and adjoining countries. The money is used to support the yeshivos and their students and families. Each week, about midweek, the letters containing this money reach the post office which is under control of the Russians, but is manned mainly by Arab workers. Between the Russian clerks and the Arab workers, the money somehow manages to disappear before it reaches the Jewish families who wait for it so desperately. The situation has become quite dismal, and our young men simply can't continue this way. Something must be done to save these poor Jewish families and the learning of Torah in the Yishuv, and you are just the one who can do this! We would like you to begin working in the post office."

Berel Meir was taken aback and began to shake his head in resistance. "Much as I sympathize with these poor families and would like to help, I feel that you are asking the wrong person. If I were to take on this post as you ask, I myself would not be able to learn Torah, which is the love of my life. Besides, to work in the post office among all those non-Jewish workers, I would be forced to change my Jewish mode of dress. How could I possibly consider such a move?"

R' Salant tried to press the young man into accepting the position, but Berel Meir was adamant. There was no way that he could take on such a post at the cost of his learning and his *Yiddishkeit*. He just couldn't risk the effect it would have on his young family.

And so the matter was dropped, at least for a few days. But then came another summons to Berel Meir, this time from the Brisker Rav, R' Yehoshua Leib Diskin.

With a heavy heart, for this time he knew the reason he was being summoned, Berel Meir answered the call and appeared before the saintly Brisker Rav. "R' Berel Meir, you cannot refuse us! The livelihood of a large proportion of the Jews of Jerusalem is in your hands and you must save these families! We have already negotiated with the authorities on your behalf and the position is open to you, now! We need a young man who is *yirei Shamayim*; you need only work a few hours daily. You can still continue to learn. Take this on as a holy duty and be blessed!"

There was no choice left in the matter. Berel Meir went to work as manager of the post office of Old Jerusalem. As expected, he handled his duties conscientiously and pleasantly, and his superiors and co-workers knew that he was the right man for the job. He was honest and reliable, and all the moneys and contributions now arrived on time and untampered with, and reached the recipients for whom they were intended. Berel Meir understood the language that the clerks spoke among themselves and thus fired any dishonest ones among them, preventing the "disease" of pilfering from developing and spreading any further. He now realized the vast importance of his presence in the post office, and he understood why the leaders of the Rabbinate had intervened.

All was operating smoothly in the post office until the political situation of the country changed and the Turkish rule came to an end. The Turks bid their farewell to the Holy Land and the British Mandate commenced its rule. The British had formed a camaraderie with the Arabs from the time of the Arab Legion. They were not especially pro-Jewish, and in fact when they later withdrew from *Eretz Yisrael* upon the founding of the Jewish State, they handed over their military installations to the Arabs.

It was up to Berel Meir to approach the British secretary in charge of postal affairs to renew his contract as postmaster under their regime. The matter was settled without any opposition. Then Berel Meir requested that an additional clause be written into his contract, for it was known that the British worked on Saturdays. It would read: "The postmaster, Berel Meir Tenenbaum, will not be required to work on the Jewish Sabbaths nor on Jewish festivals." "How will it be possible for the British authorities to know when a Jewish festival falls mid-week?" asked the British secretary dealing with the affair. "When the Jews go out wearing their *shtriemels*, the special round fur hats that you see them wear on special days!" explained Berel Meir. This too was noted in the contract, which was then sent to England for endorsement by the Government Office and the seal of King George. Berel Meir Tenenbaum was officially installed — or re-installed — in his position as manager of the post office.

Berel Meir continued his job in the same trustworthy and orderly fashion that he had worked all along, never losing sight of the real reason for his being in this post. It once happened that the festival of Purim fell exactly on the day that the letters with their contributions from Russia were due to arrive for the families of the Yishuv. Not looking to shirk his responsibilities, Berel Meir marched into the post office that day wearing his striped *kaftan* and *shtriemel* in honor of the holiday, and sat in his usual place, his garb making his presence felt even more than usual.

All went well in the post office — so well, in fact, that a certificate of commendation was sent to the Postmaster of Jerusalem by the authorities. By this time there were more Jewish clerks working in the post office than ever before.

Then the English New Year approached, and the work load in the post office became quite heavy. "This is no good; those Jews will have to do their bit!" the Secretary declared. "They can draw lots if they want to, but I need at least another three Jews to work, and that includes Saturday! And that goes for the postmaster, as well!" The Jews were forced to draw lots, and the weaker willed and less committed among them agreed to desecrate Shabbos and come in to work. Berel Meir was also informed that he was expected to work on the Shabbos before the English New Year.

It was normal for Berel Meir to arrive home quite early on Fridays. He would first lock up the post office, and then bring home the heavy ring of keys and deposit it in a special safe place in his study. Afterwards he would make his way to the *mikveh*, don his Shabbos clothes — the traditional eight garments of the Yerushalmi Jews of the old Yishuv, including the *kaftan* and *shtriemel* — and go early to *shul* to study a bit before bringing in Shabbos. This *erev Shabbos*, however, was different. Golda Rochel looked out of the window for her husband, anxiously awaiting his arrival. "Where is he?" she cried impatiently, as she bustled around, rushing with the Shabbos preparations.

Just before candle lighting, he arrived home. No clinking ring of keys was in his pocket — and he had no time to go to the *mikveh*. Without further preparation or another word to anyone, he changed for Shabbos and rapidly made his way to the *shul*. Golda had been very worried about him through the course of the afternoon but now she was left in a state of total confusion. "What on earth is going on with him? Hashem should watch over him and protect him!" she prayed with concern.

That Shabbos, Berel Meir was in a particularly spiritual mood. Those who *davened* with him remarked that they had never seen him sing and *daven* with so much enthusiasm and *simchah*. It was as if his soul was rejoicing and lifting him closer to his Creator. At the Shabbos table, he sang the *zemiros* with even more energy and spirit than ever. "*Ki eshmerah Shabbos Keil yishmereini* — If I will guard the Shabbos, Hashem will guard me!" By the time Shabbos ended, Golda Rochel still had no explanation for her husband's unusual behavior.

On Sunday morning, when he normally would have *davened* and hurried off to work, Berel Meir went to the *beis midrash* and remained there all morning. Golda Rochel made her way to the *beis midrash* to seek him out. Not wishing to enter the area where the men sat, she stood at the doorway and sent someone inside to call him out. "*Abba*," she said to him, using a name of endearment which relayed her concern. "Why are you not going to work today? What is wrong? Aren't you feeling well? Won't you come home and eat?" Berel Meir smiled a little and waved his hand as if brushing his troubles away. "It's all right ... I am coming home now to eat. I will explain matters to you a little later, *Imma*," he responded, using a similar term of endearment and trying to keep the tone of the conversation light and warm. She turned, extremely puzzled and perturbed by now, and returned home. He made his way home shortly afterwards, and sat down to eat breakfast, saying nothing further.

Suddenly, the doorbell rang loud and long. At the door stood a special messenger from the post office. He held in his hand a large sealed envelope addressed to Berel Meir Tenenbaum. Golda took it from the messenger's hand and turned it this way and that, asking her husband, "What is this? Tell me. What is going on?" He opened it to reveal the set of keys from the post office that were normally in his possession, and a cable that read: "To the Postmaster! You are hereby pardoned by the British Secretary for Posts for your misdemeanor resulting from the incident regarding Saturday. I request that you overlook my part in the matter and return to work."

Berel Meir began to chuckle quietly. "See, Golda. They came to me!" He dismissed the messenger and began to explain exactly what had transpired on that *erev Shabbos*. When Golda was satisfied that she had heard every nuance of the story in its entirety, she proudly sent him off to his job at the post office.

Later that afternoon, the secretary of posts received a visit from two of the other Jewish postal clerks, who, to their great regret, had worked on the previous Shabbos. They came to see this official to register their complaint: "For what reason did you return Tenenbaum to his post? Just like the rest of us, he was chosen, by lots, to work on Saturday. We cooperated with you as requested and came in to work. After all, you made it clear that we would be thrown out of our jobs without a penny — and lose our pensions as well — if we refused! But Tenenbaum actually had the nerve not to show up for work and now he's being received with honor!"

The secretary replied sternly, "Maybe so. However, had you both spoken as he had spoken, with his strength of conviction about his Jewish Sabbath, I might have reacted differently. He came to me on that Friday, laid the keys to the post office on my table, and said, 'I will not work on the Sabbath, for this would be a terrible wrong to my king!' 'What do you mean, Tenenbaum?' I asked. 'Explain yourself!' To which he answered in a crisp fashion, 'Just imagine that you would take your king and pound inky stamps, just as is done in the post office, all over his head, his arms and his body — until he was unrecognizable from the amount of black ink covering him. Our Shabbos has, in our eyes, the importance and status of a king, of majesty. I, for my part, utterly refuse to treat my king in this way! I know full well that this means a loss of both my livelihood and my pension, and I am sorry about that. But I will not change my mind.' And with 'A Gut Shabbos,' he turned to leave. I tried to call him back, but the fool turned away proudly as if overtaken by great joy in his conviction, as if he had done something wonderful, and off he went!"

The English secretary, a devout Christian, was not overly tolerant of Jews and Jewish practice. He failed to understand why all the Jews did not want to convert to Christianity and thus agree with his view of the world. With this ingrained attitude, he continued: "I was not very impressed with Tenenbaum's reasons for wanting to keep his Sabbath. No, I cannot really sympathize with that. But what got to me, what really upset me, was the fact that he seemed so happy to do this — to go and keep his Sabbath, foolishly throwing away his livelihood. He and his family would starve, and he would whistle away every last copper penny of pension rights! Would you believe that he walked out my door almost singing with delight! He would make all this sacrifice for his religion! For his Jewish Sabbath? Oh no! That I could not stand for! So you see, I had to take him back!"

"My father, R' Berel Meir, was someone very unique, and now you can see why," concluded Dodah Ahuvah. "He stood up for what he believed was right and he practiced his *Yiddishkeit* proudly. And thus he loved to sing in the *zemiros*, 'If I will guard the Shabbos, Hashem will guard me!'"

Bris in Bukharim

The old Bukharim Quarter lies in the area bordering Meah Shearim in Jerusalem. Although now run down, it was in its prime quite a wealthy district that was home to many established Sephardic families. Bukhara, the province from where these families originated, was in Samarkand, in the southern region of the Soviet Union. There the Jews had prospered for centuries and were free to learn Torah and keep *mitzvos* without excessive harassment. The Bukharian Jews, endowed with warm vibrant personalities, had their own special customs. They were known for their *gemilus chasadim*, and for their kindness and hospitality. It was public knowledge, for example, that in Bukhara all the poor people in town were welcome every Shabbos and festival to eat at the home of one of the wealthy and prominent citizens of the province. The Bukharian Jews' fine qualities and good name followed them from Russia to *Eretz Yisrael*.

There, in the sun-baked stone houses of Yerushalayim of the 1940s, life hummed along. The houses were built around flagstone courtyards with close neighbors or several generations of the same family living together and assisting one another in an extended family unit. The housewives would launder clothes together, prepare family *simchos* and *seudos* together and, frequently, at the close of a warm day, when the sun was creeping down into the horizon, they would sit around these courtyards with their babies on their laps and exchange stories of the world around and news events of the day.

The old houses built around their dusty gray courtyards still stand today and many of the older inhabitants remember stories that happened long ago. Some years back, a *bris milah* (circumcision) was held in the family home of one of the respected residents, a relative of R' Ben Zion Abba Shaul, honored *Rosh Yeshivah* of Porat Yosef.

The little boy was born to one of the nieces of the Rav. The young couple discussed what name to give the tender newborn. What is in a name, one can ask. Is it only a pleasant sound to the ear? Jewish sources indicate that a person's name actually holds the keys to his destiny and can have major influence on his life. There is even a recorded incident that reached the *batei din* of R' Yedidyah Frankel in Tel Aviv in which a *mohel* refused to give a child the name "Nimrod." The *mohel* claimed that although the name is of Biblical origin, it is in fact the name of an evil person, in this case one who rebelled against Hashem. (The *beis din* upheld the case of the *mohel* who triumphed over the parents!)

In pondering what to name his new son, the young father remembered an uncle called Rephael, who had died at a young age. He had been a fine young man, learned in Torah, as well as a kind and generous person. Since no one in the family had as yet used the name to perpetuate Uncle Rephael's memory, it now seemed the logical thing to do. However, the young father realized that some people might object to him using the name of one who passed on early from this world. And so, heeding his good wife's suggestion, he went to consult with Mordechai Sharabi, the famed *tzaddik* and kabbalist in Yerushalayim.

The Rav listened intently to the query posed to him and after deliberating for a short while replied, "You may name him 'Rephael,' but you should give him the name of a kosher animal as well. Add on the name 'Zvi,' a deer; it represents the quality of gentleness."

All was set for the celebration of the *bris* on the eighth day, and the *seudah* was prepared in the home of the grandmother in the Bukharim Quarter. There was an additional reason for joy, for two elderly aunts from Bukhara had just gotten out of Russia, away from the clutches of the Communist regime, and had arrived in *Eretz Yisrael* just in time to join in this, their first family *simchah*.

The *mohel* entered and started to prepare his instruments, while the men began singing traditional melodies and *zemiros* in honor of Eliyahu *HaNavi*. It is said that Eliyahu *HaNavi* once spoke out against *Am Yisrael*. From then on Hashem required that Eliyahu attend every *bris milah* as the *malach habris*. He would thus be compelled to speak favorably and in defense of the Jewish people who guard this *mitzvah* and are diligent about bringing each newborn male into the Covenant of Avraham *Avinu*.

As was customary for Sephardic Jews, one or two of the women began to ululate, as an expression of joy, and everyone who had gathered for the *bris* could feel the excitement and happiness all around them.

The baby was brought in to the call of "*Baruch Haba*!" Some explain that the numerical value of the word "*haba*," being eight, denotes the eighth day on which the *milah* is commanded. He was placed on the *Kisei shel Eliyahu*, Elijah's chair, and the *mohel* proceeded with the circumcision.

The *berachos* were then recited and the name was called out — "*Veyikarei shemo b'Yisrael* — his name should be called in Israel — REPHAEL ZVI!"

A murmur spread among those assembled as the relatives whispered to one another the name of the new baby boy. A small whimpering, then a distinct but hushed cry came from the women's section, as the proceedings of the *bris milah* concluded. People turned to see what was wrong, and found one of the old aunts, newly arrived from Russia, with tears in her eyes. She was feebly struggling to explain something to those around her whom she scarcely knew. "What is the matter, Dodah?" they prompted her.

The older woman replied, "The baby's name, is he not called Zvi? Do you know who Zvi was? Zvi was my brother! Zvi was the one that the Communists captured and killed." A collective gasp was heard in the room — and then silence. Could it be sheer coincidence that the young parents had chosen the name "Zvi" for their baby?

But that wasn't all. Suddenly, the silence was shattered by the grandmother of the little boy, a woman of great intelligence and mature good sense. It seemed as if at first she had intended to keep her peace and remain silent, but now that she had heard her aunt speak, she felt the need to share her story.

"Not all will understand, and some will say, 'It's just an old wives' tale,' but nonetheless I must speak up. Last night I had a dream, and I know that some dreams have real importance. In my dream I saw a Jew with beard and *peyos* appearing over the horizon — someone I had never seen before. Then I heard a voice proclaim, '*Dod Zvi ba l'Eretz Yisrael* — Uncle Zvi has come to *Eretz Yisrael*!' Now, what do you make of that? This has to be the same uncle that Dodah just told us about. It can't be coincidence. I'm convinced that the hand of Hashem has caused this to be. May it be a sign that Dod Zvi will stand by this child as he grows and perpetuates the names of two great uncles."

And so it was. Years passed and Rephael Zvi grew into a fine young man, learned and kind. He emulated his two name-sakes and brought joy and *nachas* to his family and to *Am Yisrael*.

The Inheritance

This is the story of Yankele Berliner, a Jew of great wealth who lived in old Berlin at the peak of its affluence. He lived in a time of widespread secularism — an outcome of the German reformation and the Haskalah movement. Yankele Berliner, with his warm affinity for Gerer *Chasidus*, had a fine reputation and was famed for his generosity and fiery piety. This Yankele was a proud Jew, but never arrogant or debasing of his fellow for the sake of his own status. He had a strong Jewish identity and would declare, "I am glad that Hashem created me a *Yid*!" Not just, "*Baruch Attah .. shelo asani goy* — Blessed are You that I was not created a gentile," but "*Baruch Attah* — that I was created a Jew!" In light of this feeling, Yankele would proudly go out on Shabbos wearing his *shtriemel* and *bekeshe*, the special clothes of the *chasidim*, maintaining Jewish identity as did our forefathers in Egypt who also retained their Jewish garments. He was never ashamed of his Jewish learning and was careful to maintain it. His doors opened readily to any Jew, no matter from where he came, and he hosted him with an open hand to provide his material wants and a patient ear to listen compassionately to the needs of his soul. Since Yankele always cared for others, it was apparent that Hashem "cared for him," and He rewarded him with great bounty.

Yankele's wife was a good woman who listened to her husband in all matters except for one — that of their only son, Henoch, on whom she doted. She, influenced by the "enlightened" *maskilim* of Berlin, allowed herself to be persuaded that the only way for her son to succeed in life and to get along in a hostile gentile environment was for him to receive an advanced secular education in all fields. Thus she provided him with the finest secular teachers that money could buy, introducing this clever child to the refinements of German thought and history, the sciences and more. These alone may not have been destructive, but the impact of the Jewish *melamdim* who came to teach the child paled in the face of the assault of the German tutors whose influence was so very dominant. One tutor in particular was captivated by this bright Jewish lad and set his eyes on him. He would talk at length with him in private, no one realizing what the contents of these discussions were until it was too late. Yankele had given in to his wife for the sake of peace. It was a terrible mistake. Henoch's tutor drew him into a circle of friends that pulled him far from his Jewish roots, and rapidly the boy became more and more distant. As soon as he was able, he insisted on leaving home to pursue advanced education in his selected field. When Henoch reached the university he detached himself almost completely from his family and home, which were by now alien to him. In his eyes, he considered himself as part of the German "elite" and fully able to study and compete with the sons of the German gentry. It broke Yankele's heart, but at this late stage there was nothing he could do to reverse matters.

So it remained until the time came for Yankele to depart to the World of Truth. His son, Heinrich, as he now called himself, was called home from the university to pay his respects and final farewell to the father he had never understood. After the *shivah*, or what seemed to him a reasonable period of waiting, Heinrich, the son who was so advanced in the knowledge of accounts and legal affairs, began to examine his father's papers.

"What a rich man!" he said admiringly with a long whistle. "My, oh my! This old father of mine had a natural talent for management and finances! What a pity that he was so uneducated! Just think how much richer and more powerful he could have been had he studied at the university! He could have even become a professor!" As he delved yet deeper into the records, a frown developed on his face. "Gora Kolwaria ... Gora Kolwaria? All these moneys dispatched to this address ... but what is it? Some prime investment of my father's? But as far as I see, there is no record of any returns, no money having been earned by this investment and returned into the account! Why? This needs investigation!" Heinrich sent letters to that address, but to his disappointment he received no answer. He tried to uncover correspondence between his father and this "investment," but there was none. He was mystified and very curious. Having checked on the map to find the exact location of this tiny town close to Warsaw, he made plans to travel there in person to inquire about the fate of all these missing funds.

He set out in style, traveling first class on the train to Warsaw. From there, he requested a place in first class to Monketov and then on to Gora Kolwaria, on the River Vistula, but was met with strange looks and stares from the Polish locals. Finally, one gentleman kindly explained to him, "There is no train at all connecting Warsaw to your stop, which is about 30 kilometers southeast of here on the River Vistula. The local Polish call it Nowy Jeruzalem, and have a certain reverence for the place, which perhaps explains their strange behavior. You have, I believe, missed the last country train in that direction for today, and if you intend to arrive before nightfall, you will have to settle for any means of transport that is available. It is only a small town, you understand. Maybe you can take a *droshke* — an open horse-drawn carriage used by the locals!"

Heinrich felt that every bone in his body was shaken out of its joints by that journey. The *droshke* had no springs, and neither the horse nor the driver had respect for the distinguished passenger that it carried. He was further disillusioned upon reaching his destination. Considering the amounts of money involved, Heinrich expected to find some large complex of buildings, or perhaps a factory that his father had built and developed in this distant place. He did not connect the investment with what he in fact found, which was a yeshivah building. In a state of near shock, he entered the yeshivah and asked for "the manager." He was greeted by the *shamash*, a *chasid* whose appearance and clothing reminded Heinrich of his father. The *shamash* viewed this young man with suspicion, and stared intently at his tailored Viennese suit with its tails and bow tie, and at his shaven face with small moustache and top hat to boot!

Heinrich gave his name, adding his father's name, "Jacob from Berlin," and said that he wished to discuss his father's business "with whoever was in charge." The *shamash* gave an exclamation of recognition — "Yankele Berliner!" — and disappeared briefly to an inner room. Soon reappearing, he ushered Heinrich into a large study lined with *sefarim*. Standing up to greet him was the holy *Sfas Emes*, Rabbi Arye Leib Alter, one of the greatest spiritual giants of the generation, the Rebbe of Gur at the time. Gur, or Ger as it was commonly called, was the name that the Jews gave to the little town of Gora Kolwaria that had been graced with the presence of two great Jewish luminaries who drew Jews into this Torah sanctuary. For the Jews of Poland had their own names in their own Yiddish language for the places of their residence, their homes in *galus*, the exile. Heinrich's journey had led him to the yeshivah where his father had once learned, and to the Rebbe he had once followed. Heinrich felt mesmerized for an instant, aware of the holy eyes that searched the inner recesses of his soul, seeking a window to enter, looking for a dormant holy spark that could rekindle the flame of *Yiddishkeit*, of holiness.

"So, you are the son of Yankele Berliner?" queried the Rebbe softly. "What is your name? Why are you here?" All of the Rebbe's queries were replete with double meanings. "My name is Heinrich," the young man answered, "and I am here to inquire about my father's estates and businesses." The Rebbe nodded silently. "What name were you given by your father, and why are you here?" pressed the Rebbe again. Heinrich was thrown off balance and did not know how to respond. He began to ask himself angrily why he had bothered to come. What did this Rabbi want of him? What could all these irrelevant questions possibly have to do with his father's investments? Gathering his composure but evading the Rebbe's original questions, Heinrich began to explain in a cultivated businesslike manner, like one giving a lecture, "I see that a large amount of money was invested in this property here, but nothing is shown on my father's records and accounts about any returns on his transactions. I respectfully fail to see, honored Rabbi —" but here the Rebbe interrupted him. "Yes, Yankele was a very wealthy man. Your father Yankele had many different kinds of investments, some with greater returns than others. Tell me, Henoch, what did your father leave to you from all of his investments?" Heinrich/Henoch felt very strange at being called by a name long discarded, and struggled to give a good impression. Proudly he recited a long list of assets. "My father left to me and my mother — everything! Hotels in Berlin, houses in Frankfurt-am-Main, banks and business interests everywhere! He had a golden touch for business! Also here, he seemed to have an investment. I do not understand." Again the Rebbe interrupted him, this time with an air of sternness, "No, Henoch, you do not understand. Now again, what did your father leave to you, his child, his son, personally?" With annoyance, Heinrich reeled off a further list of country homes and money transactions, and when he saw on the Rebbe's serious face that this was not what the man was seeking, he declared with great impatience, "I do not know what you want of me! What do you imagine that my father left that I have not told you?"

Despite himself, Heinrich felt an uncomfortable shifting in the sands of his mind. As he watched the intelligent righteous eyes searching his face, it dawned on him that he was in the presence of a holy man. Flickerings of long–suppressed memories began to surface against his will: standing before the Shabbos candles and feeling their glow; a stately table crowded with many guests reciting the Haggadah on Pesach ... And then he saw himself, a small boy in a *shul* where the men wrapped in *taleisim* were standing reverently silent, heads slightly bowed, while the *baal tekiah* raised the shofar to his lips and the piercing *tekiah* of the shofar filled every available vacuum, demanding entry into every sleeping heart. Yes, he had stood then just opposite the *bimah*, in full view of the shofar being blown, and he remembered the awesome feeling coupled with his childish excitement. Henoch twitched, discomfited. He lifted his eyes silently, more humbly, towards the Rebbe, now somehow wanting to hear more.

"Young man!" exclaimed the Rebbe in great concern for this lost Jewish child. "Yankele Berliner, your dear father, was a Jew who lived as a Jew and was proud to be a Jew. He was not ashamed to wear Jewish clothes, for he wore a *bekeshe* on Shabbos, *davened* three times a day, and kept close contact with his Jewish roots and traditions. He used his material investments for a higher purpose, *l'shem Shamayim*, to finance the Jewish poor, to further Torah education, and to support the world of yeshivos and *chasidus*. Not from his own expertise did he succeed, as much as from the *chesed* of the Master of the world. He enjoyed part of the benefit in this world but the majority of the returns on these 'transactions' await him in the '*Olam Haba,*' the World to Come. *V'hakeren kayemes lo l'Olam Haba!* He knew well why he was here, here in this world — in order to provide the money needed for the Torah community and for his Jewish brothers. Unfortunately, Henoch, not all of his investments have yet paid off. You, his only son, his beloved child, have not as yet followed in his footsteps. Where are his wonderful character traits, his *middos* of *chesed*, kindness, and *ahavas Yisrael*, love of Israel? Where has the Jewish learning and love of Torah that your father received from *his* father gone? Why have you not bothered to claim your true inheritance? What indeed did your father leave you?"

There was by then a dawning of light and understanding. The time had come to claim the True Inheritance.

True Light

It was Friday afternoon, scarcely an hour before candle lighting. The house was arrayed in readiness for the Shabbos Queen. It was then that guests would begin to arrive for Shabbos. "If he is a Yid, then he must come in!" Mother always taught us. "The door of a Jewish home must always be open to fellow Jews as welcome guests." This teaching remained with us forever. We didn't always know who these guests would be, but all would be welcome nonetheless.

The door opened to a middle-aged couple — Moshe, a short stocky man, and his wife Binah who followed close behind him, holding tightly onto her kerchief which was tied firmly around her head. Something was clearly different about these two — something was amiss, but it was difficult to pinpoint it at first. Binah seemed to be constantly be asking her husband all kinds of questions — "Which way now, right or left?" — and ordering him — "Take me to my room." When it came time to light the candles, her unsure hands felt and fumbled until Moshe took her hand in his and actually guided her hand with the match toward the wicks. By now it was clear that Binah was blind, that the beautiful aura coming from her Shabbos candles could by enjoyed by everyone but herself. Shabbos in its grandeur, the warmth and delight in the house, the table arranged with the finest that a family can find in honor of the Shabbos, and the joy on Jewish faces — how it hurt the heart to realize that Binah could only sense but could never actually see all of this. Binah had not always been blind, she explained. She had been a normal, sighted child, until that day of disaster, the day that changed her life forever. She fell out of a window of the family's first-floor apartment in the Beis Yisrael neighborhood of Jerusalem, damaging her head and her spine. She was lucky to be alive.

As the Shabbos progressed, *zemiros* were sung, filling every corner of the room, *divrei Torah* were spoken, and the relaxing meal loosened tongues as Moshe warmed to us. If Binah's history was remarkable, then her husband's story was even more so.

As a teenager Moshe had come to *Eretz Yisrael* from the Samarkand area of Russia, where the local Jewish community is predominantly Sephardic. He was not religious and he went to work in the diamond bourse in Ramat Gan as a sorter of diamonds. Honest and reliable, with a quick mind, he found favor with his employer who trusted him with the stock and other aspects of the business. Moshe prospered, and lacked for nothing in the material sense.

As is incumbent on all able-bodied men living in Israel, there came a call for Moshe to report for *miluim* — reserve duty in the Israeli Army. He was sent to a fairly lonely posting, but his tour of duty passed quickly, and he was granted leave to return home on a Friday evening. Moshe bid his farewells to all those on the base, took his backpack and Uzi machine gun, and began to wend his way over the lonely dirt path towards the main road where he would eventually hitch a ride.

As if in a dream, he saw the world spin past him in a split second. Two or three Arab terrorists who were waiting in ambush now pounced on him, grabbing his Uzi. Desperately, he managed to pull away from them and run for his life as they fired after him. He could see nothing in the pitch black, not in front and not behind, but he knew that he had been hit and was losing strength. Summoning superhuman powers, he jumped over a fence and nearly passed out. His pursuers peered over the fence and, seeing his limp frame covered in blood, left him for dead. Weak and in shock, he lay helplessly in his place, unable to move his limbs. He had great difficulty breathing and knew that his injuries were serious.

It was at that point that he had a vision — not a dream, for he was not asleep, but a revelation — something which he couldn't explain. He saw an image before him, of someone whom he had never seen before. With the "eye of his mind" he saw a venerable, saintly Jew with a beard and flowing *caftan* or *glimah,* as it is commonly called, whose hood was covering part of his forehead. The Jew called Moshe by his name, "Moshe, Moshe — get up and move from your place! You must go out to the road and you will live! When you get out, remember what I am telling you. You must come back to the Torah of your fathers and go to learn." Moshe then saw before him a *beis midrash* and inside, at the front of the room, stood a beautifully detailed *Aron Kodesh* with carved wood and gold. "Go to learn in this place, Moshe. And now, move to the road!" With great effort he stirred himself and, forcing his limbs to move, crawled in the direction of the road. There he was picked up by other soldiers who summoned help, and he was rushed to a hospital.

As Moshe sat with us at the table, all eyes riveted on him, he raised his arm to show us a line of scars, reminders of some of the injuries he sustained on that night. Skin hung onto the bone of his wasted arm making us gasp and wonder how he could work with it. Despite several operations, he nearly lost that arm, he said, but *baruch Hashem*, it is still fairly functional. Moshe sustained other injuries as well; he is truly lucky to be alive.

ᘜᕗᕀᘔ

Many weeks passed in the hospital until his strength came back and Moshe returned to the world of the living. He left the hospital and resumed his daily pattern, going back to work at the diamond bourse. In the meantime, he pushed everything out of his mind — he forgot the ambush and the danger and the pain. He also forgot the strange vision, of the saintly Jew and his instructions to Moshe. All faded into the distance in the humdrum passage of everyday life as the sun rose and set in its cycle, and all that had been was as if veiled behind a curtain. But "*Ein stam b'Yisrael* — There is no chance circumstance in Israel," and something would happen to explain it all.

At work one day, Moshe picked up a newspaper and, staring fixedly at a certain photograph, began to feel shivers up and down his spine. He asked his colleague, a religious Sephardi, "Who is this man in the photograph, this Rabbi?" and the colleague answered him, "Why, don't you know? That is the Baba Sali, Rabbi Yisrael Abuhatzeira, the miracle *tzaddik* from Netivot! He is very famous in the religious Jewish world, especially among the Jews of Morocco, the land of his birth. He does wonderful things to help *Am Yisrael!* What, you mean you have never heard of him?!" Moshe did not answer, could not begin to explain. He saw the vision once again in front of him, but could not bring himself to tell his friend how he had seen the Baba Sali in a supernatural way, for fear of how it would sound. His friend would never believe him — would say he had lost his mind. But he himself realized that this was the hand of Hashem; a directive had been issued that could not be ignored. Making an unspoken decision, he completed his week's work and made his way to Yerushalayim.

Moshe started to make the rounds of the various yeshivos for the newly religious, looking for one that was suitable for him. Each gave a different reason why he was not appropriate; one said that he was too old, another that the yeshivah was designed only for Americans and English-speaking people. Moshe was slowly but surely becoming discouraged. Finally, he arrived at a small yeshivah in the heart of Yerushalayim where initially the staff in the office seemed to be less than helpful about his entry into the program. "Go through those doors and wait for the *Rosh Yeshivah* who will shortly come to speak with you. He will then decide what is best," he was told. He came into a medium-sized *beis midrash* with wooden chairs and tables. On the opposite wall stood an *Aron Kodesh* in beautifully detailed carved wood and gold. Moshe grabbed tightly onto the table edge, his eyes thoroughly examining the *Aron Kodesh*, and muttered, "In my vision, I saw it, I saw it!"

"What did you see? Is something wrong?" came a voice from behind him. Moshe turned abruptly to face the *Rosh Yeshivah* who was standing there. Unable to restrain himself, Moshe poured out his story to the *Rosh Yeshivah* who listened with amazement — but believed him, for in our generation there are many miracles involving *chozrim b'teshuvah*. Moshe knew in his heart that this was the right place for him. He was accepted into the yeshivah and began to learn there.

Some time after that, Moshe made his way to Netivot to the home of the sainted Baba Sali. He wanted to see with his own eyes the great *tzaddik* who had appeared to him in his hour of danger, perhaps to explain to the holy Rabbi what had happened. No word of explanation was ever needed. Rabbi Yisrael Abuhatzeira passed his fatherly gaze over Moshe, looking at him with gentle eyes, and then laughed softly — as only one who understands secrets can do.

After Moshe was established in his Torah learning, he obeyed the dictum of *Chazal* that states, *"Lo tov heyos adam levado — It is not good for a man to be alone,"* and he met Binah and married her. Each one understood the impairments of the other. Moshe showed great patience in helping Binah deal with her disability.

৩৯ ৯৩

Binah sat with me on my balcony in Givat Shaul awaiting the approach of nightfall, the end of *Shabbos Kodesh.* Flocks of pigeons took to the evening sky that stretched out to the horizon over Nebi Samuel, the resting place of Shmuel *HaNavi.* The sight was so beautiful that I again felt sad for Binah who could not see it.

Binah's half-closed eyes were raised towards the heavens searching the shifting light that changed its hues from yellow to rose, the gray intermingling with the approaching black until the moon and stars began to appear. "It is now dark!" Binah announced. "Why, you can see!" I exclaimed "I can differentiate between the light and the dark," she explained. "And what else can you see?" I inquired of her with surprise, for I had thought that she was totally blind. "When the morning comes I can see the light rising up out of the darkness! It guides the night away!"

"The light rising up out of the darkness." Her words rang in my mind and the events of the Shabbos returned to me, among so many other examples of *hashgachah pratis*, the hand of Hashem working again and again to deliver each and every Jew from every trial, each from his own exile. Long and bitter is the Jewish exile, the long *galus* extending out of sight like Jacob's ladder whose end was concealed from view in its great height. My heart inquired: When will the light rise out of the darkness, when will come the morning that will "guide the night away"?

From a nearby house, children's voices learning Torah rang stridently through the night of that *motzaei Shabbos*, bringing a brightness, a smile to those who heard. There were chanting a well-known *zemer* honoring the close of the Shabbos — "*Eliyahu HaNavi, Eliyahu HaTishbi, Eliyahu HaGiladi — bimheirah yavo eileinu im Mashiach ben David!* Eliyahu the Prophet ... will come speedily to us with *Mashiach* son of David!" There was nothing else left to say. Surely, they had said it all.

Of the Covenant of
Avraham Avinu

he beautiful complex of the Yeshivah High School in Netanya was the setting for Shabbos *sheva berachos* of one of its former students. Outside the dining room, guests were enjoying the Shabbos meal, while the palm trees swayed in the cool breeze, occasionally dropping their dates onto the green lawn.

"*Tzaddik ka'tamar yifrach* — a *tzaddik* flourishes like a palm tree," the *Rosh Yeshivah*, R' Mendelson, said as he addressed the guests:

I want to tell the story of a Russian youngster who, with his mother, appeared on my doorstep one day, asking to enroll in the yeshivah. Mother and son had come directly from the airport. The 14-year-old young man had a *siddur* under his arm. The mother could speak only a few words of Yiddish and a few words of Hebrew. When she scrambled them together, she made herself understood.

"This is my son, Vladimir. I want you to teach him in your school. How much does it cost, Rebbe?" The mother addressed the Rav as "Rebbe," reminiscent of the manner in which her grandmother might have spoken with the Rav or Rebbe of her town.

R' Mendelson answered with sympathy. "We would be glad to teach your son, and will take him into the school. He can sleep here in the dormitory, and all his meals will be provided for. There will be no charge!"

"No, no! I can't have that!" responded the mother who did not find the proposed arrangement acceptable. "My Vladimir must come home every night after school. I would miss him far too much! Understand, Rebbe, we have only just arrived. I must have my son at home every night!"

"Fine," answered the Rav, "but who will be paying for his transportation to and from home?"

The mother answered with a blank stare, directed at the far wall, and the Rav quickly understood. He countered, not wishing to lose what there was to gain. "It is all right. I will arrange that Vladimir's fares will be paid. Tell me, has he learned something from that *siddur* that he holds in his hands?"

The mother shook her head. "We are not religious, nor have we learned anything about religion. In Russia, no one can learn these things. We get sent straight to Siberia for such things! You will teach my son, right? When can he start?"

The next morning R' Mendelson took Vladimir on a tour of the Netanya campus, with the intention of finding a suitable class for the youngster. It quickly became apparent to the Rav that the new pupil was going to pose a problem, as he did not fit into any class in the yeshivah. In the afternoon the yeshivah program consisted of secular studies, which may easily have suited Vladimir's previous educational background. The first half of the day, however, consisted of intensive *limudei kodesh* studies. The Gemara classes were conducted at a fast pace, with demanding and in-depth questions being thrown to the students, who responded with equally astute answers. It was clear that in a class of students his own age, Vladimir, who knew nothing of Jewish studies, would be lost. Worse yet, if the Rav of a particular class were to expend the time and energy that Vladimir required, the other students in that class would suffer. Not wishing to perform a *mitzvah* at the expense of placing additional strain upon the student body and the teaching staff, R' Mendelson came to a decision. He turned to Vladimir and said, "You will come and sit in my class. I teach the 17 and 18–year–olds. We will see what we can do to help you."

And so it was. Vladimir sat in the top Gemara class. The brightest students of the yeshivah looked upon him with puzzlement, but after the situation was explained to them, they were prepared to give it a try.

On the first day, Vladimir sat daydreaming, and remained completely silent. Any questions that were coaxingly put to him were answered with a blank stare. Then he began drumming his fingers on the desk, disturbing the others. Finally, sounds of snoring came from his corner. He had fallen fast asleep, with his forehead balanced on the edge of the desk. The Rav tried to be patient, but exasperated for the sake of the others, he insisted that either Vladimir make more of an effort, "or else go outside and play ball on the lawn!"

It seemed to R' Mendelson that this experiment was not succeeding. Vladimir diligently reported to class each day, but it was hard to tell whether he was actually learning anything. After a period of about two months, however, the young Russian miraculously began to prove himself, turning a case of hopelessness into growing potential. One day, challenged by a sharp question designed to call him to attention, he was able not only to quote the entire content of the day's *shiur* in *Bava Basra*, but to pose a question of his own, not knowing that it had originally been asked by the *Rosh*. The effect was electric. The other class members stared in awe at their new, younger, "unlearned" colleague. This was the turning point.

From that day on, no one criticized or questioned the validity of the decision to place an inexperienced Russian immigrant into the top *shiur* of the yeshivah. The boy proved himself to be a brilliant student and a sincere *yirei Shamayim*. He questioned the Rav about every aspect of each new *mitzvah* that he learned, with the goal of quickly taking upon himself all of the *mitzvos* of the Torah.

One morning, Vladimir arrived at the yeshivah and went immediately to see R' Mendelson. "I can't eat at home," the youngster said. "My mother doesn't keep a kosher home and she says she can't afford to change it." After making a few phone calls, the Rav was able to solve that problem. New dishes and utensils were bought, and R' Mendelson made himself available to help with all questions of *kashrus*.

The next problem to be dealt with was how to provide a meaningful atmosphere for the boy. He was given an open invitation every Shabbos to the homes of the Rav and other host families. In the company of such warm and special people, Vladimir was able to grow spiritually.

A short while later, the Rav felt that the time had come for Vladimir to take the next step, perhaps the most difficult one. "Vladimir," R' Mendelson began, approaching the subject with great sensitivity. "You are doing so well and yet, as you know, you have not had a *bris milah*, the covenant that every Jew makes with Hashem — from the time of Avraham *Avinu* until today."

"Yes, I know," said the lad, taking a deep breath. This was not going to be easy for him. He rushed ahead, not looking directly into the face of the Rav, and asked, "Please, R' Mendelson, arrange it for me!"

Immediately, the Rav contacted the *beis din* in Netanya which dealt with these matters, and arranged an appointment at one of the local hospitals where an expert *mohel*, experienced in performing circumcisions on older boys and adults, would perform the *milah*.

The time for the *bris milah* came, and R' Mendelson waited in anticipation to hear the good news. However, the next day, the lad appeared in school as if nothing had happened.

"Did you keep your appointment?" questioned the Rav, anxiously. Vladimir looked too good, thought R' Mendelson, to be a patient the day after surgery. "No, not yet," answered Vladimir. "Just as I suspected," thought the Rav. Perhaps it was too early to impose this on the youngster. So the Rav left it alone for a while. A week later, knowing how important this step was in making this young man a complete Jew, he broached the subject again. With a little encouragement, Vladimir asked the Rav to make a second appointment. But again, Vladimir lost courage and backed out at the last minute.

Erev Pesach came, and the young man nervously approached R' Mendelson to ask whether he could join him for the whole week of Pesach. "My parents say they cannot keep Pesach, since it is too hard for them, at their age, to eat only matzah throughout the holiday! What shall I do? Please tell me!"

The Rav began carefully, "Vladimir, I want you to join us for Pesach. But as you know, the Jews on *seder* night eat a portion that recalls the *korban pesach*. In the days of the *Beis HaMikdash*, only Jews who had been circumcised, who had received their *bris milah*, could partake of this *korban*. Even in the wilderness, on the first Pesach, the Jews had this first *mitzvah* of *milah* to perform before they were allowed to take part in the precious *mitzvah* of the *korban pesach*. How will you feel at my *seder* table knowing that if we had a *korban pesach* you would be unable to partake of it?" The young man stared longingly back at the Rav, two brown trusting eyes begging for help. The Rav understood and, feeling the youngster's inner turmoil, recognized the need to lend him support.

"Please, R' Mendelson. I want to eat from the *korban pesach*, or what represents it, and join in the *mitzvah* of Pesach properly. I — I want my *bris milah*."

And so, without any hesitation, the Rav again made an appointment through the *beis din,* at a hospital in Ramat Gan. And this time Vladimir arrived at his appointment as scheduled.

It so happened that the *mohel* was a well-known children's doctor from Jerusalem, Dr. Braverman. In his gentle and professional way, based on many years of experience, he began to speak with the youngster, calming him and helping him to overcome his natural apprehension concerning the minor operation that he faced. Dr. Braverman asked him, "Where are you learning?" The boy answered, "Yeshivas Netanya, with R' Mendelson." With a warm smile the doctor replied, "Why, I know R' Mendelson from Netanya for many years. You are fortunate to have found him! How amazing that I, his old friend, am the one who will perform your *bris milah* today!"

The youngster smiled weakly in return and nodded, his eyes gazing into the distance as if he were engrossed in thought. He then said in a small voice, "Please, Doctor, when you perform my *bris milah* for me, will you try to have the right *kavanah*, intention, and keep in mind that this is *l'shem mitzvas bris milah*? Please say the *berachah* with *kavanah*!"

The good doctor, the *mohel,* had to quickly avert his face to wipe away a tear. He was deeply moved by this youngster's sincerity and depth of character. This young man had the potential to be a true *tzaddik,* to whom it was essential that his *milah* be *l'shem Shamayim.*

After the *milah* was completed, the doctor met with his old friend and explained with great excitement what had transpired. Exchanging notes, R' Mendelson told him the rest of the boy's story. They both marveled at the integrity of the young Jewish boy.

Vladimir came to school a few days later. He said to the Rav, "Don't call me 'Vladimir' any longer. I am now 'Meir Aryeh'!" It was a name that he himself had chosen, for he wished to bring light to *Am Yisrael* and to understand all of the Torah in the correct light, hence the name "Meir." "Please, I am no longer to be called by my old name and I ask that you erase it from all my school records and from all my official documents, as if it never existed. Write in its place, 'Meir Aryeh'!"

Both the Rav and the doctor were thrilled at Meir's response. It seemed that the *bris milah* had opened the way for young Meir to make even greater progress, opening his mind to further Torah learning.

He stayed at the Rav's home for the week of Pesach, and sat quietly through the *seder*, absorbing it all. The following year, he spent Pesach with Rav Mendelson again. During the *seder* this time, though, Meir suddenly offered an opinion on a question posed in the Haggadah that was being discussed by the Rav and the other participants. "Last year," Meir reminded the group, "the Rav discussed exactly this point in great detail and explained the halachah accordingly ..." Meir clearly remembered all of the stories and explanations of the Haggadah that were expounded and discussed in all their detail at the *seder* table the previous year. His memory was crystal clear and his thirst for learning unquenchable.

The young Meir Aryeh returned to the Mendelson family again and again, over many succeeding years, never forgetting a drop of the precious Torah learning that he had absorbed from the previous occasions. He had truly "flourished like a palm tree" and developed into a *tzaddik* of our generation.

Great and mysterious are the ways of the Master of the Universe. It has been asked by many why these youngsters have to come forth from a *galus* as hard as Egypt and prove their righteousness in such a way. A marvelous explanation has been offered. It is explained that Yishmael, son of Avraham and Hagar, will come before the Holy Throne in Heaven and claim, "Look here at these so-called noble Jewish children! They make so much noise about their *mitzvah* of circumcision, at being brought into the covenant of our father Abraham. They are only 8 days old when this operation is performed. They are tiny babies who feel hardly any pain and have no free will to resist! On these grounds, they call themselves the 'Chosen People' and claim total inheritance of the birthright. We, the children of Ishmael, however, make our covenant at the age of 13, when it is much, much harder, for the child is fully cognizant of what he is facing. How can anyone possibly compare one with the other? Thus we are the worthy ones, and, by far, the more deserving of the two peoples."

Then along come the Jewish youngsters and grown men from the Russian exile who have not had a *bris* when they were 8 days old. Their parents could not have this *mitzvah* performed as Jewish law dictates. They had been prevented from doing so by the Communist regime. They were coerced against their will to ignore the teachings and ways of their fathers. But in the Land of Israel, they come of their own volition, their free will, to perform the commandment of Hashem, and they undergo the *bris milah*. They provide a mighty army of defendants for the Jewish people. As our forefathers, Avraham, Yitzchak and Yaakov, approach the throne of the Almighty, they are backed by the thousands of defending angels created by these wonderful mitzvos of *bris milah*, all performed with love, and with full cognizance. This is a defense that Yishmael could never rebut.

"See with what dedication, with what *mesiras nefesh,* Your children undertake the Holy Covenant of *bris milah*!" the *Avos,* the forefathers, proclaim to God.

"*Misboseses b'damayich*! — You were trampled in your blood." This expression is quoted in the Haggadah, describing the Jewish people as they came forth from Egypt as yet unadorned with *mitzvos*. We were granted merit for Redemption by "the bloods," the two mighty *mitzvos* of the blood of *bris milah* and the blood of the *korban pesach*! So too, it is stated by the Sages, will be the redemption still to come.

A Couple Divided

It was wonderful to listen to Dodah Ahuvah reminisce about the Jerusalem of her younger years. Life was so different in the days of the British Mandate, and Dodah Ahuvah had many captivating stories to relate.

When speaking of her wedding day, Ahuvah began by saying, "My wedding was not a run-of-the mill affair, not conventional in any way!" She became a *kallah* in 1947, at the age of 19. Her *chasan* was two years older than she.

Life for the Jews under the British was far from easy, but a bride is a bride, and a wedding is always an opportunity for excitement and jubilation! Young Ahuvah planned on making the most of the occasion, as every bride does for her special day. She bought her wedding gown at "Chic Paris," the classiest bridal salon in Jerusalem. Her headpiece and veil were designed to match the dress, and the ensemble was truly special! It cost all of three pounds sterling, a fortune in those days. She impatiently awaited the moment when she would don her finery. The British might make life hard for them, but Ahuvah was not one who caved in under pressure. Whoever increases the *simchah*, the joy, for the *chasan* and *kallah*, assists in bringing the *Geulah*, the Final Redemption, for it is as if he is adding another stone to the *Beis HaMikdash*. Thus, Ahuvah's mother did her utmost to contribute to her daughter's *simchah* in the preparations to building a new Jewish home befitting a beautiful daughter of Israel. And so, stylish dresses were sewn in preparation for each of Ahuvah's *sheva berachos*. Ahuvah, a girl endowed with lovely looks and a scintillating personality, would be a fine bride and true *eishes chayil*.

Ahuvah's parents, R' Berel Meir and Golda Rochel, lived in "Batei Varsha," in the middle of Meah Shearim. Her parents had taken a small apartment for the young couple on Yonah Street in the Geulah section, adjoining Meah Shearim. Ahuvah's *chasan* was due to arrive with his widowed mother from Tiberias, his home town, in time for the Shabbos *aufruf*, when the bridegroom is traditionally called up to the Torah and showered with candy as a symbol for a sweet life to come. The mother and son would stay in the Geulah apartment until the wedding day.

Excitement mounted as the date approached. The food for the wedding feast was brought to Golda Rochel's apartment, ready to be cooked for the Sunday wedding. The guest list was long and impressive, as R' Berel Meir was well known and respected in the city. According to the time-honored Yerushalmi custom, the parents of the bride attended the *aufruf* celebration and Shabbos *seudah* that were held in the *beis midrash* of the Chasidei Karlin in the Beis Yisrael neighborhood. The *kallah* remained at home with her close girlfriends and several relatives.

After the *chasan* was called to the Torah for an *aliyah*, the *mechutanim* and the guests embraced and exclaimed "Mazel tov!" The candies which had been thrown at the *chasan* were scattered over the floor of the *beis midrash* for the children to gather and eat. Little did the participants at the *simchah* know that a cloud was hovering over their festivities and trouble was brewing.

On that *Motzaei Shabbos*, word spread that Jewish freedom fighters had attacked British installations on King George Street, and 15 British soldiers had been killed. An immediate curfew was imposed on all the Jews of Jerusalem, and no one knew what other repercussions would ensue.

Sunday morning dawned, and as Golda stood in her kitchen with several other women preparing to cook the food for the wedding *seudah*, other family members standing on the balcony observed the British soldiers laying a barbed-wire fence which stretched directly under their window. As they investigated further, it became clear that the barricade divided the center of Jerusalem, from Shivtei Yisrael Street up to Malchei Yisrael Street. Meah Shearim and Batei Varsha were on one side, while Geulah and the apartment on Yonah Street were on the other.

Ahuvah entered the kitchen, pale and close to tears. "My *chasan* is on Yonah Street!" she exclaimed in panic. "The British military have just sealed in my *chasan* on the other side of the barricade!" The women stopped their cooking and crowded onto the small balcony to see what was happening. Gasps of shock and anger were heard all around. "Look what they are doing to our neighborhood! Do they think this is a battlefield? Don't they know that we live here? We are trying to prepare for a wedding! What will be?!"

Meanwhile, the men were discussing the best possible course of action to take. Father came into the kitchen and gathered everyone around. "You, Mamme, carry on with the cooking and don't worry! Ahuvaleh, stop crying and go rest. A *kallah* needs her strength for the wedding, and a red-eyed *kallah* won't look her best! Now, everybody — be happy! All will work out, *b'ezras Hashem*! Just don't worry!"

R' Berel Meir's bright optimism was dimmed by the bleak prospects. Ahuvah's wedding gown waited on its hanger, while her headpiece remained in the shop on the other side of the barbed wire. It was to have been picked up in town that morning, freshly ironed and finished to perfection. The wedding gown was the only dress from her trousseau in her hand; the others were in the house on Yonah Street, where she had so efficiently hung them in readiness for *sheva berachos*. Ahuvah, dressed in a simple robe, stood by the window, tears streaming down her face. Her thoughts were focused on an apartment on the other side of the barbed wire where, no doubt, a similar scene was now being enacted.

There, Shmuel, her *chasan*, leaned heavily on the window sill, feeling foolish and helpless in the face of the odds set against him. His wedding suit hung in the closet, and he allowed his eyes to drift in that direction for a moment, asking himself, "Will I indeed get married today? I have waited a whole year for this day to arrive, and now that it is here, will Heaven grant me the merit to stand with my *kallah* under the *chupah*? I am an orphan, for my father has left this world. He can be with me at my wedding only in a spiritual sense, for his *neshamah* will be there, together with the *neshamos* of all of my grandparents. I am here alone as an orphan. Will not You, Hashem, Who are the "*Avi yesomim*," the Father of orphans, permit me this new start in life, together with my *kallah*?" And so the *chasan* prayed, gazing out over the wire fence that separated him from his dear bride just a short distance away.

R' Berel Meir was not one to stand helpless, or to be defeated by barricades or curfews. He went to ask the advice of R' Werner, one of the more prominent *Rabbanim* of Tiberias who had come to Jerusalem to be *mesader kiddushin*, the rav who would officiate at the wedding. R' Werner was aware of the predicament, and admitted that he knew of others who unfortunately had the same problem. "But do not fear, and do not allow yourselves to become distraught. You will see — the wedding will take place *today*!"

The *chupah* had been scheduled for 1 o'clock, but by 4 that afternoon, the situation remained unchanged without any indication from the British authorities that their anger had abated or the situation had changed. Or, Ahuvah thought sorrowfully, that her wedding — would take place as planned. From her place at the window, she could see numerous guests clad in Shabbos attire milling around the streets on "her side," waiting for the wedding — if there was one — to take place. One of her sisters would not be able to attend the wedding for she was on the "other side," as were the *chasan's* brothers.

Another sister, Esther, could not bear to stand by quietly and witness the *kallah's* tears and distress. With the optimism and courage that she had inherited from her father, she went in search of an English-speaking friend, Mrs. Gatenoz. Together, the two went to appeal to the British captain in charge of the section. Esther spoke while Mrs. Gatenoz translated: "My sister is scheduled to get married today, but because of the barricade she cannot!" The officer retorted abruptly, "That is not my concern! Take issue with your friends who murdered my fellow soldiers!"

Esther did not give up. She cajoled and pleaded, the words bursting forth in a rush, saying, "My sister has waited so long for her wedding, a whole year in fact. Surely you can do something!"

"See here, Miss," the officer replied, "I have a fiancée back home and I have also been waiting a whole year for my wedding!"

Finally bursting into tears, to the discomfort of the English officer, Esther shouted at him, "Then you must have some heart in you! If you are in the same situation, surely you must feel for a young girl who is not to blame for what has happened, who just sits all day long and weeps because today should have been the best day of her life and now it has all been ruined!"

This tactic had the desired effect. The officer was too embarrassed to answer her to her face, but he left the room and issued orders to several soldiers stationed there. They emerged in full uniform and carrying guns. "Well, are you coming then?" said the sergeant in charge. "Where is this bridegroom? Make it quick. We have no time!"

With Esther leading the way, they crossed the barricade into Geulah. They marched at a brisk military pace to the apartment on Yonah Street where the *chasan* and his mother waited in despair. Pounding on the door, the officer shouted, "Open up! Army officer!" Two soldiers stood behind him with guns poised in case it was a trap. The *chasan's* mother cautiously opened the door, not knowing what to expect, and was surprised to see the bride's sister standing there together with the soldiers.

"Make it quick!" the sergeant shouted. "Bring the bridegroom to his wedding! Come along now, I am waiting!" The British officer must have thought he was talking to a platoon of soldiers, instead of to one frightened woman. True to his word, however, the sergeant, together with his men, marched the *chasan* and his mother across the barricade to join the wedding party. There really was "no time" — not even time for the startled young man to don his wedding suit. "What a way to go to a wedding!" remarked one of the British soldiers as they marched.

Checking to see if they had been told the truth, the military escort proceeded to the house of the bride. Once there, however, Esther stopped the British officer from entering, and insisted on going in on her own. She found her sister dejected, slumped in a chair near the window. "Quick, Ahuvah! Put your wedding dress on! Your *chasan* is here and waiting outside! Never mind anything else ... Remember R' Werner promised that your *chupah* would take place today!" Ahuvah looked up, unbelieving. "What do you mean? Now?" she asked, her face brightening. "Yes, now! Immediately!" Esther replied. Ahuvah jumped up and made haste to dress and be on her way. She could not believe it. Was she getting married today after all?

Members of the family rapidly held a conference to iron out last-minute details. One ran on ahead to arrange the *chupah* and at least a *minyan* of men. The British officer, meanwhile, wanted to be sure that Ahuvah was going to this wedding, and so he waited for her to come out. Bedecked in her wedding finery, but without a bouquet in her hands, she made her way rapidly down the steps and walked towards a relative's house where the wedding would take place.

There, in the courtyard, a *chupah* had hurriedly been erected. The family and many guests were hastily assembled to participate in the wedding. The *chasan* came to *bedek* the *kallah* with a scarf that someone had provided. "Wait!" called out the *chasan's* mother in distress. "My late husband had set aside a bottle of wine from my son's bar mitzvah to be used on his wedding day. I have taken great care to save this bottle all this time, waiting for this very moment. For his father's sake, bring the bottle of wine to the *chupah*! In the rush, I left it in the apartment on Yonah Street!"

Again the British sergeant was summoned. Having seen the situation now with his own eyes, he had softened a bit and was willing to cooperate. "Don't worry, Ma'am," he said. "We'll take care of it!" With a family member accompanying him, he rushed back "over the lines" and brought the precious bottle of wine to the *chupah*, where the *chasan* already stood, *davening*. Seeing them return, the hastily recruited *chazan* began to intone the famous moving melody to the traditional poem honoring the *chasan* and *kallah*: "*Mi bon si'ach shoshan chochim ....*" Candles were lit, held by the two escorting women, and the *kallah* began to walk gracefully towards the *chupah*. Moved by the emotion of the occasion after so much stress, the two mothers wiped away more than one tear.

By now it was 7 o'clock in the evening. The *chasan* and *kallah* did not care what time it was. They were grateful beyond words to Hashem that they had merited to reach the *chupah* on their wedding day. Everyone present did their utmost to add joy, "to be *same'ach chasan v'kallah*." The mitzvah took on an even greater dimension in light of all that had occurred that day.

Their tribulations were far from over, however, Dodah Ahuvah continued. Her *sheva berachos* clothes were all "on the other side," in the apartment on Yonah Street. So she wrote a note which they rolled up and "shot" over the divider. Their landlord, a famous Yerushalmi artist by the name of Yitzchak Back, retrieved it. Ahuvah had requested that he pack up her *sheva berachos* clothing and take the parcel to the fence and throw it across the double barricade at the prearranged time. The fence had been constructed so that there were two rows of wire with British soldiers patrolling in between. Ahuvah's parcel did not clear both rows, but fell with a thud into the mud between them and burst open.

The soldier on patrol was not a pleasant man. He considered the event a great joke, and Ahuvah's embarrassment and tears added to his amusement. Using his bayonet, he hooked her precious dresses one by one from the parcel in the mud, and flipped them across to her like a prize performer. Other soldiers standing by laughed at the fun. A crowd gathered near the fence to watch. Poor Ahuvah suffered horribly from the shame of it all.

The parcel, however, had been worth all the trouble. For when Shabbos arrived and the time came for the "*Shabbos sheva berachos*," when, traditionally, the bride goes to *shul* with her mother and mother-in-law, Ahuvah was properly attired. For a bride and groom are considered to be a king and queen and this was Ahuvah's time for majesty. Now on Shabbos, together with her *chasan*, she could feel as a *kallah* should feel.

"Come forth, Shabbos the bride, Shabbos the queen!"

To Raanana — to Refresh the Spirit

*I*n the little town of Raanana, far from the main thoroughfares of life, in a section of town where the houses were mere huts, lived the Rebbe of Raanana, R' Yitzchak HaKohen Huberman. It was to this corner of the Land of Israel that Jews came seeking advice and help, a shoulder to lean on in times of trouble, and a fountain of goodness to refresh the spirit and enliven the soul.

R' Huberman and his Rebbetzin had no children. They lived in a tiny house with walls that were aged and cracked. There were beds, a few chairs, a table held together with some nails, an old cooking stove, an aluminum sink, and virtually nothing else. The stark sparseness caught strangers by surprise, but those who were acquainted with the Rebbe and the Rebbetzin knew that they never felt anything was lacking. Indeed, material belongings meant nothing to the Rebbe. He was beyond the constraints of time and space. Late each morning the Rebbe could be found still wrapped in his *tallis*, completing his *Shacharis* prayers, with the box that contained the *kvittlech*, the petitions and tears of many of *Am Yisrael*, beside him in the corner where he *davened*.

It was known that the Rebbetzin was as great a "Yiddene" as the Rebbe was a great "Yid" — but despite the secrets that she surely knew, and the life of hardship that she willingly shouldered, she maintained her dignity and her silence. She never uttered a word, never voiced a complaint, never divulged a secret. Even as she aged, she never accepted help from anyone. More than once she was offered assistance in preparing her Shabbos gefilte fish, but she quietly refused, patiently wielding the round-handled chopper and manually chopping the fillets of fish into a fine, smooth consistency. When her time came, the Rebbetzin passed away, exactly one year to the day after the death of her great husband. Wonderful tales attesting to her sterling qualities as a faithful wife to her husband and a vital member of the community abound.

৩৵৶৩

R' Yitzchak Huberman was born on the festival of Shavuos into a well-known family of Kohanim in the city of Tomashov. His father, R' Asher Anschel, lived a life fully immersed in Torah study and Torah teaching. His mother, Zlata Esther, steadfastly provided the needs of the household through her small business. R' Yitzchak's *sefer*, *Ben L'Oshri*, was the result of many diligent years of hard work and research. It includes *chiddushim* on the Torah, punctuated by parables and stories, on both simpler and deeper levels.

Yitzchak, a replica of his father, R' Asher, was a child prodigy. By the age of 7, he was expert in *Tanach*. He was a gifted child who did not care to play with other children. There were, to his way of thinking, far more important things to engage his attention. He advanced rapidly in his studies, until his teacher recommended that he sit in the *beis midrash* and learn with the older boys. However, the teacher worried that these boys would take exception to an underaged and undersized *talmid chacham* who most likely would far outshine them in learning. So he requested that R' Asher sit alongside his son so that it would seem that it was he, R' Asher, who was joining in the *shiur*, instead of his son.

⚜

Countless troubles have been borne by the Jewish nation throughout the generations. The outbreak of the Second World War, with all its devastation, did not leave R' Huberman untouched. As the Germans stormed into the town, they burned Jews' houses and marched the occupants off to forced hard labor. R' Huberman, then a young man, was conscripted into a work detail under the command of a vicious German captain, who took advantage of every possible opportunity to beat the men mercilessly.

Gunfire was still being exchanged between the Germans and Poles near the Bulgarian border. One day, several Polish soldiers waylaid a Nazi captain riding on horseback, and killed both the horse and its rider. The immediate reaction of the Germans was a burning desire for vengeance. One German captain forced his way into a house where tens of Jewish families had crammed in ,and drove out 16 men. One of the 16 was R' Yitzchak Huberman.

"Get your shovels and start to dig a pit!" the men were ordered. "Make it six feet by six feet. Next to that dig a second pit, two feet by two feet, understood?" Silently the Jewish men dug, under the piercing gaze of the Nazi. When they had finished, the men climbed out of the newly dug pit to hear the next barked command, "Position yourselves alongside the mouth of the pit in a straight line!"

The German officer passed behind the line of Jewish men and, one by one, flicked their hats from their heads, sending them tumbling into the pit. Upon reaching R' Huberman, he discovered that underneath R' Huberman's hat was a second head covering — a black velvet *yarmulka*.

"Aha! The Rabbiner! I have found their Rabbi!" he exclaimed with a sneer. Without further deliberation, and with a face lined with hatred, he gave the Rav a shove from behind that sent him sprawling to the bottom of the deep pit. Shocked by this cruel act, those assembled peered fearfully down to ascertain R' Yitzchak's condition. The German also peered — but with completely different motives. In disappointment and anger, he realized that, yes, the Jew was still alive, still moving.

"Fetch that horse!" he shouted, his fury mounting by the minute. "The dead horse ... Run and get the carcass and throw it into the hole on top of your Rabbiner! Do you hear me? Move yourselves, Jews!"

Not one man moved. The idea was too ghastly, too diabolical to consider. One after the other, the men began to plead with the German, to beg for the life of their friend. No matter how vindictive this German was, there surely must be a shred of human decency left in him, a shred that would allow him to relent and spare the Rav such a cruel and terrible death! But, like Pharaoh, the German hardened his heart and threatened worse — either the Jews comply with his orders or he would shoot all of them.

Driven by fear, they began to drag the dead horse across the ground towards the gaping black hole. The load was heavy and the work was slow, but the Jews were grateful for any delay that would keep them from completing their task.

The horse was dragged by the unwilling entourage to the mouth of the pit. Suddenly, a senior German officer appeared on the scene. Speaking in German, he snapped at the captain, "This is not the time to bother with these accursed Jews, there is a battle raging on the front." Within minutes, both Germans were gone.

The Jews began to rejoice. From one moment to the next, utter despair became jubilation. They had seen a miracle of salvation performed before their very eyes! They helped R' Huberman up out of the dark hole that had nearly been his grave. Then R' Huberman made them cognizant of the obvious fact — this senior officer who had appeared from nowhere and vanished into thin air as quickly as he had come was an angel, a messenger of salvation.

Years later, when R' Huberman was living in Raanana, he recalled this event. A certain Rav of note was a frequent visitor of R' Huberman's, coming to glean from his *divrei Torah* lessons one could apply to real-life situations. The Raanana Rebbe, as R' Huberman was now known, admitted to him that he was still moved each morning when reciting *Mizmor Shir Chanukas Habayis l'David* right before the *p'sukei d'zimra* prayers. When he would say the words, *"chiyisani miyordi bor* — You have preserved me from my descent to the pit,"* a shiver would run down his spine. He still felt the cold bottom of that pit as if he were trapped there. He knew the fear of having a sword dangling over his head and the relief of being miraculously released from the harsh decree, and he relived the incident each and every day.

Many stories are told by those who sought R' Huberman's assistance and blessings. One well-known Rebbetzin described how she had come to seek his *berachah* for a *shidduch*. He was still wearing his *tallis* when she arrived, as he had not yet completed his morning prayers. He accepted a *pidyon* of *tzedakah* money, and blessed her that she would soon become a *kallah*. She walked away with hope in her heart — but little did she realize to what extent the blessing would be fulfilled. The husband with whom she eventually built a life of contentment and *nachas* was also a Rav who provided enlightenment to the Jewish people.

My father once had a problem with a complicated court case at the same time that a friend of his was in need of advice. They went to seek the counsel of the Raanana Rebbe. When his turn came, father spent considerable time explaining to the Rebbe the ins and outs of the problems involved, matters that had already confused many prominent attorneys. The Rebbe absorbed it all and gave his *berachah* that my father would succeed. A *pidyon nefesh* was given to the Rebbe by the two men, and they left with their minds and hearts at ease.

My father left Raanana to go to Haifa where he had an appointment with the *Beis Yisrael*, the Gerer Rebbe with whom he maintained close ties for many years. He was apprehensive, lest the *Beis Yisrael* question him about his stop in Raanana. Perhaps it was disrespectful for him to have detoured on his way to the Gerer Rebbe.

To my father's relief and wonderment, the Gerer Rebbe didn't wait for any explanations, for as soon as my father entered the Rebbe's room, he said, "Nu, you have been to Raanana, have you not? And there you discussed the law suit before you?" — to which the Rebbe supplied the details.

"And you submitted a *pidyon* in the sum of ... Correct?" R' Huberman in Raanana had no telephone, and these two great men would not waste time idly chatting on the phone in any event. Yet, there was no question that these Rabbanim knew all that there was to know about each of their *chasidim*.

CRXXCD

A recently married young man afflicted with cancer traveled with his wife and parents to visit the Raanana Rebbe. It was apparent that the young man was suffering from the effects of chemotherapy. His gaunt physical appearance revealed that he had been going through a difficult time. What could the parents possibly do to help their son? Would not the Rebbe, with his holy vision and great Torah knowledge, advise them? Could the Rebbe help?

The parents and the young man's wife were overcome with grief and trepidation when the Rebbe did not immediately receive them. Instead, he himself put his powers to work for their cause, *davening* on their behalf, and arranging that they give *tzedakah* as a *pidyon* to assist their son's recovery.

The methods and ways of great Rebbes are often hidden, but the results are evident. The Rebbe was later heard to state that he had "diverted the disease." The young man recovered, rescued from the jaws of death. "But he must volunteer time, and work with the *Chevrah Kaddisha*!" the Rebbe instructed. The young man complied and willingly volunteered his time to do the holy work of the burial society.

The Raanana Rebbe mentioned that there are certain *avodos*, holy works and hidden ways, that would enable him to give blessings which would bear fruit for all those who approached him. "I *daven* constantly that Heaven will show me how to achieve this!" His sole desire was to help his Jewish brethren.

A Rabbi, one of his frequent visitors, came to see him after the Yom Kippur War. As they were sitting and discussing the plight of the Jewish nation, the Raanana Rebbe sighed deeply, and admitted that he had been informed from Above that yet another war with Egypt was decreed on the tired and beleaguered Jewish State. He then broke off and redirected the conversation to other subjects.

The Rabbi again visited the Raanana Rebbe not long after that discussion, and anxiously asked him, "Nu, and what about the war with Egypt that you said was hovering over our heads?" To which the Raanana Rebbe replied calmly, "No, there will not be a war with Egypt after all. I *davened* for this and instead of a war involving us, Libya will go to war with Egypt." Indeed, not much time had passed before a war did indeed break out between Libya and Egypt.

☙❧

Many came to Raanana with broken spirits, and left with newfound hope for a brighter future.

In a ward of the Beilinson Hospital lay the son of a religious Lithuanian Jew. The child was chronically and critically ill. In the neighboring bed lay a child also in grave condition, whose parents were not religious. In the course of time and treatments, the parents of the boys began to talk to one another. It was soon discovered that the non-religious family knew all about R' Huberman, the *tzaddik* from Raanana, and had already consulted him for a *berachah*. "But could you please explain, how you, who do not seem to be observant Jews, have come to know and meet the Raanana Rebbe?" asked the religious parents.

The other father replied with a smile, "Listen, and I will relate my story to you. Although I am not a religious man, my father was *dati*, very religious in fact. One day he became sick and was taken to the hospital. His condition deteriorated and he lapsed into unconsciousness. We feared that he was at death's door. He was not a young man, but a father is still a father, and to us, his children, he was dear and precious whether he was young and in the prime of life or getting on in years. We knew we had to do whatever we could to help him. Someone told us to go to speak to the Raanana Rebbe. Finding him was not easy, for the little street — Rechov Allenby in Raanana — is very well hidden. The taxi driver and others laughed at us and told us that we were mistaken, that Rechov Allenby is in Tel Aviv!

"When we walked into his little house, the Rebbe greeted us as if he had been awaiting our arrival. We did not have to do much explaining, for he explained matters to us instead. The conversation went something like this:

" 'You don't need to tell me for I know that your father is lying unconscious in the hospital with pus on his brain. Is this correct?' We nodded in agreement. 'He needs an operation,' the Rebbe continued. 'Listen carefully and I will explain how this operation is to be performed!'

"The Rebbe then proceeded to supply the details of the proposed operation to remove the pus. We stood listening to this amazing Jew, seemingly detached from the secular world, by no means a brain surgeon, but who, nevertheless, was knowledgeable of every area of life. We were astonished and filled with respect. 'Do it as I have said, and your father will have a *refuah shelemah*!' concluded the Rebbe.

"We, the sons, were determined to follow the Rebbe's instructions to the letter, but were quite perplexed about how to instruct the doctors. How could we, with no technical or medical knowledge of our own, be so presumptuous as to approach a brain surgeon with detailed instructions for the surgery that we wanted him to perform? Still, we saw that G-d wanted my father to live, so we found the courage to do just that.

"I arrived at the hospital and went straight to the surgeon's office. 'I need to see the doctor!' I demanded with some agitation. His secretary told me that the doctors were in a meeting, conferring on medical cases, and could not be disturbed. However, I was too keyed up and could not be put off, for after all, it was my father lying in that hospital bed fighting for his life. The image of him in that bed, with tubes and all manner of apparatus connected to him, was all I saw before me at the time. With that picture in my mind, I knocked on the door of the conference room and walked in. The doctors looked up from their places around a long table and regarded me questioningly. The physician who was treating my father recognized me. He asked me what the problem was, why my face revealed such urgency. I felt flustered and nervous then but I plunged right into the subject and told the truth: I had come from R' Huberman who lives in Raanana. The Rebbe had told me what was wrong with my father. He had explained that he needed an operation to be performed in just such a fashion ...

"The doctor's reaction was completely unexpected. He rose from his chair and placed his hands on my shoulders in a near embrace. 'You cannot imagine what a load has been lifted off me at this moment!' exclaimed the surgeon. 'We were just discussing your father's case. This is a dangerous operation and we did not know how to approach the family with the suggestion that we perform it. We knew that you would find it a difficult decision to make. But now that you tell me that the Rebbe from Raanana has directed us to perform this operation, there is no doubt.'

"It seems that this was not the first time the doctors had heard the Raanana Rebbe's name mentioned. His vast knowledge and insight had made a very positive impression on them on other occasions as well. With this in mind they went ahead with the surgery and my father recovered, *Baruch Hashem*! He enjoyed several good years afterwards!"

⌘⌘

A laborer and his wife from Tel Aviv had a son after many years of being childless. It was apparent to those who knew him, including the teachers of the little boy, that this man was unlearned and hardly able to assist his child in his studies. However, he was a religious person, and therefore sent his son to *cheder*, to a *Talmud Torah*, to join the ranks of the children learning Torah.

The laborer went to meet with the rabbeim, teachers, of his only son at a parent-teacher meeting to discuss the boy's progress and achievements. He waited his turn among many bearded scholars, some with long *peyos*. Many were young fathers who themselves learned in *kollel*, who would sit and learn with their young sons after school, testing them on their knowledge. Even now, some of the fathers sat together, discussing points of *chinuch* and Torah subjects. In marked contrast to these young, learned men was the middle-aged Jew attending his first parent-teacher conference.

The laborer waited his turn to hear what his son's rebbi had to say. At last, he entered the teacher's room and sat down, leaving the door respectfully ajar. As he told the teacher his name, a smile spread across the rebbi's face. "You should know that your son is a genius! Without effort, almost without being taught, this very young child spouts forth *Mishnayos* and *Gemara* like a fountain — more than any other child in the class! We have never seen anything quite like this." The rebbi was a little embarrassed to continue, but seeing before him, to all appearances, a simple Jew, he could not resist. "Explain this to me, if you can. Did you perhaps teach him? Do you have a relative who helps him learn in this fashion?"

The father's face lit up with a broad smile. He chuckled a bit and replied, "No! You should know that it is not me at all. It is the Rebbe from Raanana. I will tell you all about it!" He told how he had gone to Raanana many years earlier, and explained to the Rebbe that he was a Holocaust survivor and had no children. He was the last of his lineage and there was no one to carry on his family's name after he passed on. He was only a simple man, unable to learn Torah — even on an elementary level. "After all, what was left of us, we who came forth from the fire?"

The simple man's honesty and goodness must have touched the Rebbe's heart, for he said to him, "I have something special for you. A very great *neshamah* is waiting to enter this world, a soul whose potential for Torah is splendid indeed."

"So you see, honored teacher of my son," continued the simple Jew, "this is the *neshamah* that the Raanana Rebbe promised to me. This is my son who was born due to the Rebbe's prayers."

The young fathers waiting outside the room had heard the story through the open door, and were all deeply moved. And as the Tel Aviv laborer left, they gazed wistfully after him.

A young couple once approached the Raanana Rebbe with a request that he *daven* for them that they merit children. The Rebbe smiled and stated, "Not this year," for, he explained, he had used up his allotment of *zechusim* for *berachos* in this year. "But with the help of the Almighty — next year!" Surely next year, with a "fresh quota," they would merit a blessing! And so it was.

❦❦❦

The year before the Raanana Rebbe passed from the world, to the pain of all of *Am Yisrael*, a young man came to him for a blessing to have a child. The Rebbe listened patiently and gave him a *berachah* but added, "I may not be here, but bring *arbes* (chickpeas distributed to guests at the *shalom zachar* of a male newborn) and vodka for me to make a *l'chaim* on when your son is born." Encouraged, but extremely baffled by the command, the young man left.

A few months went by, and the young man was grieved to hear of R' Huberman's passing. But indeed, his wife was expecting a baby, and he was more than joyous that the Rebbe's *berachah* had been fulfilled. His joy overflowed when she gave birth to a little boy just as the Rebbe had predicted.

Now the words of the Rebbe echoed in the new father's ears and their true meaning was apparent to him. The Rebbe had said that he might not be here, meaning that he had anticipated his demise, but that the young man should bring *arbes* and a *l'chaim* to the Rebbe. Faithfully, he journeyed to the gravesite of the Raanana Rebbe. Upon reaching his destination he took a dish of *arbes* and a bottle of vodka from his bag and laid them on the monument. "I have brought good news," he stated happily. "We have a beautiful little boy! The Rebbe gave us a *berachah* and asked that I bring the *l'chaim* — so I have come to share my *simchah* with you."

"*L'chaim*! — A blessing to life!"

Unwelcome Visitors

*L*ondon is a gray, damp city, where even the summer weather is, at best, unpredictable. Rain falling by the bucket and dripping umbrellas which hardly keep those underneath them dry are a familiar part of the English landscape. The weather is a popular topic of conversation among the British, who will often open a conversation with, "How is the weather today?" To compensate for the often unpleasant exterior surroundings, the British make every effort to see that their homes are inviting, as "every man's home is his castle." Jewish families would thus buy a buy a house in the suburbs with a garden that could be enjoyed in the not very frequent dry weather and where, in the wet weather, they could find a haven within. It was important that there always be adequate space for guests, as is the practice of Jewish families everywhere. Unfortunately, not all guests are welcome ones, as one suburban Jewish family discovered.

When Efrayim and Faigie purchased their home, they worked on the refurbishment of the interior, for like many English houses built at the turn of the century, it required modernization. They installed a dropped ceiling with spotlights in their main dining room. This room was positioned under a loft which had a small entryway from the backyard. The new ceiling increased the limited space in the loft. Very pleased with their home improvements, the family sat back to enjoy their house — especially the new dining room which they used each Shabbos, together with their guests, old friends and new.

One drizzly Shabbos day, only a few weeks after they had settled in, they were seated at their dining room table enjoying a delicious Shabbos meal when they heard sounds coming from overhead. One young boy heard the noises first, and exclaimed, "Mummy, maybe there are robbers trying to get in!" The father adjusted his spectacles and stared a little nervously at the ceiling. The mother glanced first at her husband's face and then again at the ceiling. Sounds of scraping and thumping were heard — and then, nothing. When the family began to relax and dismiss it as imagination, the banging and thumping began again, this time louder and more insistent. The father went upstairs to the bedrooms to investigate, but found no thieves or any other living soul that did not belong there. The rest of the Shabbos passed quietly but this incident was a puzzle left unsolved.

Motzaei Shabbos came. They lit their *Havdalah* candle, and Efrayim, in his melodious voice, sang the *Havdalah* prayer, *"Hinei Kel yeshuasi, eftach v'lo efchad* — Behold, G-d of my salvation, I will trust and not fear!"* — to which was added the now familiar thumping and pounding, distracting the children until the conclusion of the *Havdalah*. The family was becoming a little unnerved by these strange sounds but their investigations did not bear fruit. No one could explain where the noises were coming from.

It took them until Sunday morning, by the light of day, to reveal the source of their troubles. Faigie went into the garden for something and as she looked up she saw a small gray squirrel hopping out of the loft. It was not shy, but sat on the roof next to the opening from where it had emerged, looked at Faigie quizzically, scraped at the roof a bit with its front paws, and then with a leap bounded away into a nearby tree. "Squirrels!" she gasped. "What a *chutzpah*!" — and she ran back inside to tell Efrayim what she had discovered, that their noisy "robbers" were in fact squatters in their loft, of the gray, furry variety. Efrayim took a ladder and flashlight, climbed up, and gazed into the loft. Sure enough, they had visitors. A whole family of gray squirrels had settled in the loft, perhaps to get out of the rain. There was a father, a mother, and babies — who would be quite charming out in the woods instead of in their house.

The squirrels would not be there for long, Efrayim decided. And that same day, he called in a professional to evict the squirrels and block the entrance to the loft with wire and any other means needed.

Sitting back in their dining room to relax and laugh at the strange events of the weekend, they were far from pleased to hear the by-now familiar thumping and scraping start anew. "Oh no, not again!" they all said almost in unison. The little creatures were not going to give in so fast, and had found a way back in to their chosen home.

Over the next three months, they waged war against the squirrels, with the squirrels winning time and again. The town council's pest-control department could not get rid of them. A private firm of exterminators could not eject them. The family was at a loss for a solution. Explosive noises from cap guns would not chase them away, nor would the brooms with which the girls tried to sweep them away. The squirrel family retaliated by chewing their way through the wiring connecting the electricity to the dining room lights. When the family flicked on the switch, the lights did not go on, and the family remained in the dark!

The next morning the children delightedly pointed to two young squirrels running across the lawn. "Bet it was those two that did it!" the youngest girl exclaimed excitedly, while her father heaved a deep sigh. The squirrels literally *tanced offen kop* — danced on their heads! The family was growing very weary of the intruders.

This sort of thing went on until one day when one of the local Rabbanim came to ask Efrayim for help with some community work. He was shown into the main dining room and took a seat at the table, waiting for Efrayim to join him. He, too, was startled by the sudden loud noises above his head. When Efrayim entered the room, the Rav asked him, "Tell me, what have you got in your upstairs room that makes these strange sounds?" Efrayim grimaced and told him, "We've got squirrels! We usually enjoy having guests, but these have long overstayed their welcome!" He related at length all his sufferings with these creatures since they moved into the house. "Show me how they are entering the house. I would like to see their means of entry," said the Rav, wanting to help.

The two men climbed up the ladder from the yard to the second-story loft and peered inside.

"Wait," said the Rav. "This entrance to your loft, is this where they are getting in?" Efrayim confirmed that indeed it was. "Do you realize you have no *mezuzah* on the entrance?" asked the Rav as he began to smile. They were on the way to finding the solution to the problem.

Efrayim looked at the small entrance and inquired, "Isn't this entrance small enough to be considered a window, and, therefore, does not require a *mezuzah*?" The Rav requested a tape measure and the two of them made the necessary calculations. The entrance was large enough to warrant a *mezuzah*. "A *mezuzah* is definitely required!" the Rav declared. And Efrayim affixed one that same day.

From that day on, no further noises were heard from the loft. The dining room of Efrayim and Faigie was back to normal. The squirrels had "packed their bags" and left, never to be heard from again — at least not within the house.

The following Shabbos, a learned guest, upon hearing the tale, brought up the story found in the *Jerusalem Talmud*, of the *Tanna*, the holy Rabbi Pinchas ben Yair (son-in-law of the famous *Tanna*, Rabbi Shimon bar Yochai). He once came to a place where the villagers complained bitterly that their harvest was being consumed by mice. All attempts to be rid of them, and to stop their foraging from the harvest, proved to be in vain. The saintly Rabbi Pinchas summoned the mice before him, seeking the reason for the plague. The mice gathered before him and squeaked in reply that *terumah* and *ma'aser* had not been adequately separated (as required by halachah) from the harvest. Therefore, they had been commanded from Heaven to take up residence in the fields and to eat of the harvests. When the spiritual oversight was corrected, the physical problem that had resulted was no longer necessary, and the mice left.

"The *mezuzah* is a spiritual guard. As it is stated in the Torah: '*U-ch'savtem al mezuzos beisecha u'vishe'arecha* — and you should write it upon the doorposts of your house and upon your gates!' When this commandment is fulfilled, the Jewish home and its inhabitants are protected from all evil. And as far as the squirrels were concerned, in light of the story of the holy Rabbi Pinchas ben Yair, they were only doing their duty!" concluded the guest.

The Defending Angel

If there will be for someone but a single defending angel out of a thousand [accusers] to declare a man's uprightness on his behalf then [G-d] will grant him grace (Job 33:23,24).

The city of Safed is elevated not only in its geographical location, nestled in the hills approaching the Golan, but also in its spiritual greatness. One of the holiest cities in *Eretz Yisrael*, it provided refuge to many of the *Tannaim*, *Amoraim* and other great Jewish teachers and leaders throughout the generations. They chose this beautiful and peaceful place in which to teach their students and learn Torah in serenity.

This story is dedicated *l'ilui nishmas Menashe ben Najaya*.

The greatest of *tzaddikim* have been laid to rest in her soil. Both the Ari *HaKadosh* and R' Yosef Karo are buried here, and so are many others who were living *sifrei Torah* when they were here on earth. Jews come from every corner of the earth to pray at these holy gravesites. Nearby, is the city of Meron, where the tomb of Rabbi Shimon bar Yochai is located, of whom it is written, "It is good to rely on Rebbi Shimon in times of distress!" Many people continue on from Safed to Meron to pray at Rebbi Shimon's grave.

There is a special atmosphere in Safed, with its beautiful rolling green hills and historic streets which are steeped in Torah wisdom and ancient Jewish history. Famous, too, is the *mikveh* of the Ari *HaKadosh*, where thousands of Jews both now and in previous generations have come to immerse themselves. They hope that by immersing themselves in these special waters, the promise attached to them will be fulfilled: "Those who immerse in its waters will not leave the world without doing *teshuvah*."

On most mornings, as one descends the crumbling stone steps leading to the *mikveh* of the Ari, one can hear the strains of a melody being played. The song seems to come directly from the musicians' heart. "Who is this? What is this?" the startled visitor has been heard to inquire, for it is a sound that demands explanation. The residents of Safed know better. "It is just Gidon Prizat. He is always singing songs to Hashem near the *mikveh* of the Ari!" And as the visitors get closer, they see Gidon, with long beard and *peyos* and a large white *yarmulke*. He is singing songs describing his amazing story, of his journey from living a life at sea to discovering the One Who created him, and living a life of Torah and *mitzvos*.

Gidon Prizat, in his early 20s, was a young man in the prime of his youth. He was extremely strong and fit, both physically and mentally. He lived near the seaport of Acco. Early in his life, he felt the magnetic draw of the sea — "like a drug," he described it — and decided to work as a fisherman. He was not religious at all, and did not even have the most rudimentary knowledge of Judaism. He joined a crew of four seamen who worked on a 25-meter-long fishing boat. The craft weighed over 100 tons, and after extensive preparations,they would set out for the high seas to fish.

Each journey lasted a week or two. The crew often faced arduous conditions, fighting the unpredictable elements. They would return to shore just long enough to unload their bounty of fresh fish, which they sold to Tenuvah, the national Israeli distributor of food and produce, and then they shipped out again on another voyage. It was a life that Gidon loved, full of adventure. The vast expanse of the sea, with its ever-changing temperament, held a magnetic attraction for him. He loved the sea air and reveled in the salt and the spray.

Even during his vacations, he would set out on the water, this time in his kayak. With a carefree "shalom" to his mother, he would paddle out from the "*Chof Sussim* — the Bay of Horses" to face the challenge of the waves. This was his constant adventure. The higher and more dangerous the waves, the better he liked it — all the more to prove his mastery over the surf. He became an expert with his kayak and oars, and even entered national Olympic-grade competitions.

Twice he was awarded first prize amid thundering applause: in the 500-meter race and in the 1,000 meter. He had defeated some of the toughest competitors in Israel.

One Saturday morning, during one of his leaves, he took his kayak and bid his beloved mother the usual "shalom."The sun was shining over the sea and white crests crowned the waves as he headed out from the Bay of Horses. Gidon paddled for hours until he came to a stretch of beach that was near Kiryot Acco, Acco's suburban districts. It was dozens of kilometers from his point of departure. "Where did you come from?" called the men on the beach, who were engaged in various sports. "From the Bay of Horses!" replied Gidon. They looked at him strangely. "Why, that is miles from here!" one of them exclaimed. Gidon had been paddling for more than five hours.

A northwesterly wind was beginning to bluster in from the sea. A storm was brewing, and this boded ill for Gidon. He felt a heaviness in his limbs, but knew that there was no time for him to rest, with a storm threatening. Climbing back into his kayak, he set out again for the high seas. The waves were rising, coming up at him now. He had to pit all his strength against the rising current. He felt a strain on his heart; his throat was parched and dry. He knew from experience that his body was suffering from dehydration. "If anything happens to me, how will my mother feel?" he thought, as his mother's image flashed before him. He gritted his teeth and continued to paddle with all his might.

Gidon's mother was indeed very worried by now. It had been many hours since her son had left home. She, too, was aware of the storm coming and the waves rising, and made her way to the edge of the bay to inquire of the Arabs working in the streets of old Acco if they had seen her son go out to sea. They confirmed that they had seen him many hours ago. She lifted her eyes mistily into the distance, hoping and praying to G-d, that her Gidon was safe.

The waves were still crashing against his kayak and the Bay of Horses was still very distant. Gidon was utterly exhausted; he could scarcely feel his limbs; his mind was becoming numb from the effort of concentration; his eyes were so dry, they hurt. As he doggedly paddled towards shore, he thought he saw something floating on the water, some parcel, perhaps, something thrown from a passing ship. As he neared the object, he looked again and realized that this was no parcel or simple object. It was the limp body of a little girl, about 7 years old, he guessed. She lay face down in the water, her curly hair floating behind her. The waves washed over her, tossing her body this way and that. The current was dragging her further out into the sea. Gidon froze — for a moment his mind did not comprehend what his eyes saw. Mustering the last of his strength, he paddled towards her and lifted her out of the water. He laid her face down, behind him, in the kayak. She was blue and lifeless. Water dripped from her mouth and nose as she lay there. She had, he surmised, been in the water for a long time. Was there a chance she could be revived? With renewed energy Gidon paddled for shore.

With a burst of strength born of desperation, he finally reached the shore, jumped out, and dragged the kayak onto the sand. One of Gidon's friends was standing on the beach. Gidon took the little girl from the kayak into his friend's arms. "I am sorry. I think there is nothing left to do for her!" he gasped, "but I myself am feeling ill — on the point of collapse. I must go." And, with that, Gidon turned towards home. Once there, he went straight to bed and pulled the sheets over his head. He wanted to keep his mother from knowing just how terrible he was feeling. It took him two days to recover from his escapade.

Meanwhile, on the beach, a frenzied scene was taking place. Gidon's friend had called for help. Rescue workers had managed to expel large quantities of water from the girl's lungs. A group of curiosity seekers had gathered around, each offering his own piece of essential advice. "There is nothing left to do — the girl is gone!" one stated. A doctor was called to confirm that she was dead, so that necessary procedures could be followed. The doctor began to examine her, expelling yet more water from her lungs and body.

A woman walking along the beach observed the assembled group and heard shouts of excitement. As she grew closer, she heard snippets of conversations, and, suspicious, tried to get into the circle. She elbowed her way urgently through the bystanders, and as she saw the little girl's body a stifled cry escaped her lips. Her face crumpled and she began to scream, her hands gesticulating wildly. "My daughter! This is my only daughter!"

"*Geveret* ... Madam ... I am so sorry ... she shows no signs of life!" they each told her.

"No! No! Please! She is still alive! You cannot say that she is dead! I know for certain! I know that she is still alive! She is the only one I have left in the world! If you don't revive her, then I will die after her ... do you understand?"

Upon hearing the mother's words the doctor looked up in shock. A murmur rose from the gathered onlookers, urging the doctor to "do something!" Feeling increased responsibility, the doctor took action. He placed the child in his car and drove her to the hospital. There she was placed on a life-support machine.

Hashem, in His mercy, performed a miracle for all to see. What had appeared to be a day of hopelessness and gloom turned into a day of gladness and joy. The little girl opened her eyes and returned to the land of the living. Late that night, Gidon's friend knocked excitedly on his door, bringing him the good news.

Some days later, Gidon, now fully recovered, went into Acco with a friend. As he walked down the street, he heard someone call to him, "Please stop. What is your name? Are you Gidon?" Gidon stopped and turned, and saw a woman hurrying towards him in great excitement. "Yes, I am Gidon!" he replied. "Do you perhaps know who I am?" she asked. "I am the mother of the girl you rescued from the sea! Do you realize the magnitude of the wonderful *mitzvah* that you did? I want to repay you in some way, please."

Some days later, a large box, containing a sports bike, was delivered to Gidon's home. Enclosed was a note: "You saved my daughter's life. You gave back to me the most precious thing I have! Please enjoy this gift!" Gidon was overjoyed. The present was nice to have, but, more important, was the knowledge that the nightmare had turned into a beautiful dream — the little girl was alive and well. And Gidon had been instrumental in saving her.

About six months went by. Gidon was again out at sea, working on the fishing trawler together with the other members of the crew. They cast their nets into the waves. The nets swelled like sponges, waiting for the silvery fish to enter the web and be caught. Once the nets were full, the crewmen would work swiftly, with great skill and dexterity, to draw in the catch.

The next stage of their work was more tedious. The catch was sorted by type. The crew went through the large quantities of fish, placing each type in its own crate. The crates were then stored in the huge freezer in the ship's hold. The nets were then cast overhead again. The seamen that were not needed would retire to their bunks. They would take turns sleeping. The crew members snatched as much sleep as they could, in order to conserve their strength for the strenuous work.

The captain was in the engine room at the wheel. And it was Gidon's turn, along with another man, to work in the freezer. The temperature in the freezer was 35 degrees below zero when the door was left open, and 50 degrees below when it was shut. It was essential to complete the storing of the crates within 20 minutes, otherwise, one's bodily functions would begin to slow down and deteriorate, posing a very real danger to one's life. The crewman who was working with Gidon begged to take leave of him early for he was suffering from fatigue, and needed to sleep. "There are only a few crates left. Please finish the job for me," he beseeched, to which Gidon agreed willingly. As the sailor went to his bunk, Gidon noticed a turn in the tide. The sea was seething angrily. He increased his tempo, not wanting to be in the hold of the ship in the middle of a storm.

He turned to leave, the last crate stacked neatly in place. He reached towards the ceiling of the freezer to push open the hatch, but it was shut tight. It had swung shut after the other man left. Gidon was alone in the freezer, among the crates of cold, stiff fish. Quickly, he took the ladder and propped it against the lip of the hatch. "No problem, I'll get out of here soon enough!" he thought to himself confidently, relying as always on his physical prowess to provide a solution. He climbed the ladder and pushed against the hatch with all his might. But it refused to move. Again, Gidon heaved and pushed, with greater effort, for now he was spurred on by fear. But the door was jammed. His physical strength was of little use to him now. Descending rapidly, he then used the ladder as a mallet, hammering on all the sides of the ship, against its ribs and rafters. But the sound of the enormous engine drowned out all his attempts to raise an alarm.

Hope began to fade. Gidon, in the belly of the ship, realized that no man would come to his aid. He was in dire straits. Feeling utterly helpless and miserable, and with nowhere to turn, he realized in his last conscious moments that his physical strength was useless to him. No material force could help him. His life to this point had been full of emptiness, without purpose or reason. He began to pray to a spiritual Power to come to his assistance. He was hanging by a thread, and, although not a religious Jew, he believed in Hashem as a Higher Power. Gidon began to beg Hashem for his life. His pleas issued from the depths of his soul. *"Ribono shel Olam!* Master of the World! You can see me and only You know I am here. I once saved a little girl from death. Surely, my own poor *neshamah* now also deserves a salvation! Have mercy on me and save me now, as well, so that I and my soul do not go to waste!"

The cold began to take its toll on him. First his arms and legs felt heavy and extremely painful. Then they felt stiff. The stiffness increased until his limbs were paralyzed, without sensation or function. He greatly feared sleep and fought the drowsiness that came upon him, for if he fell asleep, he believed, that would be the end of him. Then the cold affected the trunk of his body. The cold kept inching higher, until it reached his brain. He crumpled, senseless, to the floor.

As he felt his life ebbing away, he became aware of an illumination, a welcome radiance that could be felt, almost touched, almost tasted. He was aware of delight and peace, of a sense of pure goodness that could only belong to the World to Come, in which every Jew has a portion.

Suddenly, Gidon rose from his place, revived. He was no longer in the ship's freezer, but above the whole world. He was detached, free from the physical. He perceived some of the truth that intimated the existence of the World to Come. In that mo-

---

Gesher Hachaim quotes a *Zohar* that just before passing on, every *neshamah* perceives the Divine Presence and goes joyfully to greet it.

ment, in a sensation of indescribable ecstasy and goodness, his life flashed before his eyes. Events from his childhood unrolled before him. He saw his mother as she took care of him through the years. He saw, too, the adventure of the kayak and the rescue of the little girl. He was aware of a special light and did not want to part from it. But at some imperceptible point, the radiance vanished. He returned to the state of nothingness. It appeared to him that he had died. He experienced a total blackout. He was in a void. Crew members filled him in later with the details.

The door of the freezer was opened by the crew member scheduled to cook breakfast. He had come to collect fish to fry. He gasped at the sight of the paralyzed young man lying in a heap on the slats. He ran towards Gidon wanting to gather him up in his arms. But Gidon was as heavy as an iceberg and impossible to move. "Come quickly — all of you!" the crewman yelled in panic to his friends. Within moments, the other men appeared. They each tried unsuccessfully to help. They were forced to get a winch in order raise the frozen Gidon from the freezer.

"Gidon, can you hear us?" the captain called to him, shouting into his frozen ear. He received no response. "He is surely dead!" another exclaimed in shock. The captain radioed for help to the coast guard: "SOS! Crewman feared dead! Urgent medical attention needed!" Gidon, to all appearances, was a dead man. However, they needed a doctor to issue a death certificate. A navy patrol, complete with doctor, drew up alongside the boat. The doctor came on board. "No sign of life to me, I fear, but he needs proper assessment with monitors!" stated the doctor. Gidon was taken to the hospital.

The doctors there tried to revive him. They put monitors and other sensitive equipment to his heart and lungs, trying to detect a glimmer of life. There was none. It seemed that the candle had been snuffed out. Gidon's friends began to despair. Then a specialist, due to leave that day for places overseas, entered the ward. "He is not just frozen, but shows no sign of life from both external and internal organs!" explained the intern on duty to the specialist. The specialist looked at the young man, who lay stiff and inflexible on the bed. It was impossible to stretch or straighten his rigid limbs. The doctor looked into Gidon's face and was impressed with the purity he saw there. Although the specialist was not a religious Jew, he believed in G-d, and knew that he was but a messenger of healing, working for a Higher Authority. "We cannot allow a person like this to go!" he decided. Exerting one last effort, he introduced a hairline needle into the space where oxygen enters the brain, hoping against hope to see some response. To his amazement, he felt a tiny response, or was he just imagining it?

"Cover him with sheets and nothing else. Handle him gently to avoid tissue damage. We must wait to see what happens," he ordered. The first day, Gidon showed no progress, no sign of life. Nor did his status change on the second day. Gradually, "like a frozen chicken thawing," his body warmed.

On the third day, a miracle occurred. Gidon had thawed out completely. He began to feel some sensation in his body, and found that he was gradually able to stretch his limbs. The doctors, and those around, were astounded. It was a revival of the dead. But Gidon had merited a miracle, for"Whoever saves a soul in Israel it is as if he has saved an entire world!" He merited a life for a life. The defending angel, created by virtue of his great *mitzvah*, had spoken up in his defense, and been successful.

Gidon did not return to his life at sea. After his recovery and convalescence, Gidon's father suggested that he join the family's wholesale fish business. He gave Gidon his own living quarters, signed over partial rights to the business, and gave him the keys to the office. Gidon began, falteringly, to work in a world that was totally new and foreign to him, the world of commerce. He did not feel at home in it, and did not particularly like it. In addition, his conscience gave him no rest. He had not forgotten the episode in the ship's freezer. He remembered clearly the details of what had transpired there. Hashem was with him throughout this troubling time and he began to acknowledge *hashgachah pratis* — Divine providence.

Then, with great Divine mercy, Gidon was again led in the right direction. He encountered a cousin who was working as a merchant in the same market. This young man was a *ba'al teshuvah*. "Gidon, what you need is a yeshivah!" he insisted. Gidon answered innocently, "What is a yeshivah?" The cousin looked up in disbelief at Gidon's ignorance and explained what a yeshivah is and how to go about enrolling in one.

The decision and the transition did not come easily to Gidon. There was one night that stands out in his memory. He paced back and forth in his room; sleep eluded him; his mind was in a whirl. Maybe, he thought, he should return to the sea? But no, the sea had, in a sense, turned traitor to him, it had been the instrument of his pain.

Gidon's heart was troubled, and his conscience pursued him daily. The business, in Gidon's eyes, was not successful. He stumbled around in the commercial world, but it offered him little or no satisfaction. It was then that he made up his mind. He left for Yerushalayim and, without daring to tell his parents, enrolled in Yeshivas Diskin in Kiryat Moshe. He "set sail" on the sea of Torah. His Rav and mentor was R' Ben Porat. Within a relatively short time, Gidon became a *ba'al teshuvah*, meticulous in his performance of the *mitzvos*. A full beard and *peyos* now graced his countenance.

His father came to Yerushalayim, searching for him. When his father finally found him, the reunion was far from pleasant. His father felt that Gidon had turned his back on him. "If you leave me, then you can forget me for good!" said his father, aggrieved. Gidon's new chosen path was dramatically different from his father's. Regretfully, Gidon turned to his father and handed him the keys to the business. Then he turned his face again towards Yerushalayim. He became completely devoted to a life of Torah and *mitzvos*.

There was no stopping Gidon as he rose in spirituality, higher and higher. From then on, Gidon was devoted to serving the Holy One, Blessed is He, in every way that he could. He was always trying to improve his performance of *mitzvos*. After he settled in Safed, he undertook the task of spreading his Torah message to other Jews, in his very individual style of song. There, in Safed, he married and was blessed with many children.

Still, there remained a yearning to return to yeshivah and to study full time. The renowned R' Kook of Tiberias lived in Safed at that time. He spoke to Gidon, and told him to remain in Safed, and advised him to record his songs, and even more important, to publicize the story of his life. Song is very lofty and holy. With it, one can reach to Heaven, to the palace of *teshuvah*.

So Gidon's songs spread forth from Safed and the *mikveh* of the Ari to other parts of *Eretz Yisrael*. There have even been performances on Israel Radio. The *mikveh* of the Ari and the holy atmosphere of Safed give him the necessary holiness and emotion that he needs. From his songs, we can hear his message to *Am Yisrael*.

> *King of All the Worlds!*
> *Guard Your children —*
> *Each Jew needs to retain his state of joy*
> *And to escape from sin*
> *To draw close to kedushah …*
> *Each Jew is a unique soul …*
> *He can be in the best state … sometimes the worst … but Hashem awaits the return of His children …*
> *The material world can make the Jew be more materialistic, enveloping him with its allure and separating him from his Source, only allowing him minimal understanding of the Creator …*
> *Hashem created in Man a precious vessel — but the essential emotions and basics of Judaism are kept distant in the face of this materialism …*

Those who sit in the yeshivos Hashem has raised up ...
Like flowers spreading scent ... by their work they purify
the world ...
The Jew is a great treasure, my sons and dear ones, like
a babe or little lamb that has never tasted sin ...
The Ari HaKadosh was forever happy — glad with his lot
... and from this great joy Hashem brought forth for him
greatness and kedushah ...
And I, for my part, am glad with my lot ... as I sit and sing
songs by the mikveh of the Ari ...

One day, when Gidon was singing his songs in his usual place and fashion, a group of tourists came to immerse in the icy waters of the *mikveh*. Many groups visit regularly, from Israel and all parts of the world. They are full of enthusiasm and happiness, often joining hands to sing and dance, in honor of the Ari *HaKadosh*.

Among this group was a Jew who somehow did not "fit in" with the others. "Like a lone wolf in the desert," Gidon described him. He sat, hunched up, in the corner, a shadow across his face. He did not enter the waters, but listened intently to the songs and their messages. He glanced up at Gidon as if he wanted something from him. Gidon returned the glance, trying to encourage him to speak.

Suddenly, without warning, he rose and grabbed Gidon by the sleeve. "You have just saved my life!" he exclaimed, then indistinctly muttered something.

"What happened? Tell me!" Gidon prompted him, startled. Little by little, with stops and starts, the truth emerged.

"I will tell you what happened," the visitor began hesitantly. "My life was full of problems. I became depressed, filled with despair to the point of no return. There seemed to be nothing left for me in life. In this state of mind, I traveled from the center of Israel to Safed with the intention of taking my own life. Just before I took those last dreadful steps, I heard this music floating towards me ... it was so beautiful. I decided to first hear the songs, and then go and commit the deed! As I sat and heard you sing those wonderful songs, I felt a lump sticking in my throat. It seemed to me, at that moment, that the despair and the need to die that had overwhelmed me was evaporating. And in its place was a feeling of warmth and joy! What terrible act was I about to commit? I realized that I could never do it! Your songs saved me from death!"

Now Gidon realized why his Rav had felt that it was so important for him to remain in Safed and to continue with his work. There is indeed power in song.

When the Sailing Ships Reached Port...

This story of the Levy family is well known in Gibraltar. Gibraltar was a trading post for many centuries, with its elbows leaning on Europe and its face beckoning across the waters towards North Africa. Today huge ocean liners, stories high above the waterline, traverse the Straits of Gibraltar, a stretch of water feared in times of old for its choppy seas, and dock at the Port of Gibraltar. The trading ships of the 18th and 19th centuries fought their way to the port using only their wide sails and the wind. They were without such modern advantages as telegraph, communication systems, and up-to-date maritime navigational equipment. They veered anxiously away from the pirates who "plied their trade" in these waters, in order to safely bring their cargo home.

The Levy family came to Gibraltar from Morocco. They were known for generations as a successful, fine Jewish family, who were engaged in the import and export of goods. They would purchase entire shiploads of merchandise, before the ships themselves even docked at port, and would sell the wares at considerable profit. Their wealth was not for themselves alone, for they engaged in works of charity and communal ventures as well.

Yitzchak Levy, head of the family as well as the trading company, had for many years been engaged in the import and sale of flour. When the ships laden with flour dipped their sails and came into port, it was a time of great excitement for the townspeople and harbor hands, for all were glad that they had arrived safely. Yitzchak had been most successful in this venture. Encouraged by his success, thus far, he became more enterprising, and prepurchased cargoes of flour from three separate ships, full possession to be taken on arrival in port. Originating in New York, delivery was promised by the end of February, weather permitting. Trading documents were exchanged and the deal finalized.

As the date of the ships' arrival drew near, an air of anticipation and tension permeated the Levy household. Though the weather was not unduly cold, the rains beat down without respite, and the waves at sea were high. The consignment had left its home port on time, and with G-d's help, would reach Gibraltar before Purim.

Raphael Levy, Yitzchak's son, a restless, chubby 7-year-old with a mass of brown curls on his head, was known for his sharp brain. When his mother found it hard to keep him entertained at home, she sent him on an outing with his aunt to one of the promontories on top of the Rock. "Go and look for Daddy's ships," she said encouragingly. "Tell us if you can see them on the horizon." So with a picnic lunch in hand, he and two of his friends, supervised by their aunt, went up high on the Rock, near the lighthouse. The seagulls wheeled in the air, cawing a warning to approaching vessels to take care. The children watched the waves crashing against the rocks below. Then, lifting their eyes to the horizon, where the sea meets the sky, they saw a large ship with sails unfurled. Full of excitement they began to shout, "A ship! A ship!" As they continued to stare, it seemed that the vessel was indeed approaching. But then, to their disappointment, it turned and disappeared from sight.

Other ships docked at the harbor of Gibraltar, but not the Levys' ships. By Purim, they had still not arrived. The Levy children went on another excursion to search the horizon for the missing ships, while their mother busily prepared the Purim *seudah*. They returned disheartened. They had spotted nothing on the horizon. Little Raphael announced, "Mummy, the ships must have gotten lost. Maybe they didn't know the way to Gibraltar? What will happen to the sailors, Mummy?"

His father overheard Raphael's anxious question, and answered, "We must all learn Torah with love, my son. When the time comes for the ships to arrive, they will *b'ezras Hashem* arrive safe and sound. Ocean travel has always been dangerous, as it says in *Tehillim*, '*Yordei hayam b'aniyos* ... Those who go down to sea in ships and do work in mighty waters.' You see that sailing ships have had to deal with the hazards of the sea for centuries! Concentrate on learning well in the meantime, and do not worry!"

Purim in the close-knit community of Gibraltar was a warm and merry holiday. But, as in all Jewish communities around the world, when the last of the *mishloach manos* had been delivered and the Purim *gragers* put away for another year, the women began in earnest to clean the crumbs out of their homes in preparation for Pesach.

Unlike today, everything then had to be prepared at home for the coming festival. Coffee beans had to be cleaned, roasted and ground. Eggs were washed clean in case some tiny grain of wheat had accidentally stuck to the shell or to the box. All spices and vegetables intended for Pesach use had to be checked for *chametz*. There was no refrigeration, so families had to wait until *erev Yom Tov* to bring their chickens or other animals to the *shochet*. The animals were koshered immediately and prepared fresh. This process would be repeated several times throughout the week of the festival.

The *seder* night arrived, and with great majesty, Yitzchak Levy sat regally at the head of his table. Members of the family were dressed in their finest. Little Raphael stood on a chair to ask the "Four Questions," as his mother beamed with pride. The Levy *seder* was attended not only by family members, but by many poor Jews and visitors to the city as well. Despite the stress caused by the nonappearance of the ships, no worried faces were beheld anywhere. Any anxieties or troubles were disposed of along with the *chametz*. No expense or effort had been spared to beautify the festival. This was the Levys' way, to create an atmosphere of pleasantness and joy.

During *Chol HaMoed* the children were busy making their plans for picnics. The adults, in their reserved, stolid fashion, mapped out their family visits and planned their *shiurei Torah*. In the midst of this holiday fervor came a loud, frenzied knocking at the door. A messenger had come from the dock. "The ships have arrived, Mr. Levy!" he called in a booming voice through the passageway. "Your flour has arrived. You must come to the port and sign the documents, so that the porters can begin to unload!" All eyes were on this middle-aged messenger, clothed in a fashion too youthful for his age, and speaking in a voice too loud to be polite.

Mr. Levy did not lose his composure. In fact, his expression seemed to indicate that he had been expecting this news. He gave a slight nod and answered the courier, "Kindly make inquires and inform me whether the captains of the ships will wait in port until the end of this week. It is impossible for me to take possession of the cargoes of flour during this week. It is the Jewish

Passover, and I am forbidden to own leaven during this time! In fact, I disowned this consignment, according to Jewish Law, prior to the festival's onset. Go back to the port, please, and speak with the captains. Then notify the customs and port authorities, so that they will not interfere with or disturb the ships during this time. I will wait here for their answer."

The clerk looked a little puzzled, for he knew how anxiously these vessels had been awaited, and could not fathom how the Jewish Passover could change the normal procedure. The Arab porters were all ready to unload, and would curse and complain if they could not complete their work, for then they would not get paid. He did not relish the prospect of dealing with them, or facing their anger.

Within the hour, the messenger returned to the Levy residence, where he found Mr. Levy entertaining guests at his table. The clerk felt somewhat relieved, for the reply he had received from the captains would surely make Mr. Levy realize the impossibility of his request and would make the clerk's job a little easier. "Mr. Levy, sir, I have just come back from the docks," he began, at first quietly and deferentially.

"Yes, well, and what is the answer?" questioned Yitzchak. The clerk continued with increasing volume and pomp to his voice, "The captains advise that they must leave Gibraltar for Tangiers by tomorrow morning at the latest and therefore insist that the cargoes of flour be unloaded immediately, and that you sign the papers. I have not gone to the port authorities yet since the captains refuse to tarry. I am sure, sir, that you will agree with me that it is necessary to unload now, for the monetary loss involved is enormous! The porters and stevedores are standing ready, sir!"

Yitzchak rose from where he was sitting. With an unyielding stance he placed his thumbs into his waistcoat, and with a stern look faced the pompous clerk and exclaimed, "Throw it all into the sea!"

His guests looked on in shocked silence and the gentile clerk gasped, thinking that this man had lost his mind. "Mr.

Levy, sir, be reasonable! We are speaking of three full shiploads of cargo!"

"Did you hear what I said?" answered Mr. Levy quietly but firmly. "Into the sea! All of it. And you are to stand there and make sure that my instructions are strictly followed. Is that understood!?" Whereupon Mr. Levy seated himself in full control of the situation and turned back to his guests without another word. The clerk scurried as quickly as he could out of the house, convinced that if the Levys were not insane, then they were all fools. If only he had another job, he wished!

A gentile could never appreciate the significance of Passover, of the miracle of the Exodus for the Jewish people, who cherish this festival in the face of all hardship. He could never begin to realize how serious it would be for a Jew to deliberately take possession of *chametz* on Pesach, a sin bearing a most grave punishment. Yitzchak Levy withstood the test and did the will of the Master of the world.

Shortly after Pesach, Yitzchak returned to business as usual. Now was the time for reckoning and he sat down with his accountant to assess the monetary loss of the flour that had been dumped into the sea. The figure came to 700 pounds, a small fortune in those times. Yitzchak calmly wrote it off as a loss, without a murmur of complaint.

Within the same week, news came of a pirate ship that had been captured offshore. The authorities approached several of the Jewish merchants with the proposed sale of its cargo. It was loaded with jugs of fine olive oil. This was a valuable commodity. Many of the merchants found that the asking price was too steep, but Yitzchak Levy bought it all.

The large jugs were brought into the warehouse at the dock, and Yitzchak and his workers inspected them there. "These are very large jugs!" noted Yitzchak worriedly. "There are few people, even traders, who will be prepared to purchase such large quantities! If they do, they will demand a considerable discount for bulk purchase." He turned to his foreman, a trusted employee for many years. "Go, please, and purchase glass bottles, so that we can decant the oil into them. We will then sell the oil in the smaller bottles at a greater profit!"

That week, Yitzchak, family members, and their workers labored to decant and repackage the oil. There were about 30 huge stone jugs, and two men were needed to tip them as they were emptied. There was, however, a surprise in store for them. As they reached the bottom of the second jug, Yitzchak's brother let out a shout, "Yitzchak, come quickly and see what we have found! Just look!" Yitzchak ran toward his brother. On the bottom of the huge jug were handfuls of gold coins! Everyone came running to see, their voices raised in astonishment. With the level of excitement rising, those decanting the other jugs doubled their pace, impatient to see what secrets would be uncovered at the bottom of their jugs. Sure enough, the third, fourth, and fifth jugs yielded more gold coins. The eighth, ninth, and tenth yielded coins as well. Finally, with all the jugs emptied, piles of gold coins sat on Yitzchak Levy's desk — with a total value of 700 pounds!

This was the exact figure Yitzchak had lost when he ordered the flour dumped into the sea. "Seven hundred pounds we lost, 700 pounds we have regained, without yet selling the olive oil," proclaimed Yitzchak jubilantly. Members of the family milled around the office with beaming faces, ready to declare a *Yom Tov*.

Turning to his small son, Yitzchak quoted R' Tarfon (*Avos* 2:21) with great delight: "'The Employer can be relied upon to pay the wage for your work, and know that the reward for the righteous is in the World to Come.' See, Raphael," he told his son, "you and your brothers just continue learning Torah with love, and keep all the *mitzvos* — and Hashem will take care of all your needs!"

A Pure White Dove

Many and varied are the guests who have graced the Shabbos table of the Tenenbaum family over the years. Just as many and varied are the stories that have been told at that table of Jews from all over the world. One young Yemenite woman spent Shabbos with the Tenenbaums and, after providing some historical background about the Yemenite Jewish community, enchanted those assembled with stories that she had collected from older Yemenite Jews. She felt strongly that these stories should be recorded and passed on to the next generation. "Only by understanding our history and giving over our personal stories and traditions," said the young Shabbos guest, "will our children and grandchildren be able to fully appreciate our Yemenite heritage. She then proceeded to elaborate:

The Jews of Yemen, according to tradition, can trace their roots back to 40 years before the First Temple. It was then that 70 heads of families gathered their children and grandchildren, and escaped from the Chaldeans to Yemen. These first 70 families are said to have come from the Tribe of Judah. They were followed by members of the Tribes of Benjamin and Levi (which included both *Leviim* and *Kohanim*). The Yemenite family Ayaff can trace their roots back to the tribes of Joseph (Ephraim or Menashe).

When Ezra *HaSofer* issued the call to rebuild the Temple, he pleaded with the Yemenite Jews to return from their exile. However, there were among them holy and exalted men, great in Jewish learning and prophecy, and they chose not to return. They told Ezra that they could see clearly that just like the First, so the Second Temple was also destined to be destroyed, so why should they uproot themselves and return only to be exiled again? Ezra, the holy Scribe, was angered by their response, for separating from *Klal Yisrael* and refusing to join in the glorious *mitzvah* of rebuilding the Temple is no simple matter, and he cursed them with dire poverty.

Although there are reports in the history of the Yemenite Jews of persecution and upheavals resulting in severe monetary loss, even more sorrowful was the loss of Jewish souls that they suffered. Riches, to the Jewish nation, include children, for as is written in *Tehillim*, "*Nachalas Hashem banim* — the inheritance of Hashem is children." And the form of poverty that the Yemenite Jews suffered from most during their exile was the loss of their children, both in Yemen and even more when they eventually returned to *Eretz Yisrael*. For, in Israel, in 1948, there were repeated reports of kidnapping of children from the refugee camps.

These next stories bring us the traditions, and the pain, of the Yemenite Jews in the Diaspora.

Not far from Yerushalayim, near the place where, according to one tradition, Dan ben Yaakov is buried, there is a Yemenite settlement called Tarum. There, a young grandmother in her very early 30s described the causes and conditions under which she and her family came to *Eretz Yisrael*, as well as some of the fascinating stories preserved in her family:

When we lived in Yemen, in a village outside of Suneim, life was hard, but peaceful. The more educated Jews lived in the towns, and many were renowned as skilled artisans, particularly as silversmiths and textile weavers. Most of the Jews who lived in the villages and country districts were farmers. Many stories are told of their simple piety and their ancient tradition of learning, especially their delving into the hidden, or Kabbalistic, aspect of the Torah. The Yemenites had their own *chacham*, the *Mori*, as he was known, and many learned scholars. Their pronunciation of the Hebrew language is considered by many to be the most authentic and ancient of which we have knowledge. It was for this reason that R' Beinish Finkel of Yeshivas Mir would make a special effort to hear the Torah portion of the week read by a Yemenite Jew.

The greatness of the *chachamim* could not be diminished even in death. My Savta Bina told me what her father had told her about Mori Salaam Shabazi, who lived in the late 1600s and was renowned among Yemenite Jews. His burial place in Taiz, south of Sana, was known to the locals as a site for miracles. A spring of fresh water ran beneath his grave, and people in needy of a *refuah sheleimah*, healing from illness, would go there and wash in these waters. Childless women would conceive after praying by the gravesite of the *tzaddik*. All Jews spoke with awe and reverence of the sanctity of the place.

Savta Bina's father had told her that on one occasion, when he and several other men had gone to the *kaver* to pray, an old Arab and a few of his companions happened by, bent on having some "fun" at the expense of the Jews assembled there. The silent fervor of the Jews' prayers was punctured by the Arabs' crowing and hooting, "Stupid Jews! Second-class citizens!" This was how the Jews of the time were often regarded by the Arabs, who even demanded that a Jew dismount from his horse or donkey when an Arab approached.

This particular crowd of ruffians directed their harassment not only at the living but also at the dead, in this case, the *tzaddik* who was interred there. In an vile gesture of spite, egged on by the other hooligans, the old Arab jumped onto the grave of the *Mori* and relieved himself on it. His friends burst into fits of hysterical laughter, while the Jews, too frightened to retaliate, hid their faces in their hands and shed tears of shame and anguish.

But this would be the last time those Arabs would laugh. To his horror, the old Arab found himself rooted to the spot, totally paralyzed. He called out in a choked voice, filled with panic. His friends were overwhelmed with dread. They tried to move him, but found that he was like a piece of stone, petrified like Lot's wife. He could not even change his facial expression. For two days and two nights he remained fixed in place, while his friends watched in fear, now utterly silent. Then the Jews, both out of pity for him, and sickened by the sight of his disgusting form stuck onto the resting place of the *Mori*, prayed for his release. Their prayers were answered. Robotlike at first, the Arab's limbs slowly loosened, and he slunk away, while the Arab onlookers watched, open mouthed and full of awe.

As a sign of respect, the Arabs tried to build a shrine around the grave, dragging the stones with their bare hands. The Jews warned them to desist, stating, "Mori Shabazi ordered that no building or *ohel* should be constructed on his grave." Unheeding, the Arabs continued, only to return the next day and find their handiwork shattered, the stones in complete disarray. Three times they built their monument, and even placed watchmen to guard the site. And miraculously, three times it fell down, seemingly of its own accord, and the stones broke up and rolled away.

The Jews lived in fear of the Moslem gentry. The Moslems regarded them as second-class citizens, and called them "*dhimmis*." The young Jews specifically were in jeopardy from the local princes and sheiks.

A young Yemenite *kallah*, adorned in her bridal crown, her jewelry and all her glory, was being escorted to her *chupah*, her family singing and dancing behind her. Suddenly, the local prince rode up on his horse, splitting and scattering the assembled wedding party. He scooped up the frightened bride, a girl of about 12, and carried her off, screaming, never to be seen again.

Jewish orphans were ripe targets for the Moslems. It was a religious duty to convert these children to Islam, a job that the *Imam*, the Moslem priest and ruler, took very seriously, and against which the Jewish authorities in Sana were forever fighting. Therefore, among the Jews, the death of a parent triggered unendurable anguish even greater than grief normally felt by the surviving relatives. If the family was not resourceful enough to act instantly, the mourning of the *shivah* period would be doubly felt, for the orphaned children would be lost as well. The government would simply take them into their custody, unless the orphans were married. This is why marriages between Yemenite Jews were contracted at a very young age. Sometimes orphans were hurriedly sent by escort on the hazardous journey to *Eretz Yisrael*.

The following took place at the time of the Moslem imam Yichye, who ruled until his assassination shortly before the declaration of the State of Israel. It was told to me by Rachel, a woman who had total recall of the incident:

When we heard that my cousins living in an adjacent town had lost their father, we were saddened. But when my aunt, their mother, fell ill and passed away soon after, we were overcome with grief and worry. Three youngsters were now orphaned: Yonah, a girl of about 14, Shlomo, a boy of 11, and Naftali, aged 9. The onus of caring for them fell on my father's shoulders, for he, their uncle, was the closest relative. He took them into our house and hid them in a downstairs storeroom. His chief anxiety was for Yonah, who was particularly vulnerable, considering her age. Emergency arrangements were made for her and a marriage was contracted with a distant cousin of a similar age. The authorities generally would not interfere with a married woman, and thus she would be safe from the clutches of the imam and his wardens.

Within a few days, in the utmost secrecy, without the customary music and celebration, a *chupah* was erected in the backyard. The very young couple stood underneath it somberly, realizing that their marriage was purely *l'shem Shamayim*. Still children, maturity had been thrust upon them overnight, and they conducted themselves with solemnity through it all. Yonah was thus married according to Jewish law, in the eyes of all Israel.

Still uneasy, my father tried to make arrangements for Yonah and her husband, along with Yonah's two brothers, to escape to *Eretz Yisrael*. It was a trip fraught with dangers, and the young couple and my father became more fearful as they became aware of the many obstacles they would have to face. The enormous expense involved, finding reliable guides to assist the group, and arranging for people to help them when they arrived in the "occupied" Holy Land, were just some of the difficulties that had to be overcome. Meanwhile, precious time was slipping away while the plans were being made. My father tried his best to comfort and encourage the youngsters, to strengthen them for the escape. "Be strong, *Hashem yishmor*, Hashem will guard you!" he assured them.

All would have gone smoothly had it not been for an Arab gardener who overheard the family's conversation. He saw an opportunity, not only for financial gain, but for accolades of honor from the Islamic authorities. Thus he smiled toothlessly at his trusting Jewish friends on one hand, while on the other he spewed his venom and reported them to the Arab in command, divulging what he had heard.

I still cry today when I remember what happened. I was only a child, but I still remember the thumping on our door and the forced entry of the imam's soldiers. They grabbed my father and started to beat him, threatening to kill him if he would not disclose the whereabouts of the children. But he refused to speak. Ignoring him, they sent a search party through the house and began to force open doors until they found the steps leading down to the storeroom. Mother then began to scream, "You can't take the girl, she is married! Leave the children alone!" She tried in vain to physically bar the entrance to the storeroom, but the officer in charge smirked and roughly pushed her aside. Within minutes, my three cousins were being taken. Yonah was forcibly pulled away from her young husband. They were dragged bodily from the house and placed on the waiting horses outside. "Uncle! Uncle!" they cried out piteously, but all my father could do was call after them, "*Hashem yishmor*! Hashem will guard you!" He was trying to be brave. The cries of the captured children became weaker as the sight of them faded into the distance. The soldiers galloped down the road, while we all stood at the entrance to our house, sobbing and holding on to one another for support. We were powerless to do anything against the imam's agents.

The shock and the pain took a long time to heal. My father secretly sent a messenger to the ward of the imam in the capital to discover the fate of his brother's children, just as Mordechai went each day to the palace of Achashveirosh to inquire about Esther's welfare. The messenger made contact with Yonah, who had approached him and spoken with him at great risk. She was now dressed as a typical Moslem woman, and her brothers were enrolled in Moslem schools. The boys cowered with fear when they saw the messenger, for they recognized their neighbor and did not dare to speak to him.

Yonah described how the boys had been beaten until they submitted to their oppressors. They were forced to eat non-kosher meat together with milk, and to recite the Moslem prayers. But Yonah then added a message. "Tell my uncle that a miracle was performed for me. I feel sure it was a miracle! Two women were assigned to instruct me in the ways and decrees of the Moslems. They tried repeatedly to force me to eat *treif,* but I would eat only vegetables. After a brief time, both women fell ill and died. Since then, a fear has taken hold of the Moslems, and they have left me alone. I held out against them, and although I am still in captivity, I remain a true *bas Yisrael.*"

My father received the news with mixed feelings, sorrow for the loss of the two boys, but pride and admiration for the brave young woman called Yonah. "*Yonah tehorah* — a pure dove," he called her, his eyes glistening.

When the State of Israel was founded, we all left for *Eretz Yisrael,* and had no choice but to leave the captive cousins behind. We have not heard from them since.

The trip to *Eretz Yisrael* was not easy for us for bandits wanted to attack at every opportunity. R' Alshech of Yerushalayim described the huge number of beautifully adorned *sifrei Torah* that were stolen on this journey, including one ancient *sefer Torah* dating back 900 years, to the time of the *Geonim.* Many other valuable handwritten *sefarim* were stolen by unknown factions during the *aliyah* of the Yemenite Jews. The authorities governing this *aliyah* told him that these precious *sefarim* had been burned, but there was no evidence to support that claim, and some of these *sefarim* were subsequently on view in foreign museums.

Our Sages write, "*Eretz Yisrael nikneis b'yissurim* — *Eretz Yisrael* is acquired with pain," and Jews from all the ethnic groups of *Am Yisrael* can attest to the truth of this saying. The Yemenites were not the only group among the Jews to lose their children to the gentiles. The Catholics and other Christian groups kidnapped Jewish children during many historical periods. Russian Cantonists forced Jewish boys into the Czar's army, and tried to force them to change their faith. The more we investigate, the longer the black list grows. When, please God, the *Mashiach* will come, the identity of all the lost children will be revealed. As we say the prayer *Nishmas kol chai*, we mention the attribute of Hashem, "*Ha'mefaanei'ach ne'lamim* — He reveals the lost ones." And although there are other interpretations of this *pasuk*, these children come readily to mind. Surely, the nations will pay dearly for their crime, for our children are our lifeblood!

The many Cantonist children who refused to bend to the Communist will, the young Yemenite woman who stood firm and proud as Queen Esther in the palace of Achashveirosh and all the other lost ones are truly worthy of honor.

"A pure white dove is Yonah!"

The School in
Bex le Bains

*N*estled in the Swiss mountains, in a village near the town of Montreux in the French-speaking part of Switzerland, was the Institute Ascher of Bex le Bains. Placed in idyllic surroundings, encircled by rolling green fields and sparkling fresh streams that flow rhythmically into the mountainside, this specialized center for Jewish education flourished.

What were its origins? What was its *raison d'etre*, its reason for being? And how many youngsters from all types of Jewish families thrived within its portals?

Dr. Maurice Ascher opened his institute in Neu Chatelle in 1905. Dr. Ascher had been a student at the University of Berne, where young Jewish *maskilim*, assimilated Jews, were among the student body. Many incidents and events involving these *maskilim* made it evident that "something had to be done to counter their impact on young, impressionable Jewish minds." Dr. Ascher was, apart from his secular knowledge, a *lamdan*, skilled and versed in all aspects of *limudei kodesh*. Seeing his contemporaries stumbling about in spiritual darkness — rejecting the riches and beauty of the Torah of their fathers, while trying to imitate the ways of the gentiles — was painful to him. In response to this, he opened an educational institute, initially on a university level, that would help correct the problem. Here, this young generation received Torah-based answers to their questions of faith and belief. It was one of the first schools of its kind.

It was after the First World War, under the direction of Dr. Ascher's son Shimon, that Institute Ascher became a boarding school for high school students and moved into its beautiful campus in Bex le Bains. It aimed to instill high standards of *middos*, Jewish and human values, to the younger generation. Some of the students were from religious families, and some from totally irreligious ones, but all were still young enough and malleable enough to be guided and helped to mature.

During the Second World War, Institute Ascher served as a refugee post, a "city of refuge." In the beginning, whole families found their haven there, after fleeing across the Swiss borders. Soon, however, by directives from the government social agencies and other related organizations, it evolved into a station for refugee children.

It was after the war, however, that the institute expanded and grew in fame and prestige, both in Europe and the Americas, and the children of the best families were proud to attend. It was an international Jewish school, with a wonderful summer camp. And here, apart from the top educational standards, the children received an education for life. Respect for and harmony among Jews of all backgrounds became a prime ethic, a foremost point of *mussar*.

It was not only the students who enjoyed the benefits in Bex le Bains. Due to its location, many adults took advantage of the facilities as a vacation spot and convalescent home. For miles around it was the only place which provided a *shul* and, of course, kosher food. The school raised its own chickens and cows which were milked to provide *cholov Yisrael*. Over the years, many prominent individuals were numbered among its guests.

Just after the Second World War, the Satmar Rebbe found his way to Bex le Bains. Some of his first steps as a free man were taken near the institute. There he immersed in the *mikveh* for the first time after the war, and with great joy and gratitude to Hashem, he baked matzos there for the approaching Pesach.

Other *Gedolei Yisrael*, among them R' Yosef Kahaneman (the Ponevezher Rav) and R' Moshe Soleveitchik, as well as well-known personalities from the Israeli government came to this Jewish oasis to enjoy the peace and rural beauty. Almost weekly incidents took place that remain truly unforgettable.

It was during the month of Elul, when the *shofar* is customarily blown each morning after *Shacharis*, that R' Shimon Ascher took his *shofar* in hand. It was a fine well-made *shofar*, and R' Shimon was distinguished as an excellent *ba'al tokea*. The assembled *minyan* waited in silent respect for the sound of the *shofar*, but there was none. R' Shimon took a deep breath and concentrated both mentally and physically, desperately trying to elicit the fine *tekiah* that everyone was waiting for. But a mere cough and sputter issued, and with a heavy heart he put the *shofar* away for that day.

The next day again, all waited patiently for the *tekiah*. However, it was not to be heard. Frustrated and upset, R' Shimon turned the *shofar* this way and that. He shook it and tapped it, but could find no possible reason why it should not emit the proper sound. He now cried inwardly, and asked himself if there was not some dread spiritual reason why the *shofar* would not blow and thus defeat the accusing angels. How could *Am Yisrael* achieve a true awakening to Hashem and His Torah without the sound of the *shofar*?

On the third day, as he took the polished *shofar* into his tremulous hands, he noticed two brothers who stood near the *bimah*, and his brow furrowed in concentration. He stood engrossed in thought for a few moments, as he recalled the circumstances surrounding the arrival of these boys. These two children had been referred to him by a family in Germany. They had been in the institute for only a short time. When they had arrived, accompanied by a relative, they were dressed like secular German children. They knew absolutely nothing of Jewish practices, and had not the faintest hint of any Jewish identity or background.

Many times, questions about their heritage had arisen. It had been suggested that perhaps they were not of Jewish blood. R' Shimon had brushed the rumors aside with a wave of his hand. He had trusted the relative who had brought them. He believed they were indeed true Jewish boys.

Now, however, he was not so sure and not so confident in his decision about them. Today was the third day that the *shofar* had refused to emit its faithful *tekiah*, and he felt that the fault was his.

"Please, would you two boys leave the *shul* for a minute?" he instructed, pursing his lips as one who must undertake an unpleasant task. The boys obeyed without a murmur and left the *shul*. Now, R' Shimon took a deep breath, raised the *shofar* to his lips ... and *TEKIAH!* Firm and resonant, the blast awakening the Jewish nation to repentance for over thousands of years — the sound that recalls the merit of the *Akeidas Yitzchak*, the sound that will herald the arrival of of *Mashiach Tzidkeinu*, that beautiful, welcome *tekiah* — resounded throughout the little *shul* of the institute.

No one made any remarks in the middle of *davening*, for that would be evidence of a lack of *derech eretz*. But those who witnessed the person looked at one another with amazement and relief.

After the *tefillah*, R' Shimon went to his office. He had many calls to make and telegrams to send. He spent hours writing letters, and did not cease until he had contacted every possible source of information that he could find regarding the genealogy of the two brothers. In no way did he wish to have it said that he had wrongly besmirched the names of these two children.

Two weeks later, he received a call from one of his sources. "R' Ascher? Regarding the two German boys who are studying in your institute ... We are sorry but we must inform you of the truth. After investigation, we have found that although the mother of these boys is married to a Jew, she, herself, is not Jewish."

R' Shimon now understood the incident with the *shofar*.

Madame Esther, the wife of R' Shimon's son Uri, would bake *challos* for Shabbos every week. In her birthplace, Yerushalayim, it was the accepted practice to engage in diversified acts of kindness. Madame Esther learned at a very young age how to perform such acts of *chesed*. Just as her mother always had, Esther prepared extra *challos* every week to send to needy people on *erev Shabbos*. After she married, she hoped to continue this wonderful custom in her new home in Switzerland.

Here in Bex le Bains, however, there was a problem. Who would be the recipients of the extra Shabbos *challos*? Apart from the tiny community of the institute itself, there were only the cows and the non-Jewish villagers nearby. There were no others of Jewish descent in the surrounding area. It was nothing at all like Jerusalem, where one could fulfill this *mitzvah* so easily. She felt saddened and disappointed.

It happened that one day a new *melamed*, a teacher for the children, was hired. He was a widower who lived in Montreux and had unfortunately lost his wife at a young age. For his own personal reasons, he preferred privacy. He would give *shiurim*, Torah classes, to the children of Montreux. A short time later, he began to travel to Margent, another small town, and give a class to the children in the Jewish community there as well. He delighted in this for it gave purpose and direction to his life.

One day, he ran to make his usual train to Margent, in order to arrive on time to give his scheduled *shiur*. As he climbed the steps of the platform, his heart sank, for the train had just pulled out of the station. He was greatly disappointed. With his *sefarim* still tucked tightly under his arm, he made his way to the nearest telephone to inform his students that today, unfortunately, there would be no *shiur*.

Later that evening the Ascher family, sitting together after supper, turned on the radio and heard the news: "Today there was a tragic and catastrophic rail accident! The train that left for Margent was derailed while traveling at high speed. It is not yet known how many injuries or deaths were caused by this accident, but it is feared to be a black day in Swiss rail history."

Minutes later, the telephone rang. It was the *melamed* on the line. R' Shimon asked anxiously, "Are you all right, Rebbi? *Baruch Hashem* that I hear your voice!" The *melamed* exclaimed, "You heard the news? Please rest easily and do not fear. I knew that you would worry that I might have been on that train, but *baruch Hashem*, I missed it! It left a couple of minutes early today!"

Now Madame Esther knew what she had to do. The *melamed* did not wish to take anything from anybody, so he would not be beholden to anyone or in any sense a recipient of charity. Any attempts to invite him or assist him proved futile. So one day, Madame Esther just stopped asking, and simply showed up on his doorstep with Shabbos *challos* in her wicker basket. After presenting them to him and wishing him a "*Gutten Shabbos*," she turned to leave.

"Please, no! I don't want to take ..." he began to protest.

"Now I finally know why I had to come live in Bex!" she answered, as she turned back to him. "I often asked myself what purpose I serve by living here, and but now I have the answer. You cannot refuse me, for *you* are doing *me* a favor. You are actually doing a *chesed* for me! '*Ein adam oseh chesed elah l'atzmo* — A person only performs an act of kindness in order to help himself.' You may think I have come to do a *chesed* for you, but, in fact, you are helping me do a *chesed* for myself. You see, in Yerushalayim, in my mother's house, and in her mother's and grandmother's house, they always distributed *challos* on *erev Shabbos*, and I only want to continue that fine tradition. So please, be so kind as to accept my *challos*!" And the *melamed* did so. Each week after that, freshly baked *challos* for Shabbos were brought to the *melamed* by Madame Esther.

During the summer break, children of all ages would join the other guests, and come to Bex le Bains for vacation. One summer, Mirileh, a very special young guest arrived. She was the granddaughter of R' Itzikel of Antwerp, Belgium (a descendant of Rebbe Elimelech from Lizensk), who was renowned and respected for his stature and *tzidkus*.

Mirileh, who was a thin, delicate little girl, enjoyed the Swiss mountain air and benefited from the healthful atmosphere. And a child from a family of such *tzaddikim* surely inherited some of the family's finest *middos*.

During the week, she was seated at the dinner table beside R' Ascher and his wife. It was an unwritten rule that all children finish the food put on their plate. If the portion was too big to start with, the child could request less, but had to eat it all! This thin little girl was given a tiny scoop of potatoes, an even smaller piece of fish, and a minuscule spoonful of salad. And still she found it difficult to swallow it all. The Aschers, concerned for her health, said nothing, except to encourage and coax her so that she should be healthy.

When *erev Shabbos* arrived, Mirileh heard that the institute did not always serve fish on Shabbos. It was not their *minhag*, although in most Jewish communities it is an accepted practice.

Young Mirileh's eyes grew round with anxiety. "What? No fish on Shabbos?" she asked the family in dismay. The thought was unfathomable. She had been taught that the *neshamos* of *tzaddikim* are incarnated in fish, and through the Shabbos fish, they are received into *Gan Eden*. Also, "*Mi she'ocheil dag b'dag, nitzol mi'dag* — the one who eats fish on '*dag*,' the seventh day, is rescued from '*dag*,' an acronym for *Gehinnom*."

Mrs. Ascher reassured Mirileh that there was no need to worry, her feelings were understood and respected. And indeed, that Shabbos, in merit of the young granddaughter of R' Itzikel, there was fish served in the institute.

Every Jew knows that on Shabbos we are granted an additional soul, the *neshamah yeseirah*. On Shabbos this young girl seemed, as if by a miracle, to acquire an unsatiable appetite. She was transformed. Whatever was placed on her plate, she ate eagerly and with enjoyment, in honor of the Shabbos! The ways of her righteous family were ingrained in her. She could have been called "the Shabbos child"!

◦◦◦◦◦

The Institute Ascher also accepted guests for the major *Yamim Tovim*. One Pesach, years after the institute's establishment, when many guests were expected for the holiday and all accommodations had been allocated, a man, dressed in shabby clothing and in need of a place to stay, arrived at the institute.

It was the custom of R' Shimon Ascher to place an extra chair at his table on Pesach. This chair remained empty. It served as a remembrance of our Jewish brethren of Russia who were not yet able to join in and celebrate the holy Festival of Pesach, who had not gone from "*avdus l'cheirus* — from servitude to freedom," for they were still in bondage under the Communists.

This unknown Yid, who arrived at the institute without prior notice, was from Russia. Presumably, it was intended that he fill the empty chair as an emissary of his brothers.

Madame Esther welcomed him. She saw a Jew with a beard and with *peyos* who was very reticent in his manner, and so shabby in appearance that it pained those who saw him. She arranged for fresh clothes and directed him to the *mikveh* where he could immerse himself on *erev Yom Tov*. She also showed him the room that had been prepared for him. He nodded with gratitude, but seemed amazed that anyone should bother. It was apparent that he had not expected such lodgings.

He said little and spoke to no one. In fact, he shunned attention and the company of others. But when people saw the way he *davened*, or how he secluded himself, they began to whisper among themselves that this mystery man was in fact a hidden *tzaddik*, an *eved Hashem* whose entire being was dedicated to Hashem's service.

The time for *Maariv* on the first night of Pesach arrived. it was the "*leil shemurim*, the night of watching," the time of majesty when Hashem guards each of his Jewish children. The unnamed Russian Jew entered the small *shul* to join in the *tefillah*. After the *davening*, everyone went to sit at the *seder* table. They escorted him to the special chair that was readied in honor of the captive Russian Jews, but he would not sit on it. Instead, he took his Haggadah into an adjoining room and quietly conducted his own *seder* there, while possibly lending an ear to the more public *seder* in the next room.

So it continued throughout Yom Tov and Chol HaMoed, then through Shabbos Chol HaMoed. The Russian guest would go to *shul* and *daven* together with the others, but then he would disappear without speaking at all. He would eat all his meals alone. He responded politely and with obvious gratitude to the hostess, but not once did an unnecessary word escape his lips.

The last days of Pesach arrived. The guests were already a little restless, knowing that at the close of the Yom Tov, after

Havdalah, they had to journey home, each to his own — sometimes distant — destination. The adults and the children would pass the little room where the Jew from Russia sat, poring over a *sefer*, in his own world, oblivious to the comings and goings and the general hubbub that surrounded him. Dinnertime arrived on the last day of Yom Tov, and knowing that this meal would have to satisfy them through their journey home, young and old alike ate heartily of all that was served. Supper was set in the adjoining room for the Russian guest. No one saw him, but he did partake of some of the food.

"*Havdalah! Havdalah!*" The children began to call to each other. The guests were summoned to the main dining hall to hear *Havdalah* before taking leave of their hosts and of one another. Madame Esther remembered the mystery *tzaddik*, who, no doubt, would also want to hear *Havdalah*. She went in search of him. She checked the *shul* and the surrounding grounds. She sent two children to check all the likely places, but they could not find him. Somewhat embarrassed, and not wishing to intrude on his privacy, a privacy that was obviously so essential to him, she quietly went up the stairs to his room. She timidly knocked on his door.

Speaking in Yiddish, she called out in a tone of respect, "Forgive me for disturbing, but we are going to make *Havdalah* now!" There was no sound. She repeated her request, this time louder, but no response was forthcoming. Now, feeling bolder, she turned the handle, opened the door and found a spotlessly clean room with the bed made and, apparently, never slept in. Every item in the room, including the water pitcher and the sparkling, clean glass that had been put out for the guest, sat exactly as it had been prepared before Yom Tov. Nothing had been used. Madame Esther stood in the doorway, completely dumbfounded. She knew that he was a mystery man, but this was totally unexpected. Where had he slept for the entire eight days of Pesach? If he had not used this room, where had he been? And where was he now? Her imagination flew in all directions, and her questions were endless. But no one could supply a reasonable answer to even one of them.

It was indeed a mystery — one that has never been solved.

ᏩᎾᎮᎨᎤ

Two alumni of the institute sat together one *Motzaei Shabbos* enjoying a *Melaveh Malkah*. Two candles were lit on the white covered table before them, the flames flickering in honor of the Shabbos that was now departing but leaving a portion of its *kedushah* for the coming week. "Do you remember," one young man asked the other, "how it was in the Institute Ascher in Bex?"

The other laughed a little. "Yes, I remember. I remember that the youngster who came with long *peyos* stayed with his *peyos*, for he was not allowed to cut them; but the boy who came from a very modern family whose father would object to more *chasidic* ways was not allowed to grow his *peyos* long!

"Yes! And I remember the boy without manners who sat at R' Ascher's table and shouted out 'Salt!' like one bellowing at some menial servant. R' Ascher turned his head and pretended not to hear. Then the boy yelled louder, so that everyone heard. Then, R' Ascher turned to him in that decisive fashion — very quietly, but in the way that everyone knew he was serious — and answered him, 'Here, we say, "Please," when we ask for salt and we do not yell at each other!' The message got through, for the boy turned very red and very silent!"

"Then there was the teenager who at first could not get up in time for *davening*," reminisced the second young man, "but slowly, with respect and understanding, he was coaxed into appearing each morning. In fact, young people of every kind came to the institute, but R' Ascher and his son managed to make *'menschen'* out of all of them."

"Yes, I remember!" replied his companion.

The flames flickered and danced, casting shadows on the table. The light was illuminating, continuing … It would not easily be extinguished.

The Masmid

en measures of wisdom descended to the world. Nine were taken by Yerushalayim (Tractate *Kiddushin*). It is no wonder, then, that Yerushalayim attracts men of superior ability and character. Such a sage was R' Nosson Lubart, the fiery *masmid* from the yeshivos of Poland, principally Lublin.

To merit the birth of a prodigy, a family must have special attributes. To raise such a child is a taxing and formidable task, to which anyone involved with educating extremely bright, gifted children will attest. "The child is the father of the man" is an old English proverb, and the story of R' Nosson bears this out.

Yocheved, the mother of R' Nosson Lubart, was a grand-daughter of the sainted *"Chidushei HaRim,"* R' Yitzchak Meir of Gur, on her father's side, and R' Naftali Ungar on her mother's side. In her youth, Yocheved's mother had suffered from a chronic illness which threatened her life. The doctors threw up their hands in despair. Her father, R' Naftali, was aggrieved that he might lose his only daughter, the apple of his eye.

In tears, he approached an old friend, a pious *chasid*, rich in years and wisdom, and poured out his sorrows to him. "Give me some advice. What can I do?" he implored. "I have one daughter who, like a budding flower, is just reaching maturity, but is in danger of being uprooted before she can fully blossom." The old man sighed deeply, his bright eyes filled with compassion. He gave a reply that could be given only by a true *tzaddik*, one who places the good of his friend before his own needs. "I am already old and full of days, sated with the good of life. Let me assume this harsh decree that has been placed upon your daughter. I will go in her stead so that she may survive!"

And so it was. The old *tzaddik* died, and the girl recuperated. At the end of the *shivah*, the seven-day mourning period, the old *chasid* appeared to his lifelong friend in a dream.

"You should know, my friend, that the judgment of the Holy One, Blessed is He, is not a false judgment, for Hashem does not punish capriciously. Your daughter was punished because of her behavior and if you do not take heed, the trouble could recur, G-d forbid. She goes out each day onto the balcony of your house, while a neighbor waits and watches for her, in order to admire her beauty!" The father spoke to his young daughter about this matter and she took his words to heart. From then on she guarded herself meticulously, and soon gained a reputation for being outstanding in the *middah* of *tzinius*, modesty.

Her grandson, Nosson, was born a genius. At the age of 3, he went out with his older brother who was busy reviewing a page of Gemara, repeating the subject matter again and again. The latter ignored his young charge, his babysitting job that day, as they sat on the grass. When they returned home, little Nosson proudly announced, to the astonishment of the family, "I know a Gemara! Just like a grown-up!" To prove it, he took his brother's Gemara and repeated fluently, by heart, the very page his older brother had just been learning.

So he began and so he continued. He was iron willed and steadfast in reaching his goals, never allowing laziness or fatigue to get the better of him. He would not let anyone "put him down" if he decided something was right. Study and Torah learning were his paramount joys. He cared not at all for worldly pursuits. He would debate and argue with his father. Young Nosson would also have his way in subjects that he believed he should be studying, although his father disagreed. He began to learn the *Zohar HaKadosh* at a very young age, reading it surreptitiously under the bedcovers or in other hidden places.

One day, at the age of 9, he found a copy of *Tanya*, R' Shneur Zalman Liadi's classic work of chassidic thought. He disappeared for hours. A hue and cry ensued. His mother and other members of the household organized a search party to find him. Eventually, they found him tucked away in a corner, happily reading, and not understanding what all the fuss was about! Even while he was sleeping, he was still learning. He could be observed reviewing Gemara in his sleep, his brilliant brain still active, his lips silently moving, mouthing the words of the text.

R' Nosson's family lived with their grandfather, R' Shimon Chaim, who was a brother of the holy *Sfas Emes*, R' Yehudah Aryeh Leib of Gur. To be near a Jew of this caliber was to taste a little of the Palace of the King. Nosson's mother realized this and would not allow this golden opportunity to slip through her fingers. When the zaida, grandfather, would *daven*, the mother would take her young son and station him in a corner. From there he would watch as his zaida drenched the floor with his tears, leaving a permanent impression in the child's mind of what sincere *tefillah* and true devotion to Hashem should be.

At a young age, Nosson left home for a yeshivah located near the home of one of his uncles, who agreed to look after him. Learning was his life. He did not even return home to celebrate his *bar mitzvah*. Traveling in those days was a strenuous undertaking, and he would not waste time which could be spent learning.

After his *bar mitzvah*, Nosson decided that since he was now a man, he should go on to bigger and better things. Nosson Lubart, just past 13 years of age, intended to apply for admission to Yeshivas Chachmei Lublin.

Yeshivas Chachmei Lublin, established by the *Gaon* R' Meir Shapiro, the renowned founder of the worldwide *Daf HaYomi* (the system where every Jew studies one *daf*, page, of Gemara a day, completing *Shas* within a seven-and-a-half year period), was one of the most prestigious yeshivos in Poland at that time. Accepting only the elite of the yeshivah world, its entrance requirements were exceptionally high. A young man needed to know a substantial amount of Gemara by heart, for the exam was oral and the questions completely unpredictable. The young man being examined could be "ground to a fine powder" by the Rav who examined him. Questions were asked seemingly at random on any part of the Gemara the boy had learned. The aim was to provide *Am Yisrael* with top-level teachers and religious leaders, while the other students who were not quite of the same caliber would be able to appreciate the subtle nuances of Torah learning, in order to encourage and support it.

Until that time, the majority of yeshivos relied on local laymen to help feed and sustain the yeshivah boys. If the layman was wealthy and generous, the young man ate well, and was healthy. If the layman was not prosperous, the young man would have to subsist on a lot less, sometimes at the cost of his well-being. This custom was called *"essen teg"* (eating days) in the popular idiom. Yeshivas Chachmei Lublin, however, was run on different lines, original and dynamic ones. Fresh rolls and pats of butter were provided for the youngsters every day. Laundry was also taken care of so that the boys could be free to learn without distractions. To finance these innovations, R' Meir Shapiro turned to the Jewish world at large, accepting donations in any amount.

The beautiful and stately multifloored building — which today is used as a medical school by the Polish government — was completed after many difficult years of fund-raising by R' Meir Shapiro. The yeshivah occupied the building for only about five years after its completion, before it was taken by the Nazis during the Second World War, though the students attempted to resist and defend themselves and their yeshivah.

One alumnus of the yeshivah recalled how the *Rosh Yeshivah* added a verse to one of the *zemiros* of Shabbos, "*Libi u'vesari yeranenu l'Kel Chai*," which was written by the Ibn Ezra. Frequently, this song was sung in sublime tones by the yeshivah students. R' Meir sang it not long before he passed away, about 18 months before the war began. Some say that he foresaw the tragic events that were approaching, for the verse that he added runs thus: "*Ozlas yadeinu, v'tosh kocheinu, bas kol tenachameinu, od Avinu chai* — Our hands have gone limp, our strength has ebbed away, may a Heavenly voice console us, still our Father lives."

It was to this legendary institution that young Nosson traveled. He arrived at the chambers of the *Rosh Yeshivah*, and begged to be admitted as a student. The *Rosh Yeshivah* looked at him almost in disbelief, seeing before him a young boy. He refused to accept him, adding gently, "I have a train to catch soon, and I'm sure your parents will be worrying about you. Come, I'll take you with me to the station and put you on the train home!" He escorted the boy to the local train station and together they sat waiting on the platform.

Nosson was devastated, seeing his life's dream slipping away. He began to plead with the *Rosh Yeshivah*, "Please! Please accept me!"

The *Rosh Yeshivah* gave him a sharp rebuttal, "What size shoes do you wear?" But Nosson was sharp enough not to be put down and retorted, "Do you take students into your yeshivah according to the size of their shoes or the size of their head?" The *Rosh Yeshivah* now turned and stared hard at his youthful adversary. He perceived an acuity and intelligence far beyond the norm. He parried back, "Tell me, what size head have you got?" To this, Nosson replied decisively, "One hundred times Tractate *Pesachim!*" The *Rosh Yeshivah* was smiling a little by now. "Listen," he said, "there are just a few minutes left before the train comes. I will examine you, but not on the Gemara that you have learned. Let us see if you know how to prepare a piece of Gemara with which you are unfamiliar." The *Rosh Yeshivah* produced a Gemara *Nazir* from under his arm, opened it up to a place at random, and handed it to the *bar mitzvah* boy. "You have just a few minutes now!" he said.

In less than the few minutes allotted the boy announced, "I am ready, quite prepared!" Surprised, the *Rosh Yeshivah* began throwing questions at him, not only from the page that he had shown Nosson, but from the previous one as well. Nosson replied with precision and clarity, citing the previous page to enhance his responses. "How did you know that the previous page was needed?" the *Rosh Yeshivah* asked. Nosson grinned and replied that the subject, in fact, is introduced on the previous page!

The *Rosh Yeshivah* was overjoyed. He hugged the youngster and proclaimed, "Correct! You are mine!" So it was that R' Nosson became one of the top students in the yeshivah. He was among those who learned 18 hours daily without a break. As a result of marathon standing sessions learning on his lectern, he had blistered and cracked elbows. He decided to complete the entire *Shas* in one year, learning seven *blatt* (folios) a day with all the commentaries. He had an abundant love of books, and delighted in the fact that his yeshivah possessed one of the largest and most prestigious *limudei kodesh* libraries in all of Europe. The *sefarim* reached up to the ceiling. To obtain a *sefer* from the top shelf, one had to climb a ladder. One evening, R' Nosson climbed up to get a volume, and stood on the top rung leafing through the pages. The next morning he was found still at the top of the ladder, totally engrossed in his study of the *sefer*, oblivious to the world around him.

Sleep was for lesser individuals. R' Nosson only slept three hours out of the 24. And when the need for sleep descended, he deliberately covered himself with only a very light cover so he would not fall into too deep a slumber and oversleep. Every Shabbos he would learn through Tractate *Shabbos*, along with *Eruvin* on the longer Shabbosos. He was a prime example of the yeshivah boys of the days before computers, when the mind and memory were honed into fine instruments for recording information.

The Second World War began. The yeshivah was attacked, and whoever was able to, escaped. R' Nosson was among the fortunate ones. He fled to *Eretz Yisrael* on the same ship that carried the *Imrei Emes*, R' Avraham Mordechai, the Gerer Rebbe.

Reaching Yerushalayim, R' Nosson immersed himself in his learning. His renown soon spread throughout the community as a *masmid* of highest caliber, the type of *talmid chacham* whose acuity was hard to equal. He married, and for a short time lived in Teveryah, but soon returned to Yerushalayim. Shabbos for R' Nosson meant nonstop learning and no sleep. Leisure time was for locating others of similar aptitude, in order to engage in Torah debate and development. R' Nosson found such a gem in R' Mottel Slonim. A special bond developed between them, for R' Mottel was a very wise man who loved to "talk in learning."

R' Mottel, out of curiosity, decided one day to test R' Nosson in his learning and degree of mental stamina. As R' Nosson entered R' Mottel's study, R' Mottel held a volume of the *Zohar HaKadosh* in his hand, his brow wrinkled and anxious as he leafed through the pages. He read a few lines, while he shook his head with worry. "What is your problem, why are you so anxious?" asked R' Nosson. R' Mottel replied, "I cannot find such and such a discourse!" To all appearances, it perturbed him to the extent that he had lost sleep over it. For a few moments, R' Nosson sat, his head cupped in his hands, lost in thought. Suddenly, he sat bolt upright, exclaiming sharply, "No such discourse! There does not exist such a *Zohar*!" R' Mottel began to laugh. When R' Nosson realized that the matter was just a joke, he turned around and left. He did come back later, but learning for R' Nosson was too serious a matter to joke about!

Years later, as old age approached, R' Nosson contracted an illness that ultimately proved fatal. One yeshivah boy who came to visit him asked in awe, "How many times have you learned *Shas*?" R' Nosson replied, "More times than you have hairs growing on your head and in your left *peyah*!" R' Nosson's strong, fiery nature was reflected in his vibrant sense of humor.

Another of his visitors sat and discussed *divrei Torah* with him. Due to weakness from the malady that was attacking him, R' Nosson could not, at that moment, recall the exact line and wording in the text quoted. He was overcome with distress. He was not going to be beaten, however. "So what did I do?" he explained. "Immediately after my visitor took leave of me, I sat down and reviewed that page of Gemara another 100 times!"

One day a friend brought him a new *sefer* that had just been published. A few days later R' Nosson met him on the street. His friend greeted him warmly, "How are you?" R' Nosson exclaimed in mock anger, "Robber!" Taken aback, the friend asked in shock, "Tell me, why do you call me that? What did I do?" Then R' Nosson explained. "It is because of you that I could not sleep all night! I had to read that book in its entirety! Do you not know that an old sick man like me requires a lot of rest?" And then they both laughed.

His last Succos was spent in Hadassah Hospital in Yerushalayim. At that stage of his illness, he had to take medication, something he had always tried to avoid. Throughout his life, he had been a great believer in natural foods. He disliked drugs, and he researched and experimented with herbal remedies and other natural methods of maintaining health and curing illness. But now he had no choice, however abhorrent conventional medicine was to him. Visitors to his sickbed still thirsted for more pearls of wisdom from this living *sefer Torah* but wondered whether he would be able to respond in his drugged state.

One person began a discourse on the subject of the *etrog*, expounding that the expression *"sheleimah"* appears four times in the Torah, spelling out the word *"etrog."*

> *E munah sheleimah*
> *T eshuvah sheleimah*
> *R efuah sheleimah*
> *G eulah sheleimah*

Suddenly, to the delight of those attending, R' Nosson sat bolt upright and opened his eyes. "No! There is one more! It is also written *mascorta sheleimah* (a complete wage)," exclaimed R' Nosson excitedly. A discussion of Torah matters revitalized him more than the best vitamin.

After R' Nosson passed from this world, he was brought to his resting place on *Har HaMenuchos* in Yerushalayim. Sometime after this, several *sifrei Torah* that had become unfit for use required burial, as specified by *halachah*. A suitable place to inter them was sought, as would befit their honor and sanctity. No better site was found for them than next to the grave of R' Nosson Lubart. This dedicated *masmid* had, in his lifetime, ensconced himself in the Palace of Torah, and it was therefore fitting that even in his final resting place he should be in close proximity to the *sefarim* he cherished.

A Gateshead Heroine

Before the Second World War, England was a virtual Jewish wilderness. Organized Jewish community life was sparse, with small pockets of religious activity found only in those places where the community leader was strong enough to sustain it. Outside some of the larger areas, the *rav* often served as the *shochet* and the *mohel*, for the community was lacking in Torah learning and Jewish practices. Many Jews who had fled from the scarring poverty and vicious pogroms of Poland and Russia in the period of the First World War made their way to the "golden land of opportunity" and approached the Straits of Dover. They arrived with the mistaken belief that upon reaching a new land, their key to success lay in discarding their Jewish identity. Thus they stripped themselves of all outer signs of Jewishness. Some people could not withstand the temptation of not working on Shabbos if it meant losing their jobs. Little did they realize that we Jews are like fish, who need water in order to survive. Torah is compared to water, and the spiritual survival of the Jewish people for all generations depends on Torah learning and living a true Jewish life.

Many of these refugees, in fact, had intended to continue on to America, but simply could not afford the additional expense. Not far from where they arrived in the Midlands, in industrial Newcastle, was the somber, gray town of Gateshead. A student of the Chafetz Chaim, a *shochet* named Rabbi Dreyan, settled there. Assessing the damage to the Jewish *neshamah* and lifeblood of our nation, he longed for a means to improve the dismal situation. From modest beginnings of a donation of one pound sterling and only two students, the Gateshead Yeshivah — whose Torah would illuminate the landscape and help tip the scales for Jewish religious education in England — grew. Between 1929 and 1942, the yeshivah blossomed, with a student body of approximately 40 pupils, led by influential *talmidei chachamim* such as R' Nachman Londinski and R' Eliezer Kahan of Novardok. Later, the faculty was joined by such greats as R' Leib Gurwitz, R' Leib Lopian and R' Moshe Schwab.

Who would these yeshivah boys marry? And would only the boys be privileged to receive a Torah education? Under the guidance of R' Elyahu Eliezer Dessler, a girls' Seminary and Teachers' Training College was established, in order to promote Jewish education for women. The yeshivah had a solid place on the map, and was an oasis of safety for the European refugees seeking a haven during the Second World War.

No historic treatise on the Jews can accurately measure the degree of tragedy that was suffered during the Second World War, and the degree of heroism that our nation displayed cannot be adequately described. A story is told of a Jewish cook, Sarah, who came to Gateshead during the war years. A Jewish woman was able to acquire an entry permit into Britain during wartime by becoming a domestic worker. To enter England, Sarah took a position as cook in the yeshivah, and thus weathered those difficult years. She had hidden in Holland with her son, Chaim, before escaping to England. Her husband had died and she had become separated from her daughter, whom she loved dearly. People tried to tell her how lucky she was that she was alive and well: "Try not to fret overly about your daughter — you are one of the lucky ones! Try to forget — it is possible that you may never see her again ..." But Sarah would not be consoled. Just as Yaakov *Avinu* found it impossible to forget his son Yosef — for *Chazal* teach us that one can only be comforted for one who is actually deceased — so Sarah could not be persuaded that her daughter Masha was not alive. Sarah continued her search, month after month, with great determination. She hoped and prayed that one day, from behind those black clouds of war-torn Europe, some good news would reach her.

One morning, as Sarah stood at her stove stirring a huge pot of soup, the young mailman came by on his "wartime transport," his bicycle, with a letter. It was from one of the many search organizations that she had contacted. It read: "We have information that we believe involves your daughter, whose description and details fit a young lady we have identified. There is a group of youngsters, boys and girls, that have been rescued by a Christian organization. They have been brought to a country town near Portsmouth, where they are receiving a Christian boarding-school education ..."

Sarah turned off the gas under the soup, sat down and began to laugh and cry at the same time. She held the precious letter in her hands and called out, "Look, look what I've got!

Thank God! *Baruch Hashem*! Look, look, she is alive! She is alive!" and she laughed almost hysterically, the tears streaming down her face. "I will see my Masha again! My Masha will come back to me!" She could not wait for this wonderful moment of reunion. Members of the yeshivah staff heard Sarah's outburst and rushed in to see what had happened. "Look!" she cried, holding out the letter. "My Masha is alive and well! I knew it all along!" The kitchen buzzed with excitement and emotion. There was laughter, followed by singing and clapping.

"Who was the one who led you to her?" asked Rivka the housekeeper.

"Do you remember Mr. Israel, the religious businessman from Portsmouth?" replied Sarah. "He is now staying in the country with his family to escape the bombings. He is a wonderful man with a dynamic personality who has many connections. He helped me gain entry into Britain, maintaining contact with me through my brother-in-law, David. It was through his efforts that we discovered Masha's whereabouts. You can't imagine how many Jews he has helped during this war!"

Through Mr. Israel, Sarah made contact with Masha, and arranged for her to come to see her in the yeshivah. Sarah counted the days until she would be reunited with her daughter. Meanwhile, official negotiations were made with the organization that had given her refuge.

Frost and bitter cold filled the early morning on the day of Masha's arrival. Sarah had saved up precious wartime rations and had managed to do the nearly impossible — to bake a beautiful cake. The atmosphere throughout the yeshivah was festive — everyone joined in her *simchah*. The doorbell rang and the tension mounted. Rivkah, the woman who worked with Sarah, motioned encouragingly for Sarah to open the door.

Sarah ran to the door and opened it to admit her daughter, her arms outstretched to welcome Masha in a warm embrace. But the sweet wine turned to vinegar. The girl walked in with a blank expression on her face, ignoring Sarah's open arms. She was accompanied by her uncle, Sarah's brother-in-law. She stood stock still, wooden, and stared unmoving into Sarah's face. "Masha, my Masha — don't you recognize me? I am your mother!" cried Sarah. But Masha stood stiff as a board. Finally, she answered in an icy cold voice, in short staccato sentences that betrayed much personal trauma. "What do you want? I don't know anything about you. When I looked for you, you weren't there. And you people are all Jewish! I have a new family now! All the nuns are my friends!" And she turned on her heel and pushed her way out the door, leaving the attendant company devastated and her mother crying openly. It appeared as if the Christian missionary group had virtually brainwashed her — they had rescued her physically from the Nazi evil, but were holding her soul in their clutches.

Masha clearly remembered her brother Chaim. She reestablished contact with her brother and her Uncle David. They, in turn, reinforced this contact with gifts and other enticements. Still, Masha would have nothing to do with her mother, her people, or her Jewishness. Without hesitation, she retreated into the other world that had captured her.

"What will we do, David, what will we do now?" Sarah cried to her brother-in-law. David stared back grimly, but could not answer. Sarah felt beaten and diminished. It was as if a part of her, a limb, had been cruelly amputated without anesthetic, and she would never come to terms with the loss. To have lost a child — then to have found her — then to lose her yet again to the gentile missionaries in a legalized kidnaping was too much to bear. "Yaakov *Avinu* lost Yosef to the *goyim*," Sarah was heard to rationalize, "but when Yosef was discovered living in Egypt, Yaakov exclaimed, '*Od Yosef Chai!* — Yosef is still alive.' He was still a Torah Jew, faithful to Torah and mitzvos. But my Masha — what about my Masha? She too is still alive!" insisted Sarah, never giving up on her daughter's return.

How to bring back the old Masha — with her warm receptive manner, and love for her people, family and heritage — was a problem with no easy solution. Not only would she not return, but the missionary group made every effort to put obstacles in the family's way, to prevent them from making further contact with Masha, who was now their "property."

Sarah and her family turned again to Mr. Israel, hoping that somehow he would find a solution to the problem. After long deliberation, he informed them that he was making further inquiries into the case. He had heard previously of instances where the missionaries had carried out "rescue work" on the Jewish refugees, but with ulterior motives in mind. There was another story of a young woman from Poland fleeing from the Nazis, who begged the nuns for refuge. She was given the choice of safety, with conversion to Christianity, or facing the dangers of the night and dying a Jewess. Placing her trust in Hashem, the God of her fathers, she fled from the danger of "*shmad*" — forced conversion — and survived the war, her faith and her soul intact.

Mr. Israel had an idea formulating in his mind. But at the present time, he regretted that he could not speak about it. The success of the operation depended on secrecy. "*Yeish berachah al davar ha'samui min ha'ayin* — There is blessing on the matter concealed from the eye," say *Chazal*.

Thus he did not discuss his plans with anyone. Apart from any other considerations, had the story leaked out, his own integrity as a prominent member of the *kehillah* and the good name of the Jewish refugee community could be damaged. Silently, he researched the case and made careful plans.

It was a cold December day, close to the winter holidays. One of Mr. Israel's informants told him that the convent school which Masha was attending would be performing in a London theater during the holiday period and she would be dancing a solo during part of this performance. On the appointed evening, in the pouring rain, Mr. Israel's chauffeur-driven Rolls Royce sped towards London with the businessman seated in the back. To the outside world he appeared to be a business tycoon on his way to an important meeting, a fine model of an upright citizen. But when it came to saving a soul in Israel, he never hesitated to place that image on the shelf. *"Kol ha'mekayeim nefesh achas mi'Yisrael ... k'ilu kiyeim olam malei* — Whoever saves a soul in Israel it is as if he has saved an entire world!"

Stopping the car at the back of the theater, they heard sounds of a band striking up a gay melody. Mr. Israel sent his driver to speak to one of the theater employees who stood in the doorway smoking a cigarette. They spoke in low tones discussing the progress of the show. Money exchanged hands. Then the word "Now!" rang out clearly over the sound of the loud music. The driver returned to the Rolls Royce and took a blanket from the back seat. Disappearing through a side door of the theater, he made his way along a maze of corridors, following behind the man who had been bribed to guide him. As previously arranged, he paused and waited patiently until the music stopped and the sound of applause was heard. A door opened and a young girl in dancer's dress and ballet slippers appeared backstage. At a nod from the guide, Mr. Israel's chauffeur quickly grabbed her, threw the blanket over her head, and escaped with her to the waiting vehicle. Minutes later, the Rolls Royce was speeding to Portsmouth, to the home of the Israel family.

To hold Masha illegally, and against her will, was no simple matter. The refugee organizations tried to trace her. At the beginning, there were tense telephone calls between them and Sarah, for they refused to believe that she had not had a hand in the girl's disappearance. Search parties and other forms of investigation were undertaken by them but, thank Heaven, they failed to make the connection between Mr. Israel and Masha. Meanwhile, she had to be "detained" for a period of time in Portsmouth without outside contact or interference.

Time passed; however, the scars of war and the work of the missionaries left the girl with a mental barrier against her mother.

Nothing could persuade Masha to return to her mother. Many were the painful occasions when Sarah tried to visit her daughter, only to return defeated in spirit, feeling helpless and without an answer for the future. Doctors and other professionals were consulted, and they advised her that only patience and understanding would help. Finally, with a very heavy and broken heart, after much soul-searching and deliberation, Sarah realized that she and her family had lost a daughter. But she courageously decided that if Masha was to remain a dedicated daughter of *Am Yisrael*, she must be restored to *Yiddishkeit* — if not through her own mother, then through a suitable foster family. Masha did not cooperate willingly at first and rejected outright the first family who took her in. Many tears were shed by her poor mother, who watched all of this from a distance. "*Karov Hashem l'nishberei leiv* — Hashem is close to those broken in spirit." The heartache and pain that this mother felt at her daughter's rejection, first of her and then of the family who so desperately tried to rescue her on Sarah's behalf, were acute beyond words. However, Sarah's tears and struggling were not in vain. The second Jewish family who fostered Masha made an outstanding success of the venture. With concerted effort on their part and all those other devoted Jews who were involved, they saw Heavenly blessing and aid in their holy work, and Masha finally accepted them and her Jewish identity. She grew into a fine, observant, Jewish woman. She married and made her home in America, where she, in turn, brought up a good Jewish family.

Some heroes make history and their glorious deeds are on every person's lips. Silent heroism like that of the *tzaddekes* called Sarah is known only to those standing very near — and to Hashem Himself — who realize the deep suffering and dedication involved in such decisions. For how many people would forgo their own personal delight in raising their own child in order to ensure that future generations would remain true Torah Jews?

Mighty Tree From Ribnetz

ears ago, I needed a tailor to sew a suit for my son to wear at his *bar mitzvah*, so I hired a Russian tailor. Mr. Doboski, a short, middle-aged gentleman with spectacles arrived at our home one evening to take my son's measurements. As the initial stiffness between us eased, he became quite friendly with my husband and son. As he worked, he talked, and shared many interesting vignettes of personal history.

"You know, I was a neighbor of the Rebbe of Ribnetz. The Rebbe was the local dignitary, and the Jewish townspeople in Ribnetz were proud of their connection with him." The tailor was especially proud, as he boasted, "He was the *mesader kiddushin* at my wedding, and he personally wrote my *kesubah*."

The tailor spoke of the Rebbe with affection, with words that came from the heart. "In the biting cold of the harsh winter, we would watch him go to the Nestov River, on the outskirts of town. There he would break through the layer of ice on the surface and immerse himself in the frigid waters. Such *mesiras nefesh* and dedication to the Almighty is rare.

"He was a true *tzaddik* possessed of *ruach hakodesh*, who always knew a man's thoughts. He owned a tiny *sefer Torah* that he had written. He was apprehensive for the Torah's safety, fearful that the Soviets would seize it. As I was preparing to emigrate to Israel, being one of the fortunate ones to obtain an exit visa, the Rebbe entrusted the *sefer Torah* into my care. It is a small *sefer Torah*, but very beautiful."

We hungered to hold this special *sefer Torah*, and begged him to bring it with him the next time he came. He readily agreed.

At the next appointment, he brought it, the personal *sefer Torah* of the Rebbe of Ribnetz. It was small and perfect. The Vilna Gaon also had a small, compact *sefer Torah* such as this, which was ultimately brought to Israel from Europe by a prominent family. It was the *sefer Torah* that had always accompanied the Gaon on his travels. Perhaps this one as well had been a traveling companion to this *tzaddik*.

Who was this Rebbe of Ribnetz?

His name was R' Chaim Zanvil Abramovitz. He was the son of Moshe Abramovitz, from the city of Yas in the Soviet Union. Orphaned at an early age, he was raised up by his uncle under the tutelage of the Schtefarneshte Rebbe, R' Avraham Matisyahu. He was an outstanding pupil, and by the age of 18, there was not a single *Rashi* in all of *Shas* that he could not recall at will. He enjoyed a close association with the Skulener Rebbe. He was renowned locally as well as throughout the Jewish world. His later years were spent in the United States, where he formed strong bonds with many American Jews. He departed from this world at the age of nearly 100 years.

The Rebbe's life story was one of great interest to us, and we endeavored to find out all we could about this fascinating man. By a stroke of good fortune, we encountered R' Baruch Kuperman in Yerushalayim. R' Baruch not only knew the Rebbe, but was a member of his "inner circle" in Russia for many years. R' Kuperman's father, Shimon, had been a prominent official in the Communist regime, and in 1946 Shimon first approached the Rebbe to consult with him.

When he was a young man, the Rebbe's fame was yet unknown. Thus, he was able to live and study privately and unnoticed, in the village in the Carpathian mountains, on the border with Bessarabia, where the Communists were not yet entrenched. The Rebbe was able to remain hidden, serving as the local *shochet*, learning Torah and keeping *mitzvos* as his fore-fathers had. Thus, Shimon Kuperman sought him out when he was passing through the area. On that first visit, the Rebbe was startled to see a uniformed official at his door. But it soon became apparent that this official was a Jew, "one of ours." After several meetings, seeds of friendship blossomed and flourished. R' Shimon had the privilege to go into seclusion with the Rebbe for six months, serving him, and *davening* with him.

"My father witnessed things there that he can never tell anyone about," said R' Baruch. "Where the Rebbe was concerned, even a tree could make up a *minyan*. For the Rebbe could commune with souls and perceive that which others could not. He would fast every day except for Shabbos and *Yamim Tovim*. When he recited *Tikkun Chatzos* from the depths of his noble soul, he would dress in sackcloth, descend to a cellar, and weep over the exile of the *Shechinah* and the destruction of the Holy Temple. His *Tikkun* would shake the roots of the earth and the pillars of the skies."

As the years passed, the Rebbe's fame grew and he gained a loyal following of Jews. For the most part, they were simple, unlearned people, the "*seridei charev*," the fragments left by the sword. They were the ones who survived after the realigning of the political map. For these religious souls who remained in Russia, life under the Soviet Communist regime was far from easy. In many regions of Russia, a virtual reign of terror was in effect against all religious groups, especially the Jews. The Jewish arm of the Communists, the "Yevsektzia," implemented Communist ideals, and tried to totally stamp out Jewish religious life. To observe Torah and *mitzvos* in the Communist "paradise" required determination, courage and *mesiras nefesh*.

The Lubavitcher Rebbe held the Ribnetzer Rebbe in great esteem, and even sent a letter of approbation to Lubavitcher *chasidim*, encouraging them to seek the Ribnetzer's counsel. In addition, he personally sent the Ribnetzer Rebbe a *kapote*, a *gartel* and a *yarmulka*.

The Rebbe's house in Ribnetz was once flooded and the extreme weather conditions forced him to move up into the Carpathian mountains for a year. The Jews of Ribnetz were heartbroken, for the Rebbe was beloved by them. He was their Rebbe, their pride and glory. They feared he would move elsewhere, and implored him not to leave them. Their persistence succeeded and the Rebbe returned to their town.

He would not surrender to the Communists nor give up observing any *mitzvah* of the Torah. The locals, for the most part, were in awe of him and a little frightened of him as well. In the early days, when the Rebbe would immerse in the Nestov River, the local gentile peasants would come to jibe and make fun of him as they watched him break the ice and jump into the freezing water. To their great chagrin, however, their laughter froze upon their lips, for they remained paralyzed on the riverbank in the sub-zero temperature long enough to teach them a lesson. After this, they left the Rebbe alone.

As the Rebbe's fame as a saintly person spread, there were occasions when the gentiles of the town would ask him to pray on their behalf. Even some atheist Communists came to him with such requests. When the daughter of the gentile deputy mayor of the town lay sick, without hope for recovery, a message was sent from the deputy mayor to the Rebbe: "Please, will the Rabbi offer prayers on behalf of my daughter?" The Rebbe asked Shimon Kuperman. "Is he a righteous *goy*?" The answer was in the affirmative. The Rebbe prayed for her and the young woman recovered. As a result, the Jews of the town gained a strong ally.

R' Shimon himself succeeded in doing the impossible, right under the noses of the Communists. Not only did he remain a re ligious and practicing Jew, but he raised his sons to be observant Jews as well. This was extremely dangerous, but he did it nonetheless. R' Baruch Kuperman described how, as a young man, he would put on *tefillin* on a train full of Communists. There were several classes of accommodations on board, and the second-class passengers had bunks which offered some privacy. There in his bunk, he would seclude himself and put on his *tefill-in* without being seen. Then he would nonchalantly walk out into the corridor, find an unobtrusive corner, and complete his *tefillah* without being disturbed.

R' Baruch Kuperman, who was an accomplished mathematician, was given an eminent position in the field of education; he was appointed administrator of several schools. He was highly regarded by the Communists, who saw him not only as a person with a finely honed intellect, but also as a friend, for Baruch was blessed with a cheerful personality and an ability to warm the hearts of those around him. Little did they suspect his inner, concealed identity, that of a religious Jew who did not conform to Communist ideals.

He, too, drew close to the Rebbe, and marveled at the Rebbe's insight and acuity both in secular and religious matters. Initially, his visits were infrequent as the journey was long and arduous. When after a 12-year hiatus Baruch was visiting in the area, he went to see the Rebbe. He was ushered into a small room into which 20 people were crowded. The Rebbe, whose memory was extraordinary, raised his warm eyes to acknowledge Baruch and then welcomed him with a handshake and a verbal greeting spiced with a rich double meaning: "*Gam Baruch tiheyeh!* — Also Baruch should be blessed," or very literally, "Also you should be blessed!" The Rebbe knew exactly who Baruch was, despite the lapse of 12 years and the hundreds of visitors he had received in between. From this personal attention extended to him, a warm affectionate bond was forged, as it was with so many others who came to the Ribnetzer. It was thus a natural progression of events that when Baruch needed help with a problem, he would turn to the Rebbe.

The year 1968 was a time when no Jew could safely consider leaving Russia. In order to apply for an exit visa, one had to first notify his employer of his intent. By doing so, he ran the risk of dismissal or, at the very least, demotion. He would be ostracized by those around him, rejecting the nectar and honey of the Communist system that had nurtured him! A palpable fear, even terror, often accompanied such an application.

The Rebbe stood at Baruch's side as he handed in his application for an exit visa. And the Rebbe warned him, "They are *groisse banditen* — great bandits! The Soviets will not readily relent."

Baruch's request caused a sensation in town. Among the Jews, a whisper rose and rolled like a wave, "It is the Rebbe! The Rebbe is with him on this!" Baruch was the first in his community to make such a request. As a result, he was demoted from his position. His first application for a visa was rejected, but with the Rebbe's encouragement Baruch reapplied.

Baruch wanted the visa so he could emigrate to the Land of Israel. His elderly parents' letters, always intercepted and read by the censors, beseeched Baruch to join them in the Holy Land. In addition to all other considerations, R' Kuperman knew that he was sitting on a time bomb, for his young son was now of school age. This child showed great promise in all *limudei kodesh* studies and his father was helping him develop his potential by teaching him privately at home. Should he begin to attend public school, however, certain problems and dangers would arise. He would have to attend school on Shabbos and would be forced to write, thereby violating the Shabbos. He would be brainwashed into accepting the Communist ideologies, and would be pressured to join Communist youth groups. If it were discovered that his parents were Jews, observing Torah and *mitzvos*, the dangers would instantly multiply. With all this in mind, Baruch made the long and difficult journey to Ribnetz, turning once again to the Rebbe for advice and support.

As Baruch neared the Rebbe's front door, he was filled with trepidation. As he entered the Rebbe's room, the Rebbe turned, his *tallis* wrapped around him. Baruch immediately plunged into his inquiry, but did not need to explain at length, for the Rebbe understood. The Rebbe urged his friend to be strong, and advised him, "It is a matter of *kibud av ve'eim*, honoring one's parents. It is also *pikuach nefesh*, a danger to life. In this case, it is the spiritual life of your dear child who learns Torah at home, and who would be in grave danger if he began attending a Communist school. Your safety could be threatened as well. *Lech*! — Go! Resubmit your application!"

In the midst of all of this, Baruch's wife discovered that she was expecting a baby. When the local doctor insisted that the baby would not be healthy, and may not even survive the pregnancy, she came home, heartbroken, and informed her husband of the doctor's diagnosis. Without hesitation, R' Baruch took his wife and set out for the Rebbe's house.

The Rebbe listened with a furrowed brow. After giving the matter thoughtful deliberation, he said to Baruch and his wife, "*Ich nem das auf mich*! — I take this one upon myself." All would be well, he promised. The child would be born alive and well. Knowing that a *berachah* should "rest upon something," R' Kuperman took out a ruble from his pocket and presented it to the Rebbe. The Rebbe held it tightly in his hand for a minute, and then returned it, motioning to Baruch's wife to take it. The

Rebbe then blessed her with "*zara chaya v'kayama* — a live and viable child."

Broaching the subject of his other problem, Baruch asked, "What of my exit visa?" He was hoping with all his heart that the new baby would be born in the Land of Israel. But the Rebbe shook his head, "*A lange maayseh*! — It will be a long, drawn-out episode." With this said, Baruch and his wife returned home.

As expected, the next application was refused. Baruch informed the Rebbe of the refusal, and asked him if he should write to higher officials in Moscow. The Rebbe dissuaded him from such a move. "No, you must move quietly and with stealth, only through the local authorities. Tell me now, how is your wife feeling? *Zara chaya v'kayama*! — She should bear a live and viable child." The Rebbe's blessing was reiterated with enthusiasm and warmth. The affection the *tzaddik* felt for every one of his followers was apparent, especially for the children of the members of his "inner circle."

The weather was gloomy and the ground wet with puddles of mud reaching to the knees when Baruch's wife went to the hospital to have her baby. It was clearly a scary situation. She clutched tightly onto the ruble that the Rebbe had given her, but kept it hidden from the hospital staff who would most likely scoff at matters of a spiritual nature. She prayed with strong emotion that all would go well, as does every Jewish daughter in time of need. She trusted in Hashem's help and in the merit of the Rebbe's *berachah*.

Soon the hearty crying of a baby was heard. A boy had been born to the Kuperman family. The doctors were amazed that the baby was alive: and while the infant was not well, there were only minor problems with the newborn's health.

After the baby was born, Baruch's wife searched under her pillow for the ruble that the Rebbe of Ribnetz had given her as a symbol of his *berachah*. She could still mentally recall how she had received his special blessing and had drawn strength from it throughout this trying time. But now, to her great disappointment, the ruble was not to be found. It had simply disappeared. Apparently it had "done its work" and was no longer required. Nevertheless, it hurt her to have lost it, for it had meant so much to her over all these months, and she would have liked to retain it as a memento. But now she had the little baby, *baruch Hashem*, here in the crib beside her, and that surely meant that all the *tefillos* had been heard ... *zara chaya v'kayama*!

Under Communist rule, when a person applied for an exit visa to Israel, he was classified as a rebel and traitor. Baruch should therefore have been dismissed from his post and ostracized by everyone. But he was a highly successful teacher who prepared pupils for the very competitive School Matriculation Certificate, which determined university entrance. Since the school where he taught had a large enrollment of children of the elite Communists, not only was he not fired from his post, but he now realized that this was why his request for a visa was being denied. The children of these officials needed to receive the very best education from the most competent teachers available. This was the overriding consideration. Communism is based on everyone being equal, but "some are more equal than others."

In the summer of 1972, Baruch's brother Eliyahu from Samarkand came to visit. The city of Samarkand was known as a safer place for Jews to live, as the local government there was slightly more lenient concerning religious issues, and therefore it had many Jewish inhabitants. Baruch's hometown, on the other hand, had almost no Jews and was a wasteland of *Yiddishkeit*. Eliyahu, a Lubavitcher *chasid*, knew that Baruch regularly traveled to the Ribnetzer Rebbe. Eliyahu had brought many *kvittlech* for the Rebbe from the members of his community. He would stay with Baruch for a few days, and then, after Shabbos, the two brothers planned to travel to Ribnetz.

Eliyahu was amazed to see his brother's preparations for Shabbos. "Where do you get wine for Kiddush?!" he asked. "No problem. We buy grapes and squeeze them!" "And the *challos*?" "No problem, my wife bakes!" "And to go to *toivel* on Shabbos morning as I am accustomed?" "We can go at 6 in the morning to the lake when there is no one there!" And so it was with many other *mitzvos* that were performed under the most trying circumstances and with the greatest *mesiras nefesh*.

But Eliyahu found it very hard to follow Baruch's system. "You are living like this, virtually among *goyim*. Why don't you go and live among other Jews? Be part of a *kehillah*," Eliyahu said. "Surely the Ribnetzer Rebbe would agree that you should move from here!" And on this note, the brothers set out together after Shabbos for Ribnetz. Eliyahu was most confident that his view was correct, and that it was not right for a Jew, however observant, to live separately from his brethren and the mainstream of Jewish life. He expressed this sentiment emphatically, "I thought at first that we were going to Ribnetz for *me*, but now, having seen your circumstances, I know that we are going also for *you*." And thus they traveled to see the Rebbe.

The Rebbe spoke a Romanian Yiddish and it was not easy for him to comprehend the Russian Yiddish spoken by Eliyahu. Eliyahu knew that he would have to make a great effort to make himself clearly understood without trying the Rebbe's patience. As Eliyahu approached the Rebbe with the supplications, the *kvittlech* he had from the Jewish community of Samarkand, he was not prepared for the sharp, piercing glance that the Rebbe gave him. He had not even broached the subject of Baruch leaving Stanislaw, when the Rebbe got up to confront him. And in what seemed to be near anger, he exclaimed. "No! Baruch need not leave Stanislaw. He keeps the *mitzvos* wherever he lives!" After which the Rebbe sat down again, apparently calm, but he seemed cold and distant.

The Rebbe then listened to all of the requests that were put before him, seeming to the outside observer to be almost disinterested. Eliyahu felt stricken with guilt that he had somehow taken a wrong step and aroused the Rebbe's ire. "Who knows if he will take seriously all the requests that I've brought from my community?" he worried, sickened in his heart that perhaps the journey was in vain and that those who had sent him would in some way suffer as a result of his failing. His anxiety was unfounded, however, for within a short time after his visit to the Rebbe, tens of families from Samarkand miraculously received exit visas. They all left the country together, a virtual "*Yetzias Mitzrayim* — redemption from Egypt."

⊚⊰⊱⊚

One day, a young man with an urgent need to learn mathematics for university entrance came to Baruch. His need was especially pressing, for if he was not accepted into the university, he would be drafted into the Russian army. Baruch was a bit suspicious initially, so he questioned the young man about his family background. "My father is the *shochet*, Chezkel!" answered the youth. This was R' Chezkel's son? That explained the young man's plight. If this young man, a bit irresponsible in his youth and not strong in his *Yiddishkeit,* would enter the army, what would become of him? What would happen to this *neshamah*, blowing aimlessly in the wind? Although not terribly academic, and perhaps not one of those who would normally be accepted to the university, he desperately needed to get in. Between university and the military, university was the lesser of two evils. Baruch turned to the youngster with a suggestion. "I go often to the Ribnetzer Rebbe. Perhaps you would agree to join me?" The young man consented.

They arrived in Ribnetz to find a long line of women with live chickens in their hands, waiting for the Rebbe to *shecht* these birds for them. The Rebbe turned in greeting to Baruch and the youth who accompanied him, and before Baruch could speak or introduce the boy, the Rebbe exclaimed, "Chezkel's son!"

The young man was dumbfounded. True, his father was a *shochet*, one of the very few professions left to religious Jews

under the Communist system, for ritual slaughterers were needed to provide meat. But he, the son, not a religious boy, had been
ground in the mill of Soviet education and looked like any other
Russian youth. No one had notified the Rebbe of their coming.
How could the Rebbe have known that he was Chezkel's son?
The Rebbe knew who he was and who his father was. The
youngster was dumbfounded and began to stammer. "Rebbe, if I
don't get into the university or get a visa to *Eretz Yisrael*, they
will take me into the Red Army, G-d forbid!" The words tumbled
out of the boy's mouth almost unbidden, and he was surprised at
himself. The Rebbe heard the boy's plea. He removed the *tallis*
from over his head and, not just smiling but laughing out loud,
stated to the youngster, "All of you will travel — just wait and
see!"

Now the teenager was even more startled, for no one in his
family had even contemplated the possibility of leaving Russia
and emigrating to Israel. It was not even a dream. His parents
were aging and had never considered leaving at this stage in their
lives. And now the Rebbe was telling him that Chezkel the
shochet and his family would be leaving for *Eretz Yisrael*! They
had not even discussed emigration! It was unbelievable! Baruch
looked at the boy almost enviously. "See, you have succeeded in
acquiring everything!" Then he turned to the Rebbe with questions on his own agenda.

It was time to leave, but the Rebbe warmly called to them,
"I have not yet taken leave of this youth! Wait!" Then shyly, and
with new respect that was growing and developing from within,
the young man asked the Rebbe, "Who will organize the exit
visas and emigration procedures for all of us? Don't forget, my
parents are elderly!" The Rebbe answered firmly but with encouragement, "You are young and energetic. You are also
educated, and know enough of the Communist bureaucracy to
handle negotiations. You will be the one to arrange everything!"
And so it was.

In the meantime there was another hurdle to overcome, that

of the university entrance exam. The young man did not live in the same town as Baruch, but in a distant village. Baruch arranged that the boy spend time with him. Thus he would be able to tutor him and somehow get him through the examinations. There would be oral math, written math, Russian composition, and an oral physics exam. No partiality whatsoever would be accorded to a Jewish boy. After all, this was Russian "equality." Still, the Rebbe had given his *berachah*, so he would undoubtedly succeed despite the difficulties.

Baruch did his "homework," and extended himself to help the boy. He went to the school in question, and spoke to a teacher there who turned out to be a distant relative of his wife. She agreed to help Baruch and the youth and provided them with books from which to study. On the day of the examination, she stood by the young man's side to give him confidence. He was able to pass the written math exam. The next problem would be the oral math exam which was scheduled to be given on Shabbos. Baruch counseled the youngster, "Go to an outside telephone, not ours at home which I know is tapped. Call your mother and ask her to send a telegram to read, 'Mother not feeling well. Come home!'" This he did and his mother sent the cable. The 19-year-old took the cable to the proper authorities at the school who grudgingly canceled the Saturday exam, and arranged a private exam for him on Thursday instead. Miraculously, he passed.

Baruch's wife, who taught Russian language and literature, wrote a sample essay for him on a particular subject. Amazingly, on the day of the test, just that topic appeared on the exam sheet! The guiding hand of Heaven was certainly with him, with the help of the *berachah* of the Ribnetzer Rebbe.

On the fifth of December, the young man received a cable regarding his exit visa: "Yitzik: Sabba said it would be so — first time you would be refused — so it was!" This was a cryptic message, obviously referring to the instructions of the Rebbe. His first application to leave Russia would be turned down but he should reapply.

The boy just managed to receive passing grades on his exams and he entered the university. He was not interested in studying, but if he had to choose between the university and the Red Army, studying won, hands down. However, what would he do when it was time for the next set of exams? Would he be able to prevail? It was all a bit worrisome.

January came, with its vacation, and a phone call and another cryptic message: "Sabba said that we would leave — and so it is!" The cause for anxiety had evaporated into thin air. The exit visas had come through just in time. R' Chezkel and his family would be off to *Eretz Yisrael*. His son had been rescued from the Red Army. Everyone would be safe. No wonder the Rebbe had laughed!

The Rebbe lived in Ribnetz in relative peace for many years. Then the KGB began to make trouble for him. Baruch and other *chasidim* feared for the Rebbe's future and pressed him to leave. "Who will *shecht* for the families here? Who will look after them?" the Rebbe worried. It bothered him deeply that these simple Jews would be left without a shepherd, for they were all "*tzon kedoshim* — holy flocks of sheep." But the harassment of the KGB became more intense and the danger more imminent. Jews were intercepted on their way to Ribnetz and threatened with violence. It was the start of a campaign mounted against the Rebbe and his followers.

One day, Baruch received a message from another *chasid* of the Rebbe. "The Rebbe is leaving! It is not just a rumor, not just a story! He has left for Kishinev!"

In Kishinev the KGB were known to be "better at their job." They confiscated *sifrei Torah* and *sefarim*. They kept a register of names of suspected *chasidim* of the Rebbe. Baruch knew that the Rebbe would be vulnerable in a place like that and in need of protection and support. And, if the Rebbe were truly leaving Russia, it was unthinkable not to be alongside him now. And so, Baruch traveled to Kishinev.

Trying to find the Rebbe, he followed his instincts, and made his way to the *shul* for *Shacharis*. Planting himself quietly in a corner, he took out his *siddur* and began reciting the *seder korbanos* before the morning service. Two respectable-looking Jews with beards approached him with commiserating smiles but hard, blank, cold eyes. "*Shalom! Fun vannen kumt a Yid?* ... — From where does this Jew come?" Baruch did not reply immediately, wanting first to complete his recitation of the *korbanos*.

"*Tzaddikim Yidden!* They don't even talk when *davening korbanos!*" they jibed at Baruch. Baruch understood well that these Jews had sold their souls to the KGB and were working as its agents against their own brethren. His icy stare bored through them like the weather in Siberia, and he snapped, "Just give me form number three (establishing place of residence) and I will fill it out for you!" The two turned quickly on their heels and disappeared. They realized that Baruch understood what they were.

Soon after they left, the Rebbe entered the *shul*. He did not tarry, nor did Baruch, for they knew that it was dangerous to converse there. It was a even a danger to speak words of *tefillah* to Hashem in those days. They took a taxi together to a safe place. When the cab dropped them off and drove away, Baruch's heart sank as he realized that his *tallis* and *tefillin* had been left in the taxi. He began to panic, and worried that they would be stolen or destroyed. How would he replace them in Russia? But the Rebbe simply smiled. A messenger was dispatched to locate the taxi with the missing *tallis* and *tefillin*. The messenger returned about two hours later with the bag under his arm. "The driver was very upset!" he reported. "He had been driving around for the past two hours looking for a fare, and yet no one hailed him. Not that he would have known or realized but, maybe the *tefillin* on the back seat had something to do with it?"

Baruch turned to the Rebbe and asked, "Rebbe, when are you

leaving for *Eretz Yisrael*? When will I see you again? Are you leaving now?" The Rebbe smiled but did not reply. He clasped Baruch's hand tightly and then they parted.

When the Rebbe arrived in Israel in 1972, he was greeted with joy by many fine Jews, among them the parents and family of R' Baruch Kuperman. "When will my children come to *Eretz Yisrael*?" asked the old Shimon Kuperman. He felt a sharp pang at the thought of his children so far away, in a land of oppression, and wondered if he would live to see them again. His best, most vibrant years were already behind him. If only, G-d willing, the years of his old age would be golden years, spent reaping the rewards of *nachas* from his children and grandchildren. Each hour that kept the elderly father and grandfather away from his loved ones was painful.

The Rebbe answered gently, with a tone of consolation and encouragement. "Little Shalom is already learning Gemara, the first chapter of *Bava Metzia*, *Sh'tayim ochazim*." Then the Rebbe watched the lines on his friend's face soften, and saw the pleasure enter the old man's eyes, as he understood that his grandchildren were following the Torah path.

☙❧

"Rebbe, Rebbe, will you come to a *chanukas habayis*? Our sister is moving into her new apartment and your *berachah* on the occasion of her *simchah* would be so greatly valued and appreciated!" invited one of Baruch's siblings.

"After Chanukah!" The Rebbe smiled warmly. "But wait for Baruch to enjoy your *simchah*. He is on the way!" The family knew better than to ask questions, and they held their breath in anticipation. One of the youngsters ran out to tell the others, "Uncle Baruch is on the way! The Rebbe said so!"

They did not have to wait very long. The very next day, a telegram arrived at the Kuperman home in Israel reading, "EXIT VISA RECEIVED! BARUCH."

That Purim was especially lively. There was a sense of joy that pervaded the atmosphere and seeped into the walls of the new apartment. This was the long-awaited *chanukas habayis* which "initiates" a home in the way it should continue. The family combined this celebration with the *Seudas Purim*. Through the power of the two occasions, that house surely merited to carry joy within it for generations. Baruch and his family bounded up the steps of the apartment building with great excitement. They were being reunited with their family and, yes, with the Ribnetzer Rebbe, too.

He embraced his father and each family member, and clasped the Rebbe's hands like a long-lost son. Baruch's gray-blue eyes surveyed the room, taking in every corner, examining every face, for it had taken him and his family so very long to reach this moment! The family and all who joined them were intoxicated without even drinking wine. A special spiritual exuberance pervaded the gathering. The feet danced and the hands clapped as melodies of praise and thanks filled the room. It was an unforgettable Purim.

In the midst of all the festivities, little Sholom, the baby born as a result of the Rebbe's blessing, picked up the Rebbe's *shtriemel* and placed it on his head, acting as small children are wont to. There was a temporary moment of unease. Seeing his son, Baruch halted instantly in his tracks, feeling anxious lest the Rebbe view this as an act of *chutzpah* on the part of his child. He glanced back at the Rebbe who caught the look in his eyes, understood his fear and reassured him, "No matter, you will see, he will grow in time to become a *talmid chacham*!" The Rebbe always spoke the truth. The young man today shows promise still to be developed.

It is said that a *tzaddik* is like a tree of the field. The Rebbe is now gone, but his life's work, the young saplings he planted in Ribnetz and elsewhere, still sprout and grow.

"Like a tree deeply rooted alongside brooks of water ... that yields its fruit in the right season ... and all that he does will succeed ..." (*Tehillim* 1:3).

A Rock Where the Levanter Blows

r. Nehori, a respected citizen of Gibraltar, joined us one evening, together with another member of the community. They revealed to us a special corner of the Jewish world, and described the traditions and Jewish teachings passed on to them through stories showing the history of Jewish life in Gibraltar. It came as a shock to hear that Mr. Nehori passed away shortly after reviewing and correcting these stories. These are stories of the hashgachah of Hashem, of the merit of fine Jews like Mr. Nehori, stories of chizuk. The zechus of the mitzvah of bringing these stories to life belongs to him.

The Rock of Gibraltar rises steeply from the coastline confronting Morocco and its North African neighbors. Even in midsummer, the levanter — a strong easterly wind accompanied by overcast or rainy weather — can blow across the Rock and along the narrow streets of the towns, rattling the windows of the gray-white houses until they seem about to shatter, and bending the surrounding palm trees almost in half. It has been so for centuries. Due to its strategic position, Gibraltar has been a pawn in the hands of several kings on the historical chessboard. First it belonged to Spain, and Queen Isabella donated the bells for the famed Bell Tower during the time of the Spanish Inquisition. Then possession passed to the Moors, and finally to the British, who possess it still, much to Spain's chagrin. Each nation, during its rule, left its cultural stamp on the place.

Its position was not only of interest to foreign powers, but also to Jews who sought refuge from the terrors of the surrounding world. The first Jews to settle there were traders from Amsterdam, Spain and Morocco. In 1474, before the Expulsion from Spain, a group of Jews actually leased the Rock for four years from the Duque of Medina Sidonia. The influence of the Jews in commercial and administrative affairs in this region continued throughout the years. The Jews dealt in commerce, chiefly with Morocco.

Gibraltar was a natural choice for the Jews after leaving Spain, for it closely resembled their homeland. Jewish commerce flourished there until 1713 when, under the Treaty of Utrecht, the negative Spanish influence again forced the Jews to leave. They found refuge in the prosperous Moroccan city of Tetuan until 1727 when they were readmitted to Gibraltar, after the Spanish breached the Utrecht agreement. Business again flourished for the Jews of Gibraltar.

The slave trade was very profitable for the gentile traders dealing with Africa, but the Jews never took part in it. Instead, they relied on these trade routes to help other Jews in Portugal, Spain, Morocco and Europe.

Christopher Columbus, by all evidence, was himself a Marrano, a secret Jew. He is reputed to have headed his letters with a *beis hei* inscribed in Rashi script. His wife was Jewish. He left Spain on his famous voyage at 11:30, with the ships' holds loaded with Jews, knowing that at 12 o'clock the Spanish Inquisitors were due to board and inspect his ships for "illegal cargo."

Over the years, the Jews of Gibraltar have amassed their own personal treasury of traditions. Their hospitality and good-heartedness have given them an honored name in the Jewish world. Generations of fine, observant Jews were raised here. In addition, many great Rabbanim, who were renowned for their righteousness, made this place their home, and four magnificent synagogues were built.

With some members of our family in *kollel* there and some working there, we discovered, firsthand, the warmth and kindness natural to the Jews of Gibraltar. Several stories were told to us by the senior members of the community. These stories are quite dear to their hearts and are worthy of being retold here.

One of the great Rabbanim of Gibraltar, R' Avraham Israel Menashe, came originally from Morocco in the 1840s and led the community faithfully for many years. He taught Torah both to the younger and older members. He himself led an exemplary life.

It is said that few Jews have the merit to pass from this world on *erev Shabbos*, for at that time the Heavenly Court no longer sits in judgment, and such a soul is therefore ushered directly into *Gan Eden*. R' Avraham Israel Menashe passed away on *erev Shabbos*. With this great merit in mind, the members of the *chevrah kaddisha* and the heads of the community acted with haste to see that the funeral would be that day. They made the strenuous trip, on foot, to the Jewish cemetery which is situated nearly at the top of the Rock, carrying the coffin up the steep path. They accompanied the deceased with the customary prayers and chants, straining to reach the summit of the mountain, for the roaad was long and difficult. Shabbos was approaching quickly, and each man fearfully whispered to his friend, "Will we get there in time? Will there be sufficient time to dig the grave?"

As they continued their climb, an additional problem was voiced: "It is befitting that an honored sage such as our Rav be buried in the area set aside for the *tzaddikim* of the town. But it is nearly full, and we will have to be very enterprising to find a way to extend it!" Many great Jews had been laid to rest there, including HaRav Shlomo Abudraham, of the same family as the *gedolei Tzefas*, and HaRav Yosef el Malach of the synagogue Nefutzos Yehudah. Would there be room for R' Avraham Israel Menashe as well?

They did not need to fear. They reached the plot of the *tzaddikim* and placed the coffin on the ground. Then, to the utter amazement of all assembled, the ground between two neighboring graves split, leaving a space the exact dimensions required for R' Avraham Israel's coffin. The other *tzaddikim* had "made room" for him! "Look, just look what has happened!" cried out the members of the *chevrah kaddisha* in awe. "We knew that our Rav was a great man, but if only we had known while he was alive that he was such a great *tzaddik*, we would have honored him even more!"

❧❧❧

The Jews may have been at the mercy of the political winds, but Hashem accompanied them in their exiles, and they possessed great wealth and wielded remarkable influence even under foreign rule.

Eliezer Benoliel was called "El Nino de Oro, the Golden Boy," and is listed in the 1784 census as one of the four richest men in his region. Despite this, his son Yehudah, or Judah, as his father preferred to call him, began his business career at age 16 as a mere shopkeeper. "My son, my Judah, start small in order to become great!" was his father's shrewd advice. Judah was destined for greatness and he did not remain behind a counter for very long.

Judah Benoliel became a business tycoon, with many influential friends including kings, heads of state and even the pope. Judah used these contacts to protect his fellow Jews, and to influence decisions of state for their benefit. He, along with Nathan Rothschild and two other partners, used their money to help finance the British war effort against Napoleon. British officers were then paid in gold coins, and so were Judah and his partners. The payment for their "assistance" was a quarter of a million pounds in gold coins. The day they received this payment was indeed a joyous one.

Then another day of joy came to the Benoliel household. A little boy was born to Judah's brother, and he was named Eliezer after his grandfather. On the day of the *bris*, both the little one's father and Uncle Judah danced for joy in front of the new arrival who cried lustily, not sharing the happiness of the adults at all. "Come, let us weigh him!" called the boy's mother. He was a fair-sized infant, over three kilos in weight. Unlocking a chest in his study, Judah counted out gold equivalent to the weight of the infant, and distributed it among the poor that day.

Judah's money built a yeshivah in Tetuan, Morocco, married off poor brides and supported orphans. One day a messenger came breathlessly to Judah's door, holding a scroll on which were written plans for helping the Jews of Tangiers. The Sultan of Tangiers had taken it upon himself to destroy the synagogue and initiate a pogrom, to satisfy the Moslem princes who had gotten themselves badly into debt with the Jewish moneylenders. Judah did not wait. He intervened with diplomatic finesse and money, calming the political furor, until the Sultan and the princes allowed the matter to rest. To this day, Judah, a "lion" among his brethren, is remembered for good each year on Yom Tov, in the synagogue of Tangiers.

On 24 Teves 1837, there was a terrible earthquake in Safed in the Land of Israel. The ground shook and trembled violently. The city of Safed became not just a pile of rubble but a terrible tragic graveyard for about 90 percent of the population. A member of the British Consulate informed Judah of the disaster. He, in turn, informed Sir Moses Montefiore. The two of them, together with others, raised the money to rebuild the holy city of Safed.

Judah Benoliel passed away in 1839 and was brought to rest in the Jewish cemetery of Gibraltar. Some of his descendants still live in Gibraltar.

෧෯෬

The cemetery of Gibraltar gained renown as a holy place, and thus members of the community went there to pray in times of need. In 1777, during the siege of Gibraltar by the French and Spanish, members of the Jewish community went to the gravesites of the *tzaddikim*. There they beseeched these *tzaddikim* to intervene before the Heavenly Court on behalf of the Jews who had, in the past, suffered so much at the hands of each of these nations. They prayed: "May it be G-d's will that the British should be victorious" — and so it was.

Life, however, was not always smooth under British rule, as the Jews of Gibraltar discovered. In the 1840s, there appeared on the scene a certain governor aptly named Gardener, who was not kindly disposed towards the Jews. Despotic by nature, he would impose his will and drown out all other opinions, rather than seek a peaceful resolution to any problem. This anti-Semite tried to interfere with longstanding Jewish trading rights, causing the Jews much trouble with the Gibraltar Chamber of Commerce. Then he decided that the only plot in the whole of Gibraltar suitable for growing vegetables was the Jewish cemetery.

The anger and outrage of the Jewish community was disregarded. Gardener, knowing what his decision meant to the

Jewish citizens, viciously ignored them, and snickered at the delegations sent to prevent him from going ahead with his plan. He sent a platoon of soldiers marching up the hill, armed with picks and shovels, to dig up the tombstones.

As the first men to arrive raised the picks above their heads, they mysteriously collapsed. Being British, however, the soldiers kept a "stiff upper lip" and were not easily dissuaded from their task. The next group of men raised their picks. They passed out and died. British onlookers, seeing what had happened, ran back down the hill in a state of panic. They reported to the governor that "there — that place kills off men! We're not going to fight dead men, we're not!" But Gardener was a stubborn and cruel man who would not relent, so he sent another platoon up the hill to prepare the ground for the planting of his vegetables. When this third platoon was assigned to go up the hill, they went only after much coercion. Sadly, not all of them returned.

The heads of the Jewish community were so pained by all the attempts to desecrate the Jewish cemetery and destroy other Jewish rights as well that they sent a delegation to Britain to present the case personally before the Minister of Colonies. They were totally successful in their endeavors. The Ministry took charge of the cemetery, as a preserved historical site, and continued, together with the Jewish community, to maintain it.

The Second World War erupted, and Gibraltar again became a place of strategic importance for the Allied forces. British soldiers posted near the top of the Rock came breathlessly back to base to report, "In that cemetery! Those Jews up there! Their dead are praying!" If at first those who bore the reports were subject to blazing scorn from their colleagues, subsequent reports were treated with greater respect by the officers in command. "Yes, it's strange, but we have heard of this before. Yes, there are voices up there praying! It can only be for the good of all of us, for the Jews are loyal subjects. May it be granted that their prayers be heard."

Passing through Gibraltar a few years ago, Rabbi Abecasis, from Tetuan, Morocco, brought with him another story, one recorded in the *genizah* of the cemetery of his town. Whether it has ever been retold before, I do not know.

The *chazzan* of the community in Tetuan, a young man, had a superb voice whose strength and clarity filled the synagogue. When he led the congregation in prayer, his ringing tones melted every heart until each member was aroused to sincere *tefillah*.

One *Rosh Chodesh*, a member of the Moslem gentry was visiting in the Jewish Quarter, possibly to see one of the Jewish merchants of the town on some business matter, and happened to pass by the synagogue during the morning service. He stopped in his tracks, enraptured by the bell-like voice echoing from within. Following the sound, he approached the entrance to the house of prayer. His glance fell on the young man standing before the holy Ark, leading the congregants in the recitation of the *Hallel* with great fervor and concentration, oblivious to the danger that lurked at the entrance.

The Moslem gentleman went immediately to the pasha and described with great enthusiasm the prize he had found. Subsequently the news of his "discovery" was passed on to the Moslem religious authorities. "This young man could sing for us in court. Furthermore, with his great talent, he could work in the mosque with the muezzin and call people to prayer. Yes, indeed, we need him as one of us!"

As the young *chazzan* concluded the *Kaddish* of *Shacharis* the next day, he turned around to find an armed guard awaiting him. Forcibly, he was marched to the Moslem section of the town, where they took him into the mosque and locked him in the muezzin tower. Fearful of what these fiends might do to him, he sat on the ground and wept, asking himself why this had happened, what it was that Heaven required of him. Whatever transpired, he decided, he would remain a Jew, the same Jew who loved Torah and *mitzvos* with all his heart, and had inspired others through his *tefillah*.

Summoned before the local pasha and the Moslem authorities, he entered silently, but stubbornly. They had given him no food or drink throughout the day, not that he would have accepted it, for fear of touching forbidden food. "Sing for us, young man, we want to hear your voice!" they commanded. But the *chazzan* of Tetuan remained silent. His voice had been dedicated to the holy work of singing in Hashem's house, and now he strengthened himself not to profane it.

"You will sing for us, my son, and we will make you great. You will convert to Islam and sing in the mosque and before the royal court of the king. Wealth and fortune will follow you and your family. Do not be stubborn and foolish. Take heed now, so we need not compel you. We have our ways of 'helping' you to decide, surely you realize that."

The young man was righteous, from the finest of Jewish families, and a true *yirei Shamayim*. He understood all too well that their methods of "helping him" could prove deadly not only to himself, but also to his family.

He forced himself to reply, "How can I fulfill your request, honored lords, for I am a Jew. How can a Jew, one of those that you despise, sing before you in court or in your religious services? Release me and let me go home for I am not worthy!"

"Sing for us first, young man. We command that you sing!"

But the young man pleaded tiredness, tension and strain. He had neither eaten nor drunk the whole day. He needed sleep. Within his heart, however, he kept recalling the verse, "*Eich nashir es shir Hashem al admas neichar* — How will we sing Hashem's song in a foreign land?"

The next day, imprisoned in the tower, the young *chazzan* of Tetuan did not wait to be coerced to convert to their faith. He quickly recited the *Vidui*, and accepted upon himself the yoke of Heaven with the words of "*Shema Yisrael.*" As he finished the word *Echad*, he threw himself from the tower, and joined the ranks of the Heavenly Choir.

The Moslem guards ran towards the body in great consternation. The members of the court were in a quandary as to how to save face before their own people and before the Jewish "subordinates." Thus, they picked up the young Jew's lifeless body and buried him in the Moslem cemetery, claiming that he had already joined their faith and assembly by virtue of his presence there.

The Jews, not fooled at all, waited until the first possible opportunity presented itself, and under cover of night, they sent a party to rescue the body of the *chazzan* from the grip of the Moslems and to bring him to *kever Yisrael*, to be buried as a Jew.

Enraged anew at the action of the Jews, who cheated them of their new "Moslem" singer, both in life and in death, the pasha sent a team of soldiers with bloodhounds to the Jewish cemetery to uncover the fresh grave. They reached the grave with loud expressions of triumph and glee. But the victorious march was cut short.

An enormous boulder, a meteorite, fell from the sky, next to the grave of the *chazzan*. By merit of this *tzaddik* who had died *al kiddush Hashem*, the pasha's soldiers instantly dispersed with screams of fear instead of victory, fleeing like dogs on the run.

"How indeed will we sing Hashem's song in a foreign land?"

If one thinks, "These are simply stories told by old grandfathers at teatime — surely they cannot be true!" then take into consideration that at least one of these tales involves someone who is still alive and retells his own story even today. Of the rest of the characters in the stories, their children, grandchildren and others closely connected are vibrantly involved in the retelling, for the events are alive and fresh to them.

A former citizen of Tetuan, now a grandfather living in Jerusalem, recalled the events of his youth, nearly 50 years earlier. He still has family among the Gibraltarians who remember his story and give it its due respect.

We will call him Menashe, to preserve his anonymity. When Menashe was a young man, in the prime of his strength, he was walking one day down the *mellah*, the Jewish Quarter of Tetuan, when he suddenly felt ill. Faintness overcame him and he was forced to stagger to the nearest seat. Neighbors came quickly to his aid with glasses of water and damp cloths to revive him, but to no avail. Further medical examination revealed that the unfortunate young man had been stricken with polio. In time, his limbs weakened, and because of the limited medical knowledge and treatment available for such diseases at the turn of the century, there was nothing to be done for him. He became paralyzed.

Great was the grief of his family and friends, who saw a fine, strong young man suffering so terribly. He had to be carried from place to place, for his legs would not support him. He required complete care. All feared for his future.

His parents did not sit calmly by and accept their son's fate. They worked without respite to find relief for his malady. They approached the *chachamim* of Morocco, many of whom were renowned for their greatness in both the *Toras HaNiglah* and *Toras HaSod* — the Revealed Torah and the Hidden Torah. One of these great men recommended that they take him to pray at the graves of the greatest *tzaddikim* of Morocco, and allow him to spend the night adjacent to their resting places. "But he is a *Kohen* and is thus prohibited from entering a cemetery!" one of the relatives objected. The *tzaddik*, however, waved his hand and insisted that in view of the danger involved to Menashe's life, and in light of the fact that no impurity is attached to *tzaddikim* such as these, an exception could certainly be made.

A strained and painful journey was undertaken by Menashe, accompanied by his male relatives. Together, they visited several of the holy places of Morocco. As instructed, his relatives left him to sleep overnight alongside the grave of a great Rav. While Menashe slept, two men stood guard nearby.

The young man fell asleep easily, fatigued after the long and arduous journey. His relatives watched as he slept through the first part of the night. As the night wore on, they saw him stir a little, as if somewhat disturbed, and mutter loudly, but indistinctly, as if in reply to something he saw in his dream. His body shifted closer to the grave. Then, as his relatives looked on in sheer amazement, Menashe sat up, rubbed his eyes, stood up unaided and staggered away.

"Menashe! Are you all right? You are walking! Menashe, what happened? Why did you mutter in your sleep?" The questions came pouring out of everyone's mouth.

"Come, we must leave here. I am a *Kohen*, and must not remain in a cemetery!" Menashe replied. And with this, Menashe walked, on his own, out of the cemetery.

Once outside, he turned to them and explained briefly, "I saw the Rav in my dream. He asked me why I was sleeping in the cemetery next to his *kever*. I explained that I had been stricken with the dread disease polio and could not move my limbs. He instructed me with great urgency to get up and leave immediately. 'You are a *Kohen*, of the holy seed of Aharon, and for you to remain here is prohibited. It is an *issur*. Rise now, on your feet, and go! You can do it! Go!' And with the vision of this great Rav before me, a sight that was both wonderful and awe inspiring, I had no choice but to listen. So I got up and walked out, as bidden." Menashe was still pale and shaking slightly from that vision he had seen. But he was cured.

From that time on, all his limbs functioned normally. The paralysis had miraculously left him. And most important, he merited to see his children and grandchildren walking with him in the Holy City of Yerushalayim.

In Baron Rothschild's Gardens

y aunt who lived in Bayit Vegan told of an "adventure" she had soon after her arrival in *Eretz Yisrael*. Often people do not realize why they are directed to a certain place at a certain time. But there always is a purpose. And she explained:

When I first came to live in the Holy City, I took many bus tours with the purpose of fulfilling that which *Chazal* state: "Whoever walks four *amos* in the Holy Land merits reward." So together with my two grandchildren, I explored many interesting and historical places. Some were exceptional in their beauty.

Some were holy places, deeply moving in their religious and historical significance, whose true holiness a Jew can only feel and understand from within his soul.

One of the less holy, but quite interesting, places that we visited was Ganei HaNadiv, the garden park memorializing the famous philanthropist Baron Edmond de Rothschild, in Zichron Yaakov. Beautiful landscaped grounds were spread out on all sides, flowers bloomed in vibrant colors, and tree-lined paths led up to the gates. We stood still for a moment, my grandchildren and I, drinking in all this splendor. Then, together with the other tourists, we passed through the gates to the Baron's gravesite. Here the gardens burst forth with additional delights; with fountains, miniature waterfalls and water lilies in a forest-like area.

As we enjoyed this panorama, undeniably a joy to the senses, a man's deep voice cut through the peaceful atmosphere, as he said in a rich Polish Yiddish, "*Dus heist geleibt!* — This is what I call living!" Tuning in to his sarcasm, I burst out laughing, for this was an obvious jab at the senseless extravagance in honor of Baron de Rothschild. For however great a philanthropist he had been in his lifetime, he surely had no need for all of this beauty now. It seemed to me that the Baron's good deeds and generosity to the Jewish nation and the world were and still are the true living tribute to his name. So, what is this beautiful garden doing here? What is its purpose?

Thinking about this brought to mind the famous account of the Baron's righteous ancestor, R' Meir Amschel Rothschild, in whose merit, it is told, the Rothschilds became wealthy.

R' Meir Amschel worked as a *shamash* for HaRav HaGaon Zvi Hirsch Horowitz, the *Av Beis Din* of Tchortkov. R' Meir Amschel was a poor man, but known to be totally honest and G–d fearing. It was common practice for members of the community to give the Rav moneys they had collected for various purposes. The Rav would safeguard these moneys in a secret place in his house known only to himself and his *shamash*.

One day, a sum of money was needed, and the Rav instructed his trusted *shamash*, R' Meir Amschel, to retrieve the required amount from the secret place. He returned promptly, but empty-handed, stating that he had searched but the money was not to be found. The Rav checked and found the hiding place in disarray, as though someone had rummaged through it looking for something, and the money was indeed nowhere in sight. The Rebbetzin was called in. She glared suspiciously at the unfortunate *shamash*, for she did not trust him as her husband did. The Rav was loath to suspect R' Meir Amschel, who had been completely trustworthy for as long as he had known him. But tongues began to wag among the townspeople and demeaning looks and snide remarks were cast in his direction. It was obvious that many suspected him of taking the money. Our Sages caution against both slandering and putting a man to shame, and equate the latter with the shedding of blood.

While the commotion was still raging, R' Meir Amschel suddenly disappeared without a trace, and residents of the town nodded their heads in righteous self-commendation: "Certainly we were right — just look how he left town."

But the *Av Beis Din* of the city was not at peace with himself for he believed in his *shamash's* innocence. He pleaded before G–d that the truth emerge. Between Purim and Pesach, when the house was cleaned from top to bottom, the "stolen" money was found. Some say it was concealed within the pages of a Gemara, some say the non-Jewish maid admitted to taking it — but clearly the *shamash* was innocent.

The Rav was sick with anxiety at having allowed this wrong to be perpetrated. His heart ached. He could not learn Torah or concentrate on community matters. Without telling anyone, the day after Pesach he took his staff and his coat and left town in search of the blameless *shamash*, R' Meir Amschel Rothschild.

In each town and Jewish community that he visited, he gave a *derashah*, a Torah discourse, which included an account of how he had suspected his innocent *shamash*, who had fled in the face of shame and public ostracism. He, R' Zvi Hirsch, was begging forgiveness publicly and seeking R' Meir Amschel, an upright and honest Jew, in order to compensate him for the agony caused him and the damage done to his good name for suspecting an innocent person of wrongdoing is one of the 24 sins that can hinder a man from doing *teshuvah*.

So it went, day after day, town after town. Then, one day, from among the assembled was heard the unmistakable voice of R' Meir Amschel himself. He called upon his holy and revered Rav to forgive *him*, the unworthy *shamash*. For although R' Meir Amschel had long ago put the incident out of his mind, he felt that he must have been guilty of some grave transgression in the eyes of Heaven that had resulted in his being falsely accused.

Each reached out towards the other to make peace and reconcile. And then the Rav gave the famous *berachah* that would impact on all future generations of the Rothschild family: "All men will trust you, R' Meir Amschel, in all your dealings, especially business; you will be exceedingly successful and all the world will be honored through you."

So, that was the secret of the Rothschild prosperity. Now it all made sense. Surely only Divine guidance and bounty would be the lot of the recipient of such a blessing.

❧❦

Turning to face the man who had awakened these thought in me by his sarcastic remark, I asked him in Yiddish where he was from, using the traditional Polish Yiddish idiom, "*Fun vie kimt a Yid?* — From where does a Jew come?"

"*Fun Poilen* — from Poland," he replied. "Now I live in the United States."

"My parents were also Polish," I informed him.

"Oh yes?" he answered politely, but with little interest, as he moved on, his wife close behind. We were all feeling the heat of the day, and the fatigue that it prompted. I glanced at the couple, noting that they were most likely in their late 60s or early 70s.

I decided to try again and said, "My father was born in Warsaw, and my mother was born in a small town near Molawa that you have probably never heard of." His steps drew slowly to a halt and he turned back to me, showing unusual interest in what I was saying. It was common for people to recognize my father's name, for he was from the large Jewish community of Warsaw. But no one had ever before shown interest when I mentioned a nondescript little Polish town like Molawa.

"Yes, I know Molawa!" he exclaimed.

"Lipowietz or Lipofze?" I asked quickly in excitement, naming the two small towns outside Molawa.

The man turned so pale, he seemed about to faint. His wife murmured something anxiously and rummaged in her bag for some refreshment. However, he soon recovered and inquired in a loud voice, "Your mother was from Lipofze? Tell me, who was she?"

"My mother's maiden name was Itzkowitz," I replied.

"What? Tell me, are you Lemel's granddaughter?" he asked, his excitement growing.

"Yes! yes! My mother's father was called R' Osher Lemel!"

The mention of my grandfather's name conjured up a vision of another time, and I recalled stories that had been recounted about him. He was a simple farmer, and a *chasid* who had sent his sons to learn in Yeshivas Gur in Warsaw. A powerful man, physically and mentally, he had an iron will that could not be conquered, and he was willing to stand up against anyone or anything, including the elements. He was a Jew of the Diaspora, one who had to contend with the hardships of eking out a livelihood from the soil. Although he was not a *talmid chacham*, when he sat in his house or under the open skies to recite *Tehillim*, he could split the heavens with the power of his prayer.

Within our family, a story is told of the time when a non-Jew owed him money and, out of spite, refused to pay. The Polish gentile then challenged him to a duel on horseback, sneering, "If you want your money, come and get it! You Jews don't know how to fight, but I will teach you! If you win, you can have your money back!"

A significant sum was at stake and R' Osher Lemel decided not to allow the *goy* to emerge unscathed without a challenge. It was not only the money involved, but Jewish pride and self-respect as well.

With the townsfolk surrounding the combatants to bear witness, R' Osher Lemel rode out on his horse, wearing his customary leather-patched trousers, the wind tugging at his beard and *peyos*. He held a stave in one hand, and the reins of the horse in the other. The Polish farmer rode out snarling, the smell of vodka reeking from his breath, a long stave in his hands, and hostility tightening his face.

The Jews on the side called out in Yiddish to R' Osher Lemel to ignore the remarks of the *goyim* and to be strong. *"B'shem Hashem na'aseh v'natzliach!* — In the Name of Hashem we will do and succeed!" they cried. Each one *davened* and cheered him on, both with words and unspoken prayers.

R' Osher Lemel smiled a little as he raised his stave and quickly brought it down on his opponent's back. The gentile, infuriated, raced with his horse, swinging his stave in all directions, but in poor control. The vodka he had swallowed with his meal was interfering with his ability. He had overindulged. The two horses nearly collided, but R' Osher Lemel managed to ride away in time. Now the *goy* tried another ploy, for he realized that this Jew was stronger than he had expected. He took a stone out of his pocket and attempted to hurl it at the horse's hooves, in order to injure the animal and unseat its rider. Seeing that fair play was never intended in this fight, R' Osher Lemel maneuvered his opponent into some overhanging trees. The *goy* tried to charge, but became entangled in the low branches, where R' Osher Lemel unseated him with a heavy blow. The Pole landed in a heap on the ground and R' Osher Lemel held him down. "I want my money, now! Hand it over or this is the end of you!"

R' Osher Lemel retrieved his money and Jewish honor was vindicated.

R' Osher Lemel's eldest son, Avrom, fought against the Germans in the Resistance. He inherited some of his father's grit, as did other family members in that generation.

My new acquaintance remembered him. "I was Avrom's best friend! We did everything together. I was a *bcn bayis* in that house!" Memories of his youth flooded back, myriads of happy events that had long since been forgotten. Recollections of these happy times had been erased by the war.

My aunt also remembered, "Avrom was my mother's older brother. He, his wife and 12 of his 13 children were murdered by Hitler in the Holocaust." More memories ... painful ones.

From this visit to the resting place of Baron Rothschild began a renewal of history. "Here, let us start again. It is time to renew contacts between families!" proposed the visitor from the States. My aunt was more than a little excited by this unexpected "find." She fished in her bag for her notebook and pen, and the families exchanged addresses. "You must come to visit us in the States!" the wife offered. My aunt invited them to Bayit Vegan. And indeed, the visits were made and a friendship was established.

My aunt concluded in her own words, "For my part, I believe that miracles happen more often than we think. Perhaps also what originally appeared to be senseless extravagance surrounding Baron de Rothschild is neither senseless nor extravagant. There is a continuing influence of *chesed* that generates from that place, and it is indeed fitting that it be so beautiful."

Flour for Torah

Without flour, there is no Torah;
without Torah, there is no flour.

he kosher bakeries owned by the Grodzinsky family are among the well-known landmarks of Jewish London. This small "kingdom of bread" dates back to 1888, when Harris and Judith Grodzinsky arrived in London with their two small children and Judith's parents. They came from Varanova, in the district of Vilna, where the family had been bakers for as long as anyone could remember. Settling in the East End of London, they started out by baking wedding rolls, or *bulkelach*, with oil, and fine white flour and Judith's loving expertise. It was her recipe and her impetus that started the ball rolling, with her husband selling the products from a pushcart in Wentworth Street Market. Their popularity grew, and very soon they were producing 400 to 500 tasty *bulkelach* a day.

At the turn of the century, a whirlwind of vicious pogroms in Lithuania, Russia and Poland instigated the Jewish migration to both the United States and England. The influx of Jewish immigrants helped the business flourish. They acquired a premises on Fieldgate Street, in the East End of London, and hired a master baker who worked with three sets of double-decker coal-fired ovens. They produced delicious loaves and placed two special stickers on the top, as did all the Jewish bakers then. One sticker was from the Jewish Bakers' Union, long since gone, and the other bore a picture of Harris Grodzinsky and the company's name and address.

In 1904, Harris Grodzinsky passed away, leaving Judith to run the business together with her 18-year-old son, Abby. The business was developing nicely, and Abby married Bertha Jeidel from a town near Frankfurt-am-Main. They had five children, the eldest of whom was a son named Harry. Sadly, Abby died in the 1918 flu epidemic, and Bertha was left to cope with the family and the business single-handedly.

By 1937, they followed the trend of the Jewish migration from the East End to the northwest, with a chain of kosher bakery shops serving the growing population, and both boys with pushcarts and horse-drawn vans undertaking the deliveries. At 4 o'clock each morning, between the receding night and the dawning of the new day, the vans could be seen trundling out to reach the small grocery shops that dotted the Jewish neighborhoods of London. Judith's great-grandsons, Harry and Reuven, were now active in the business. Reuven remembered how Harry had called him up one day and told him that he would have to drive one of the vans and make the rounds for the deliveries. He had no idea how to drive a horse-drawn van, and did not know how he would manage. The horse was a very capable chauffeur, however, and drove Reuven comfortably to every address on the route, stopping briefly outside each customer's house so Reuven could make his delivery. The horse then led him back to Fieldgate Street!

The Grodzinsky's bread was of excellent quality, and Hashem blessed the work of their hands. Soon, there was not a Jewish home in London that was not familiar with the bread, *challos*, and other fine baked goods from their bakery. As Harry grew more experienced in the business, he branched out into other "areas" as well. After the Second World War, Harry went to assist in the D.P. (displaced person) camps. In much later and happier times, he developed a strong friendship with the Ponevezher Rav, head of Yeshivas Ponevezh in Bnei Brak. The Ponevezher Rav was more than just a good friend; he also acted as *shadchan* (matchmaker) for one of Harry's sons who was learning in a yeshivah in Jerusalem.

As for Harry, he loved to do *chesed*. It was an integral part of his nature. A warm, happy and modest man, he liked to do his *gemilus chasadim* without the world knowing about it. One of the many charity projects that he quietly undertook was to supply bread to the local yeshivos for free. His only condition was that a representative of the yeshivah be responsible each day for picking up the bread.

Some yeshivos declined his merchandise, for various reasons. Harry thereupon gave them the money needed to cover the cost of bread for the day. However, among those who did accept this generous offer of "the staff of life" was R' Moshe Schneider, *Rosh Yeshivah* of the yeshivah in the Stamford Hill section of London.

The venerable R' Schneider enlisted the help of two reliable yeshivah boys for two separate tasks involved in the running of the yeshivah. One *bachur* was to collect the bread from Mr. Grodzinsky. The other was to be the *vekker* who would awaken the boys in the early morning for *tefillah* and *limud Torah*. Both did their jobs faithfully for many years, affording their *Rosh Yeshivah* a feeling of satisfaction and *nachas ruach*.

As an expression of his gratitude, R' Schneider gave each *bachur* a special blessing. To the one who went to get the bread each day for the yeshivah, he gave a blessing for material wealth — that he would merit to maintain the House of Israel with material support. To the other, who rose early to awaken others, R' Schneider gave a blessing that he merit to awaken the hearts and direct the souls of Israel.

Years have passed, and the beloved *Rosh Yeshivah* is no longer with us. But his good works still generate more good works, and his blessings have come true! The *vekker* of the yeshivah is today a well-known Rav and Torah personality living in Yerushalayim, R' Moshe Sternbuch. The "bread collector" is a famous orthodox Jewish millionaire, Moshe Reichmann of Toronto, Canada. Some say, however, that the "bread collector" had once been heard saying that it was his misfortune that he had not been given the other task in the yeshivah.

The Shochet from Moscow

*L*ong before the Iron Curtain dissolved into nothingness, many groups and delegations visited the Soviet Union from all parts of the West, to strengthen and spread Torah and *mitzvos* among our Russian Jewish brethren. No one dreamed that the Soviet Communist threat would depart from the earth "not with a bang but with a whimper." Many individuals and groups operated with *mesiras nefesh*, often in secrecy and in disguise. Their aim was to disseminate Jewish education to a dispersed community that had become separated from their Jewish roots when anti-religious edicts and other hardships were a mortal threat to Jewish life.

Many are the stories that have been told about the dedication and the perseverance of Russian Jews who struggled daily to retain their Jewishness, to perform *bris milah*, to observe laws of family purity, bake matzos for Pesach, learn Hebrew, and more. The Jewish spirit can never be subjugated and, therefore, these courageous brethren fought the vicious Communist onslaught by retaining as much of their Jewish identity as was possible.

One *Erev Pesach*, a religious boys' choir, the Pirchei of London, visited Moscow. Ostensibly, their visit was classified by the Russians as "a cultural tour." However, the British singing group had their own quiet intentions. They had brought along with them young married men, who had been trained in yeshivos, to give Torah lectures, inspire, and to ignite fresh enthusiasm in everyone they encountered. Ignoring Russians who could have interfered with their efforts, they boldly proceeded with their schedule. Young and old came from near and far to hear them sing, and especially, to experience the wonderful *Kabbalas Shabbos* that they *davened* in the age-old Moscow *shul*.

The old *shul* of Moscow is renowned for its beautiful edifice and for its history. Prayers still echo from its crevices and the cracks still reverberate with sighs. Although the Communists had driven the Jews out of their houses of study and places of prayer, many prayers, bottled up and sealed in Jewish hearts, begged for expression. You could see the desire in their eyes. But because of fear, the Jews had forgotten how to pray. The old people, the ones who remembered what it used to be like, who had not heard so impassioned a *tefillah* offered within the old *shul* walls for nearly 50 years, were emotionally stirred and began to weep. The young people there comprised the generation which was comparable to the fourth son described in the Pesach Haggadah — the *she'eino yode'a lishol*. They had never witnessed Jewish learning, for their learned ancestors were deceased, and their other forebears had become alienated from Torah life. There was no one left for them to ask and thus they no longer know *how* to ask.

Now, these young people were trying desperately to find what their souls yearned to be part of.

At the end of their stay in Moscow, the leaders of the group quietly organized the distribution of *kosher L'Pesach* food parcels for those who had requested them. After they had handed out the last parcel, an old man approached them. They motioned to him that they were finished. There was no more left; they were extremely sorry.

"Wait! — *Vart a minut,*" he cried out in Yiddish. "You can't close up yet!" Mottele the *shochet* explained his plight. "If you don't find a parcel for me, then you doom me to near starvation throughout the Pesach week. Other than potatoes, I will not touch anything. I am a *frum* man, a Lubavitcher *chasid,* perhaps the only remaining *shochet* in Moscow!" As the young Englishmen later stated, they had come to Russia to give *shiurim,* but Mottele was about to teach them a lesson they would never forget. He was a walking *mussar sefer.* Mottele continued his story.

Mottele had remained in Moscow after the Communists had come to power. All attempts to drain Yiddishkeit from his Jewish veins had proved unsuccessful, for he had continued in his time-honored Jewish ways and had secretly supplied kosher meat to the remnants of the observant community. However, Mottele was a Lubavitcher *chasid* and he never gave up hope of escaping the Soviet shackles and arriving at 770 Eastern Parkway in Brooklyn, to bask in the warm radiance of the Rebbe. He therefore applied for an exit visa for himself, his wife and his daughter. He was rejected, and made to suffer ostracism, loss of employment and worse because of his request. He never lost hope, but applied time and again. Finally his request was granted and the longed-for exit visa was in his hand, gazed at with delight by the family and with near jealousy by his Jewish neighbors. The *shochet's* family made their preparations and began their long trip, via Vienna, to their destination.

Mottele the *shochet* arrived in New York. The dream of his life had been achieved, and his heart soared with praise and thanks to Hashem for His salvation and bounty. He was now able to meet the Rebbe, his Rebbe, in person. How long had it been since he had had participated in a *farbrengen*? How many years had passed since he had sat with other *chassidim*? Not wasting a moment, he hurried to the Rebbe's house and waited impatiently for his turn to speak with the Rebbe.

The Rebbe received him welcomingly and gently. He asked his name, and from where he was. Hearing from where Mottele had come, the Rebbe spoke to him with praise and words of comfort. The Rebbe knew of Mottele's ancestors and was able to supply details about the family that the *shochet* had long forgotten, for the Rebbe was famous for his remarkable memory. But then, unexpectedly, the Rebbe asked, "Whom have you left in your place as *shochet* in Moscow?"

Mottele was dumbfounded, unable to answer. Stuttering, he replied that he thought there was another *shochet* somewhere in the region, but he was not sure ... not sure if other *shochtim* were reliable ... and how many were left in Russia ...

The Rebbe was adamant, "Then you must go back! You cannot leave your Jewish brethren without kosher meat and the teaching of Yiddishkeit that a man of your standing is still able to impart to the members of your community. You must not leave the ship without a captain! R' Mottele, I know it is hard, but you must go back!" With great effort, Mottele left the Rebbe's presence.

Mottele's troubles were not yet over, for when he faced his wife and daughter with the news, they burst into tears. "You cannot do this to us! We have struggled and suffered enough!" exclaimed his wife, "and I, for my part, cannot return." His daughter added, "Papa, do you not want me to get married? How long did I wait in Moscow, seeking the *chassan* who never arrived? Did you not always tell me that I must wait until we reach New York to find a *chassan*, a fine religious young man, a *chassid* like yourself? Where will I find such a young man in Moscow today? I must stay here, but I cannot remain in this big city alone. Papa, please, you will have to think of something!"

Mottele had been taught never to question the teaching of a sage, of a *tzaddik*. He buried his personal feelings in the face of the needs of the community. He did not even go back to tell the Rebbe of his family's emotional response. With a heavy heart, he gave his wife a *get*, kissed his daughter good-bye, and returned to Moscow.

So, this was the Moscow *shochet*, this shabbily dressed, graying man, a paragon of *yiras Shamayim*, who now stood before them. One English youngster, envious of the *shochet*'s obvious spiritual stature, said, "Surely everyone can achieve this *madreigah*, spiritual height!" His friend, however, sharply retorted, "If so, then surely every person should work on himself until he in fact achieves such a *madreigah*!" Looking at each other, each one was left with a nagging question in his heart, "Would I, who has had all the modern advantages of the finest Jewish education, have been able to withstand the test, the immense *nisayon*, that this *shochet* has withstood?"

"A living *mussar sefer*, a *tzaddik* in his generation, this *shochet* from Moscow!" they unanimously agreed.

Esther

The last night of Chanukah was a cold winter evening, and the family had gathered in my home for one of our traditional get-togethers. While the cold wind blew outside, we sat in the study comfortable and warm. The dancing flames shone brightly and created an aura of coziness. The children sat on the floor, spinning a *dreidel*, while the adults, caught up in the atmosphere of the evening, began to do some "spinning" of their own, and started to share family stories and memories. The life of my grandmother Esther unfolded like a history book.

Esther was an old-fashioned woman who emigrated from Poland to England in the 1930s. She is remembered clearly by all as a quiet woman who spoke little and accomplished a lot. Often it was her eyes that did the talking. Optimistic and intelligent, she had a worldly wisdom from which one could not help but learn. Her spontaneous cheerful laugh made everything brighter, even when times were far from sunny. Esther's story is one of someone who lived not for herself, but for those around her.

She came from a very poor family. But, in her view, the lack of material objects was compensated for by the abundance of spiritual riches. Esther's father, R' Avraham Kopper, was known as the Torcziner *Iluy*. He was a child prodigy who demonstrated great potential in Torah learning. One of Esther's brothers had a razor-sharp mind as well, and it was hoped that he would follow in his father's footsteps.

R' Avraham Kopper had written a *sefer* of *chiddushei Torah* which he was never able to publish due to a lack of funds. When his cousin, Shaya Blatt, left for England, R' Avraham begged him to take the manuscript and publish it there. Shaya, however, was also extremely poor and his emigration was being sponsored by others. He feared that he would not be able to afford the cost of the project and begged to be relieved of the responsibility. So it was that this *sefer*, along with many other treasures of our people, was lost in the Holocaust.

When Esther was of marriageable age, around 16 or 17, the family began to seek a suitable match for her. Her *shidduch* was found, a young man named Mendel Gayer who came from a well-known family. Some of R' Mendel's cousins said that they descended from R' Zushe of Hanipoli. Other cousins claimed they descended from Rebbe Zushe's elder brother, R' Elimelech of Lizhensk, the *Noam Elimelech*, one of the great chasidic masters of his generation. Nobody is certain of the exact lineage, but the family surely had strong sturdy roots. Young Mendel was a fine Torah scholar. He was also studying to be a *shochet*, so *b'ezras Hashem*, he would eventually be able to support his wife and family.

⚜

After they were married, the young couple was supported by both sets of parents, according to the custom of "eating *kest*," eating meals at the homes of their respective parents. Shortly after their wedding, Esther and Mendel went to her mother's house for dinner. Soon after they arrived, one of her brothers grabbed his hat and jacket and ran out of the house. "Where are you going?" she called after him in surprise. "Is this how you treat your sister, the *kallah*, when she comes home to visit after her wedding?" He waved behind him and called back briefly, "Be seeing you!" Esther and Mendel sat down to the table, set with steaming soup and stew, and were treated as very important guests. "Where is Moshe? Why did he not stay to eat?" Esther asked her mother innocently. "Never mind, it's no concern of yours," came her mother's reply.

At the house of Mendel's parents, the young couple witnessed a similar scene more than once. Upon their arrival, a family member announced, "I am not hungry, thanks!" or "I have already eaten," and then would leave. The truth suddenly dawned on Esther. In order to feed both her and her husband, someone else in the family had to go without a meal that day. Esther was deeply disturbed by this shocking fact. She could not let anyone suffer on her account. It went totally against her nature as a "giver" to be on the receiving end and to allow someone else to suffer deprivation for her sake.

So she began to play the same game. She would make excuses to her parents and in-laws, saying that she had a stomachache and couldn't eat, or that she had already eaten.

However, she rapidly lost weight and began to look wan and sickly, arousing grave concerns about her health. The truth came to light, however, and she revealed the reason why she had not been eating. Her young husband and family quickly realized just how serious this situation was — not just for the young couple, but for everyone else as well. At that point, a plan was formulated which would alleviate the strain.

The First World War was taking its toll on all of Europe, and especially on the Jewish population. The acute economic stress was one of the major factors that forced the Jews to emigrate and find new homes in the *goldene medinah* of America and in Great Britain. Thus, Esther, Mendel, his brothers and his parents prepared to leave the Polish soil where their families had lived for generations and to set sail for uncharted territory in Great Britain.

The good news was that there were jobs to be had in London. One could earn enough pay to provide the needs of his family. Unfortunately, the price for this economic stability was steep. Countless tears were shed as families embraced for the last time and parted, knowing that there would be no money to spare for return visits. At that time, the ocean seemed an endless expanse, an insurmountable barrier.

England's Jewish population was still quite small at that time and did not increase dramatically until the influx of Jews from Eastern Europe before, during and after the Second World War. Mendel got work both as a *chazzan* and as a *shochet* in England. There was no religious education available for the small population of Jews, and since Esther and Mendel feared the influences of a non-Jewish education, they kept their daughter at home until age 7. Only then did they allow her to attend the non-Jewish school where she was only the second Jewish student in attendance. Her command of the English language was poor when she began school, and the teachers labeled her "the refugee child." The language barrier proved to be an even greater problem for the adult immigrants, who had to deal with earning a livelihood while trying to master the language of their adopted country.

Esther settled into her role as an Orthodox Jewish housewife in a completely foreign environment quietly but cleverly. She also took it upon herself to help the newly arrived immigrants become acquainted with their new homeland. Working on a very limited budget, she turned her home into a one-woman soup kitchen.

The Bloomsbury Shelter for Men in London's East End was the first stop for Jewish immigrants after disembarking from the boats. Upon arriving at these shores, most could not speak English. For the most part, the men had come alone, seeking employment to prepare the way for their families. All were hungry for a meal. Day after day, small groups of these immigrants were to be found in Esther's kitchen, sitting around her table where she would serve them a simple, nutritious and greatly appreciated meal.

The word soon spread. "Good meals to be had in Rebbetzin Gayer's house!" They kept coming and she kept cooking! How did she manage to constantly feed all those poor souls? No one really knows. But just as she had always put others first while in Poland, she was doing the same in England. Now she placed the Jewish immigrants at the top of her priority list. In order to cope with the added expense, she had to prepare most everything herself. Her only luxury was a "charlady" who, for about a shilling, came once a week to scrub the endless flight of stairs in the old English townhouse where they lived.

The Jews who came "off the boat" formed a club of sorts. They would meet in Esther's kitchen at mealtimes, and exchange news and information. This became an opportunity for them to help one another and offer advice and suggestions about living in a new world. Along with these men came the stories — priceless gems that reflected their own situations and bolstered their courage to continue. Every Jew helped another so that they could all survive.

A tale was told of a Jewish immigrant who wandered around London's East End in search of the old Jewish center, trying to locate some of his "landsmen." In his broken tongue he begged the locals to help him find "VITTERHAPEL STRIT — PLIS!" When this elicited only blank stares and furrowed brows, he began to feel a little desperate. Then, thank G-d, he met another Jew. "Reb Yid!" his new-found friend exclaimed. "You should be asking for WHITECHAPEL — not VITTERHAPEL!"

Another major problem which all the newly arrived Jews faced was that of finding work. This problem was multiplied because of Shabbos observance. No provision was made for an employee who kept Saturday rather than Sunday as his day of rest. Many tried becoming "Shabbosnicks" — working five days a week, getting fired, then looking for another job the following week. Those who were more enterprising opened their own businesses.

Some less fortunate individuals ended up working for unscrupulous individuals who would exploit them. A simple but observant Jew came to the Shatzer Rav, R' Sholom Moskowitz. His tale of woe was typical of many others — he was cracking under the strain of trying to keep Shabbos as a Jew should. Under great pressure, he finally succeeded in finding employment of a very menial nature, working for an irreligious Jew who had agreed to let him have Shabbos off. However, he had to pledge to work extra hours in the evenings and on Sundays, plus other hours of overtime yet to be arranged.

When Shabbos finally arrived, the cherished Shabbos for which this simple Jew had sweated and slaved all week long, he managed to go to *shul,* come home and make *Kiddush,* and then collapse into his chair. He fell into a deep slumber, from which none of the family could rouse him. He was exhausted to the breaking point. Thus, he slept through Shabbos, awakening to find that he had virtually missed it. And so it was on the following week; finally he came weeping to the Rav.

"No *davening,* no Shabbos *zemiros,* no Shabbos meal! What

can the One Above possibly think of a Jew such as me? For this disgraceful way of life, I needed to leave the Old Country, the 'Alte Heim'?"

The Rav responded by comforting him. He assured him that his *sheinah b'Shabbos* — his extended, involuntary Shabbos sleep — was a result of his enormous effort to guard the Shabbos and keep it holy. Therefore, it must be as cherished by Hashem as if he had meticulously kept Shabbos in all its details on a very high spiritual level.

ဆ•ော

As the wife of the *shochet*, Esther was entitled to certain cuts of meat as part of her husband's salary. She sold some of this meat and made a nice profit, part of which she sent to her family back in Poland. She, who had worried for her family's well-being and had refused to eat their food when there was not enough to go around, now shouldered their financial burden by supporting them from her minuscule budget. At the beginning of each week, before she set aside her own housekeeping money, she would sit at her kitchen table with a stack of envelopes. Each one was marked with the address of family members living "back home." An English shilling, and certainly an English pound sterling, was worth a considerable amount on the exchange in a poor country like Poland. Thus, those who had earlier sustained Esther and her husband were now being sustained by them. She felt consoled by the fact that she was able to help them, even from this distance, from this faraway place where there was no organized Jewish community, no Jewish schools (except for Hebrew school in the evening for her daughters) and certainly none of the neighbors, cousins, aunts and uncles that she had left behind.

And so each week a pile of envelopes would be prepared, each with a letter, a word of encouragement and a little money. A sum for this one, a bit more for that one, depending on the circumstances. Then she would faithfully make her way to the post office where the elderly mail clerk awaited her arrival before closing for the day.

The dark days of the Nazi Regime were filled with excruciating pain not only for those directly involved, but for Esther and all those like her who had relatives they had left behind. Esther prepared her last batch of envelopes and took them to the post office. She laid them on the desk before the clerk, who looked at her with great sympathy. Heaving a sigh, the woman handed them back to her saying, "Sorry, I can't take these today. Those rotten Germans — they've gone into Poland. This awful war! Your letters won't get there now. I'm really sorry."

Esther returned home, heartbroken. She had made a major effort to help her family, with the thought that one day she could help "bring them over" as immigrants. But time had run out.

But Esther persevered. She built a new life for herself in England. He selflessness stood her in good stead and she was able to help herself by helping others. She kept on building — and lived to see the blossoming of a new generation, some living in England, some in the United States and some in the Land of Israel; some learning Torah, some prospering in the business world and one, the leader of a major Jewish women's organization in the United States.

How much more could a good Jewish grandmother ask for?

It Is Good to Give Thanks to Hashem

The school years in the Polish "*Gymnasia*" were exceptionally sweet for Tzipporah. The daughter of a Rav, she had a quick, bright mind that rapidly absorbed all she was taught. She preferred learning rather than merely staying home and lazing around as some girls did, especially during the summer. Children looked forward with great anticipation to the warm summer months, when the air was fresh and clear and the orchards were full of ripening fruit trees. It was at this time that Tzipporah's mother and the other Jewish women worked at a hectic pace to prepare preserves for the grueling, cold winter months ahead, and even for the Pesach festival that would follow. The youngsters would frolic in the brightness of the season, and participate in hikes and various other outdoor pastimes.

Tzipporah, however, did not share in many of the activities, for they were often scheduled on Shabbos. The *Gymnasia*, although a Jewish school, was not a religious one. The renowned Sarah Schenirer had begun her pioneering work in education for observant girls by establishing the "Seminary" in Cracow, which gave rise to a small but expanding network of schools in Poland. These schools, however, had not yet reached the Polish-Lithuanian villages, and in Tzipporah's town there was no choice but to attend the *Gymnasia*. "The Rebbetzin," as the girls nicknamed Tzipporah, stubbornly and correctly refused to lower her standards by even a millimeter. Her father was the Rav of the town, and their home the clearing house for all community problems — halachic and otherwise. The religious upbringing that Tzipporah received at home provided her with the strength and backbone to "swim against the tide," both in her youth and later in life. And so the seasons passed, and it seemed that life in this little town would have remained the same forever. Babies were born, grew up, married, had children, and the cycle would begin anew.

On the third of Elul in the year 1942, life became anything but routine. The German soldiers, who already occupied parts of Poland, moved into the town. They dragged out Tzipporah's father, his son-in-law and 19 other Jewish community leaders, and publicly executed them. The bodies were then dumped in a swamp and abandoned.

Thus began the reign of terror. Their routine existence became a nightmare. People lived in fear, praying to G-d for their very survival. In the gray dusk of dawn, the Jews in town went to *Selichos* prayers and soaked the ground with their tears, not knowing what tomorrow would bring.

Tzipporah and her family had physically survived this terrifying ordeal, but their minds could not rest while the body of their dear ones and those of the 19 other Jewish men remained in the bog. After these men had been so cruelly murdered, the survivors' overriding concern was to perform "*kevuras meis mitzvah,*" and bring these martyrs to Jewish burial. The only way this could be accomplished was to approach the German Command in the larger neighboring town of Molodezna, and request permission to bury the bodies. The journey would be fraught with dangers, as the roads were full of German military units as well as civilian German gangs out to kill any Jew who was unfortunate enough to come within their grasp. Jewish life was cheap! Still, the women would not give up. Tzipporah, along with two of her sisters, waited for dusk and then made their way on foot, in the relative safety of the fields, in the direction of Molodezna.

Their journey led them to a field. The farmer who owned it was in the middle of his potato harvest. Tzipporah's sister, her clothing soiled and her eyes red from fatigue, approached him as he was carting his potatoes to the silo. With humility and trepidation in her voice, she asked permission to take refuge and sleep in the silo. The farmer was uncouth, but a simple and fair man, and he did not feel threatened by the three women refugees. "You may sleep here," he indicated to them, "but you must not stay too long."

The next day the farmer approached the bedraggled women huddled in the corner of the silo. "You can't stay here much longer," he warned, jerking a thumb in the direction of the distant town. "They are coming! I can't take the risk. I have a family of my own!" His warning was echoed by some of the Polish day laborers who arrived to work in the fields — there were German soldiers searching for victims.

The women continued their long trek, 120 kilometers in all, and finally reached Molodezna. Approaching German headquarters demanded an act of courage in itself, and requesting a meeting with the commanding officer bordered on outright insolence. Tzipporah and her sisters, however, conducted themselves with great dignity. Speaking clearly and meaningful-ly, they said: "Despite the occupation and all that it involves, it is an act of humanity to the living and the dead to permit the relatives to conduct proper burial of those executed." The commanding officer must have been impressed by them, or possibly he was caught by surprise at their unexpected appearance in his office, but he granted his permission. The sisters returned home the same way they had come, and the bodies of their relatives and the other victims were retrieved from the swamp and buried in the Jewish cemetery.

For the next year, the people of the town existed in a state of limbo. They realized that the situation was treacherous. The Germans would not permit them to live indefinitely. Yet at this moment there were few options open to them. Then, one of the citizens of the town received a message from a young friend, a youth who had joined the Russian and Polish partisans in the forests on the Russian border. It read simply, "Why are you all sitting and just waiting for the end? You can join us, the partisans. There are many others like you — at least here you will stand a chance!" It included directions to a distant town on the Russian border.

The news spread like wildfire through the town and many left as soon as they possibly could. The Rebbetzin and her family — Tzipporah and a second unmarried daughter, a widowed daughter with two children, and a married daughter with a 3-year-old son named Baruch, whose husband was in another town — left the town together with other neighbors and headed in the direction of the fields. For safety reasons the group tried to stay together, but had to maintain a rapid pace to ensure that their flight remained undetected.

The pace they set proved too much for Tzipporah's widowed sister and her two small children. "I can't keep up, Mama! I can't manage! What will I do?" They coaxed her to keep trying, fearing for her safety, but they knew that they could not slow down the rest of the party. At a loss for any other solution, they cried, then embraced her and the babies and watched as she turned back, weeping, towards the town.

When it proved impractical for such a large group to travel together, they split up into several smaller groups. Night was rapidly approaching, and a chill winter wind was blowing. As hiking in the dark in the unfamiliar fields would be too dangerous, each group began to worry about a place to rest. It was then that Tzipporah recalled the silo in the potato field where she had once taken shelter. She led the way there, the group following close behind.

That night was not a night for sleeping or dreaming, for a nightmare of a storm was all around them. The rain beat down incessantly in icy spears against the ground. Little Baruch screamed as the skies were rent by lightning, and the sound of thunder rebounded from the horizon. Nonetheless, in the distance, but still audible above the noise of the storm, the sound of gunshots was heard. The group in the dark silo cringed at the sounds they heard, waiting apprehensively and impatiently for daybreak.

The following morning, as early as possible, they continued on their way. Some farmhands they encountered confirmed their worst nightmares — "Germans! Aktion!" The Jewish group redoubled their efforts to distance themselves from the danger behind them. They had to contact the partisans. There was no other way.

Trekking, footsore and weary, with little Baruch and the other children being handed from one to another, they covered 15 kilometers a day, until they reached their destination on the other side of the rolling fields.

The Rebbetzin held tightly in her hand a note with an address, their only hope for the future. She knocked on the chipped wooden door of a small house, and watched as it opened slightly and a pair of eyes peered out from the dim interior. The door opened and there stood a man who was obviously not Jewish, tufts of white hair framing his face. He heaved a sigh at the distressing sight of the exhausted women, one holding in her arms a small child suffering from cold and exposure who moaned slightly from time to time. "Come in quickly!" he instructed, and as the group entered he closed the door behind them. They had, *baruch Hashem*, found the right address. This man would lead them to the forests, where the partisan groups were hiding.

The forests were thick and dark, and since they were close to the Russian border, the winters were cold and damp. Mud oozed underfoot. Hunger and fear constantly churned in the stomach. Only a sparse diet of what could be begged or bartered from the neighboring farmers or scavenged off the surrounding land sustained them. The partisans continued their defense work and the groups of refugees that followed behind them felt a certain sense of protection.

The Germans were not accustomed to the rough terrain and bitter winter conditions, and were wary of the forests, knowing that the partisans could freely attack them there. Once the summer came, however, the Germans plunged in to comb the woods, seeking out the "terrorists" and all those accompanying them. The summer, which had once been the favorite season of the year for Tzipporah and her friends, was now a painful, miserable time for the whole group. Their only hiding place was the swamps, for the Germans would not consider venturing into them. The small groups of Jewish refugees would spend the daylight hours wading knee-deep in thick mud, in order to survive yet another day. At night, they were able to sleep on an island of solid ground in the middle of the swamp.

One night during the first winter on the run, Tzipporah's father appeared to her in a dream. He was seated at a table, with other Jewish men she could not identify, and by his side sat a young man, a *yeshivah bachur*. Tzipporah's father turned to her, smiled, and said, "Look, Tzipporah, I have found a fine *chasan* for you. He is 18-years-old and already a *talmid chacham*. Your other sisters have found their *shidduchim*. Now it is your turn." Although Tzipporah was pleased to see her father in the dream, his message to her was disturbing. In her heart she thought: "But surely my father must know that such a *yeshivah bachur* is hardly right for me! I am a modern girl — certainly a religious girl, but educated in the *Gymnasia*!" Nonetheless, Tzipporah remembered the dream well, and especially the face of the young *yeshivah bachur*, which was etched in her memory, but she told no one about it. Being practical by nature, she did not allow her imagination to run wild, and put the dream out of her mind.

Life in the forest was grueling. Tzipporah recalled how once, in the summer of 1943, the Germans came too close for comfort. Intense in their searches for partisans in the woodlands, the Germans came upon the group. A partisan nearby shouted an order for the group to go to the left. Tzipporah blundered and went to the right, isolating herself from the group. Within minutes, bullets ricocheted all around her, while she ran on blindly, in terror. Only by a miracle, for no other word can describe it, was she able to avoid the enemy fire and hide, and later to reunite with her group. Thus were their days spent throughout those two dangerous and traumatic years, always fleeing from the Germans, following behind the partisans.

In the summer of 1944 the Russians advanced on Lithuania and, together with the Allied forces, engaged the Germans in a three-pronged attack. Finding themselves ensnared in a trap, the Germans retreated, with many of them taken prisoner. Conditions improved and Tzipporah, her family and others returned to their town, where they remained until the end of the war.

In May 1945 the war ended in Europe, and the world began to rebuild. In Lodz, a center was established for all the yeshivos and the fragmented families of the refugees. It was to this center that Tzipporah and her family came. Tzipporah was included in a group with other young girls. They were housed together and given assistance until the time came for them to be relocated. The group was organized and led by a religious woman, the daughter of one of the Polish Rebbes.

One of Tzipporah's young friends came running to her one day, waving her hands excitedly. "Hey, Tzipporah, I have wonderful news for you! I have just the *shidduch* for you! Now is the time for rebuilding families. Why wait?" She had a young man from Radin in mind. Although he looked nothing like the *yeshivah bachur* in her dream, Tzipporah married the young man from Radin. In time, after the wheels of bureaucracy had turned, they received papers and emigrated to America. Her mother and sisters also emigrated, first to America, and in time to *Eretz Yisrael*.

Time passed; Tzipporah raised a family, her husband at her side. He was a Rav and educator, and later worked as a *shochet* as well. He was an upright man, who earned every penny honestly. Tzipporah became a teacher and was successful. The scars of the war years faded somewhat. "*Rav lach sheves b'eimek habacha* — Too long have you sat in the valley of tears," and new strength came with new life.

More good years passed, but then her world was shattered again. Tzipporah's husband became sick and, after a prolonged illness, passed away, leaving her a young widow with growing children to support. Yet her strong inner core would not let her down even now. She complied with her husband's request to make his resting place in Yerushalayim rather than in the United States.

Tzipporah then took stock of her life, counted her blessings and rallied her strengths to the task at hand. She continued to teach, and with the help of G-d, provided both a yeshivah education and professional training for her children. Then, one by one, they married. After their weddings, her two daughters moved to

Israel. After assessing her situation and seeing that most of her family was now settled in Israel, she decided to follow suit.

Tzipporah became a grandmother, and assumed the role of "Bubbie," stepping in to assist her daughters who were working to support their husbands in *kollel*. But even with her grandchildren to keep her busy, as time went on Tzipporah felt a vacuum that her children could not fill. All of them were involved with their own lives and families, and she was left feeling alone.

Tzipporah remarried. His name was Yitzchak; he was a widower several years her senior from a fine established Yerushalmi family and a respected *talmid chacham*. Yitzchak had had a wonderful marriage with his first wife, and they had raised a fine family of young Torah Jews. All his children were now married and busy raising their families, just as Tzipporah's own children were. In time, a mutual feeling of respect and loyalty developed between the new couple.

A short time after the wedding, Yitzchak had a dream. He saw a man who gave him a message that was short and to the point: "Look after my Tzipporah; she has been through a great deal!" Yitzchak awoke, a little startled by the dream, but did not wish to act in haste. He could not forget that face ... something seemed familiar ....

Feeling his way with great care and sensitivity, Yitzchak approached his wife about the matter. He took an old album of photographs and laid it on the dining room table. He sat down comfortably in the large carved armchair at the head of the table and called to Tzipporah, "Come sit with me. I wish to show you some photos of my family. Have you any of your family to show me? It would be a good way for both of us to learn about each other's lives!" In this manner, he encouraged her to tell him of her life before they met.

As they sat leafing their way through the pictures of the past, laughing a little and commenting on what they found, Tzipporah stopped short at a picture of a young man. "Who is this?" she inquired with amazement. "Why, that is me as a young *yeshivah bachur*," replied Yitzchak calmly. Then came his turn to be amazed as he picked up a photograph from her collection. "Who is this?" he asked, indicating the portrait of a Jew of noble bearing. "That was my father," explained Tzipporah. The aura of incredulity deepened, and it was as if the last piece of a jigsaw puzzle had been set in place.

The aristocratic Jew that Yitzchak had seen in his dream was Tzipporah's father! The picture of the *yeshivah bachur* that Tzipporah now held in her hand, raising it slightly in wonderment before her eyes, was identical to her memories of the young man that her father had chosen as a *shidduch* for her in the dream so long ago in the forest! They were amazed and incredulous at their discoveries. "*HaKadosh Baruch Hu mezaveg zivugim* — It is only the Holy One, Blessed is He, that can determine a match for a marriage!" quoted Yitzchak to his new wife.

"So is the will of the One Who created all in a wondrous fashion, and governs His world in ways greater than our minds can begin to fathom. It was all '*bashert*'!" concluded Tzipporah. With a heart filled with joy at the *chesed* they had witnessed, Yitzchak began to sing. Intoning a melody that he had composed to the psalm "*Mizmor Shir L'Yom HaShabbos*," he sang the words "*Tov l'hodos LaHashem* — It is good to give thanks to Hashem!"